tHE POWER to bEND SPOONS

tHE pOWER tO bEND SPOONS

INTERVIEWS WITH

CANADIAN NOVELISTS

EDITED by bEVERLEY dAURIO

THE MERCURY PRESS

The publisher gratefully acknowledges the financial assistance of the Canada Council
for the Arts and the Ontario Arts Council. The publisher further acknowledges the
support of the Department of Canadian Heritage through the BPIDP.

Cover design by Gordon Robertson
Aspects of page design after work by Katy Chan
Composition and page design by Task

Printed and bound in Canada by Metropole Litho
Printed on acid-free paper
First Edition
1 2 3 4 5 02 01 00 99 98

Canadian Cataloguing in Publication
Main entry under title:
The power to bend spoons : interviews with Canadian novelists
ISBN 1-55128-058-2
1. Novelists, Canadian (English)–20th century.★ I. Daurio, Beverley, 1953-.
PS8081.P68 1998   C813'.5409   C98-932197-5
PR9189.6.P68 1998

Represented in Canada by the Literary Press Group
Distributed by General Distribution Services

The Mercury Press Toronto, Ontario CANADA M6P 2A7

CONTENTS

There was one story that shook our neighbourhood to its foundation. It was called *Saved, or the Bride's Sacrifice*, and concerned two beautiful girls—Jessie, fair as a lily, and Helen with blue black hair, and lustrous eyes as deep as the night. They each loved Herbert, and Herbert, being an obliging young fellow, not wishing to hurt anyone's feelings, married one secretly and hurriedly by the light of a guttering candle, in a peasant's hut (Jessie), and one openly with a peal of organ and general high jinks, at her father's baronial castle, (Helen).

This naturally brought on complications. There were storms, shipwrecks, and meetings in caves, with the tide rising over the rocks and curlews screaming in the blast, there were plottings and whisperings; a woman with second sight and one with the evil eye. And did we love it?

I can remember staggering along through the snow behind the sleigh reading the story as I walked, and when I drew near home, members of the family would come out to shout at me to hurry...

— Nellie McClung, *Clearing in the West* (1935)

fOREWORD

THE TITLE OF THIS BOOK is borrowed from the title of the first piece in culture critic Frank Davey's essay collection, *Canadian Literary Power*. Davey, in turn, was quoting bpNichol:

> ... all we have is the power to bend spoons...

which presents a complicated, metaphysical view of what writing can do. Is fiction an illusion, a complex of insiders' prestidigitory tricks? Or is writing actually a strange, dirigible force, the focus of winds of ideas and emotions that must be reckoned with in the real world? Here is Frederick Philip Grove, one of Canada's most mysterious modernist novelists, describing quite definitely what he believes about fiction:

> Novel[s]... deal with *socially significant* things from the main stream of life... both characters and happenings must be more or less typical for a given society. They must be normal, natural growth of given conditions actually existing in our midst. In reading them, we must be living the lives depicted as if they were our own.
> [emphasis in original] ("The Novel," *It Needs to Be Said*, 1929)

Trends and attitudes may dive and flutter, but a country's literature is built, layer by layer, over time. The Canadian novel, from its beginnings in the disguised-identity story *Wacousta* (1832), trudges across the landscape of a fairly dreary hundred-and-twenty years until it meets the magic of Sheila Watson's *The Double Hook* (1959), the novel that dug out the last roots from the colonial tree and liberated Canadian fiction, at last, to begin to become itself. Although the Canadian novel wobbled in the interim, from the wondrous (Sharon Riis' *The True Story of Ida Johnson*, for example) to the unambiguously stilted and tenebrous (*Auntie High Over the Barley Mow*, a scraggly fat volume from the 1970s McClelland and Stewart lists is surely down with the lows of this period), it was around 1990 that the Canadian novel seemed to solidify in presence and strength. Suddenly, a selection of powerful, varied novels was being published every year.

The blossoming of the Canadian novel means that, unlike thirty years ago, there are hundreds of Canadian novelists whose views should be explored in critical works and in interviews. *The Power to Bend Spoons* can offer only a selection of voices, and its editor is highly conscious of how many writers are not represented here, from Jack Hodgins to Rohinton Mistry, M. Nourbese Philip, Kristjana Gunnars, Cecil Foster, Lee Maracle, Anne Michaels, Ruby Slipperjack, Barbara Gowdy, Austin Clarke, Hiromi Goto, Linda Spalding— and many, many, many more. Perhaps it will be possible to collect these interviews by writers in a future volume of this series.

As Janice Williamson, one of Canada's foremost practitioners of the interview form, observed, "[V]oices in dialogue refuse the closure of correct arguments or final analyses." Fiction is slow to be made, its quiet art one of long-term introspection, a constant, thoughtful adding and revising; the interview is quick in action, off-the-cuff in answer, curious, Puck-like, and interrogative. Interviews with novelists can capture different angles, refractions, views of fiction's construction that emerge from consideration and hindsight, rather than from the conflagration of passionate involvement, offering explication, as well as contradiction: about the novel, about life, about what matters.

In this volume, the reader will meet many different kinds of practitioners of the novel form— impassioned, calm, clinical, intellectual, cataclysmic— and a variety of attitudes, including the desire to foreground or diminish the importance of social and political issues in fiction. Highly self-referential, and libidinous, and swooning approaches to writing are represented, as well as the autobiographical and the observational— all seeking beauty and that which is most complex, daring, and vital in fiction. Across this array of approaches is stretched a web of the important concerns of Canadian novelists these past few years, and a variety of tones, moods, and predilections, from the technical and spiritual issues discussed by Douglas Glover, to the idealism of Veronica Ross, the bluntness of Margaret Atwood, and the lyrical politics of Dionne Brand. *The Power to Bend Spoons* brings together Janette Turner Hospital on chimerical geographies, Joy Kogawa on the meaning of character, Althea Prince on community stories, Timothy Findley on extremes of violence, Lola Lemire Tostevin on Catholic childhoods, Michael Ondaatje on how he writes novels, and a cornucopia of others.

Phyllis Webb, in *Talking* (1982), said that the search for Canadian identity is not the search for definitions, but the search "for signs and omens." Ethereal, granite, fey, iridescent knowledge of ourselves is evoked in these pages, in voice against voice, twined into implied agreements and arguments between positions, in these writers' love of words, in the sense of hands clenched on desks or opening like roses over keyboards or paper. No one agrees with anyone else, yet the voices, taken together, form a vast choir, so that each is also right, echoing anthropologist Wilson Duff:

"I can see how to think now: in unfettered analogies. I have found my mood and think it is my country's mood..."

Beverley Daurio

The Body of Our People

JEANNETTE ARMSTRONG
by Victoria Freeman

JEANNETTE ARMSTRONG is an Okanagan writer whose works include *Slash, Breath Tracks,* and *The Native Creative Process* (with Douglas Cardinal). She is the director of the En'Owkin International School of Writing in Penticton, BC.

VICTORIA FREEMAN ¶ Do you think there has been any movement on the issue of cultural appropriation?

JEANNETTE ARMSTRONG § Over the past year or so there has been some good dialogue about it, as well as some sorting through the anger.

One good thing is that a number of the Native Canadian writers got together in a series of forums to dialogue with one another, because there were people coming from a diversity of backgrounds and cultures attempting to speak about cultural appropriation in relation to all of them. A meeting ground was arranged by Margo Kane, through a Canada Council Explorations grant. It was one of the best forums that I've attended. There wasn't an agenda. Every person who was invited was asked to give their thinking on the question of cultural appropriation and copyright. After everyone had spoken, people would comment on other people's points of view, so there was a layering of thinking. It was an Indian meeting.

People tuned into each other's perspectives and thoughts and examined them in an almost organic process, so that by the end of that first forum there was an alignment of thinking. That process itself was extremely powerful and a beautiful thing to watch; it was an example of Native people's ability to harmonize their thinking with one another without dispute and without discord. A book is being compiled from that forum; Theytus will publish it.

The issue was explored not only by writers but also by people involved in the performing and visual arts, because the question of copyright was also at issue, especially for the artists of the west coast, whose family crests and symbolic emblems are owned by the families.

There is great difficulty in bridging the two cultures where legal matters are concerned. The expression of copyright law for the protection of intellectual ownership is always defined in relation to the individual whose creativity is expressed in that work. It precludes the idea that a cultural group can express one mind and one creative thought, which is the case in some of the creative arts of Native peoples. In a sense the law says that a cultural group cannot own its own idea, its own expression, and cannot have the right to determine the use of that creative configuration. If that cannot be expressed and protected and be perpetuated in terms of legal practices, then we have a serious problem with multiculturalism in Canada.

One problem is that it's very difficult to precisely define for legal copyright the ownership of a specific design. I'm thinking of things like the Cowichan sweaters. In relation to words, it's even more difficult...

Those were some of the issues we have had to try to grapple with: how do we as a cultural group try to present some serious discussion on these issues and how do we actually bring about legislative changes?

At the forum, one of the storytellers was explaining how stories are transferred from one generation to another, explaining that those stories are stories that are sanctioned to be told only by those people who are given permission by the cultural group and by the family and by the people who have been the teachers of this person. That person is the holder, the carrier— the owner, in essence— of the stories. Ownership is defined differently; as the carrier, the preserver, the storyteller is in a sense the owner, but in a sense everyone owns the stories and has the right to access... He or she is the custodian, but decides how and when those stories are told and how they are disseminated and under what circumstances and in what context.

What has been happening over the past hundred years has been a deliberate suppression by our people of very important pieces of cultural knowledge, which custodians have had to keep secret, so the stories wouldn't be stolen, so therefore very small numbers of our people have had access to them... Many people at the forum were expressing concerns that this situation was not going to change, and there is the fear of of losing those stories and the context in which they are used and delivered.

On the one hand the stories are being kept by those people who are being given the right and responsiblity to look after them; on the other hand you have unscrupulous people who repeat various kinds of stories, Native and non-Native people who may have been privy to some of those things. Those stories are repeated out of context, out of alignment in terms of their intent, then they've been reprinted by some ethnographer. The intent of the story has been totally corrupted, without the cultural context that it emerges from... and a great loss occurs in that gap.

FREEMAN ¶ That loss really hasn't been focused on in most discussions about appropriation. Can you tell me what is being lost?

ARMSTRONG § The thought and philosophical worldview underlying a cultural system which did a number of things that seem to be important in terms of knowledge today— the connectedness to the environment and to the land in a way which preserves and promotes regeneration for the next generation... the cooperative systems that encompass and move always outward to include and align with anything that remains counter-active.

That's where the greatest losses occur, in those systems and customs— the stories reflect and embed the philosophical ideals, the underlying infrastructure. When those stories are left out of the knowledge base of all of us, we all lose [i.e., not only Native people]. We just continue on in our direction of destruction of each other and the land without other ideas to help us to ground ourselves and make the changes that may be needed in each of us individually.

The loss of those stories constitutes a much larger and more critical loss than simply the loss of a few books. That loss to any society— the loss of knowledge and information— is immeasurable. Every piece of knowledge gives us more to be able to put our best thoughts together with.

FREEMAN ¶ There's another level of it, too, isn't there, that the stories also contain the energy of the people. There is some kind of energy that a cultural story contains that is passed on specifically to the people of that culture.

ARMSTRONG § Cultures, groups of people who can be identified as a culture, have evolved a way of being and a way of thinking, and that way of being is not a singular individual thing that belongs to one individual. That way of being is something that is embedded in the consciousness of the people, and constitutes all of the various ways that we interact with one another as conscious beings, whether through the various arts, or ways of structuring our societies, our homes, our families. In a really complex sense culture contains the very life force of that cultural group.

When the gaps start to happen, the life force of that people as a group begins to diminish. The life force becomes fractionalized and weakened, and in a sense the people die through the culture dying. When the thinking of the people becomes lost, we see the effects, in terms of the deaths. The statistics can show you that assimilation doesn't work.

FREEMAN ¶ Are you saying in part that a culture is a group mind? And that individuals within that culture are not strong unless they have been nourished by that group mind?

ARMSTRONG § Yes, a group being. We have words for it in our culture. We don't see people as individuals within a cultural group. In our language we call it the body of our people. As a cultural group we are the body of one being that needs all pieces of it to function properly and all those pieces of it could correspond to the eyes, the ears, the nose, the brain, and those are representative of the different things people do within the society. Those are all important parts of the whole being. The whole being operates very fluidly and in a healthy way when those parts are intact. When some of those parts are missing and are replaced from parts of another being, it doesn't operate as well because those parts are displaced, out of context. They don't have a clear whole connection to all the other parts. If you can look at it from that allegorical perspective you can sense what we talk about when we say all of the parts— the language, the philosophical ideas, the ceremonies, the processes, the family structures, and so on— need to be there for that culture to survive and thrive.

When those gaps occur, the whole being is endangered, all of the people in that cultural group are in danger of vanishing. I don't just mean assimilation, because they don't fit into the other cultures...

FREEMAN ¶ What struck me while you were talking— you are going to laugh— was that the description that you are using is the same description that western scientists have belatedly discovered in describing the earth as a single organism.

ARMSTRONG § Yes.

FREEMAN ¶ I don't know a lot about how storytellers told stories traditionally. Did they not only tell old stories but put new things together to make new stories appropriate for a particular time?

ARMSTRONG § I can only speak for the Okanagan. In the Okanagan the storytellers never were restricted to telling the old stories. Old stories were always handed down to storytellers and storytellers should know all the traditional stories, should have that understanding of all the old stories, to make the new stories. The new stories that emerge from our people have come from storytellers that know all the stories, but also are immersed in the culture in a really specific way, different than other people. The storytellers in our culture moved around from community to community and family to family. They were travellers. I guess you could say they studied life and all the goings-on of people. They mixed with people, listened to them, continuously. So all the stories the storyteller told were also stories of the people in a contemporary sense. The last storyteller that we had, Harry Robinson, moved around continuously. He observed all the goings-on of his community, all the thinking of the people, in all different kinds of contexts. He knew the heart and the thought of the people. He knew that historically as well. And so he had contemporary stories, and recounted contemporary stories to our people.

Some of the contemporary stories that I listened to and some from other storytellers— there are still two storytellers walking around out there— the contemporary stories that they tell take from the thinking of the people, the heart of the people, the actions of the people, and some of them are like the old stories in the way they are structured, the way the sensibility works... That process is something only those storytellers are given the responsibility to do.

FREEMAN ¶ Can anyone else tell their stories?

ARMSTRONG § If someone were to recount one of the stories that Harry orginated, in our society, they have to acknowledge that— they have to say "This is Harry Robinson's story" or "This was given to me by Harry Robinson." When I speak to the people or any of the elders speak to the people, we say: "This is not something that I originated, this was told to me by my grandfather," and you'd name his name, and it was told to him by his uncle and so on. So there is a strict protocol about who originated which stories and how they came. Then there are the stories of antiquity, but again you recount who gave you that story, who passed on that story to you. And then they know who passed on the stories to that person.

FREEMAN ¶ Are there any guidelines that a contemporary storyteller has to follow? Are there any topics that are off limits?

ARMSTRONG § In our culture, there's nothing that's off-limits. The storytellers that I know will tell stories of a wide open nature within our own culture, but outside of that, even with other Native groups, there's a line that's drawn in terms of what can be told.

FREEMAN ¶ Would an Okanagan storyteller ever tell a story from another Native culture?

ARMSTRONG § Yes, they would say "This is a Shuswap story, this is how I heard it and this is the Shuswap that told me," or "This is a Nootka story and this woman, her name is such and such, told me the story." And it would be told in exactly the same way. In some cases I've been told that on the west coast you have to have permission before you can even do that. So my practice is that if I want to repeat stories, I ask the teller if that is something that I can tell my people.

There is another level of cultural appropriation and its impact on contemporary culture. I'm talking about the stories that are written about Native culture by non-Native people. What's at issue there is the ability of those non-Native writers— without malice in most cases— to draw a picture of Native contemporary lifestyle and thinking and so on which creates a false image in the mind of the reading public, and which creates problems for contemporary Native people.

Many Native people, young people, have been fostered out and have not had any kind of access to truth within their culture and do not have access to their own people's thinking. Or people who are second- or third-generation urbanized Native people. They find it necessary to ground themselves in their culture, so books that give a false identity in terms of values and philosophical worldview and indeed in terms of how people interact with one another are dangerous to those people. When they interact with Native people who are steeped in the traditional cultures, a sense of imbalance and disorientation occurs. We've seen that happen to our people when they've returned from fostering.

What that says to me is that Native people themselves need their own stories emerging. Beatrice Culleton's *April Raintree* is a good example of that. Jordan Wheeler's *Brothers in Arms*. Some of the stories in Thomas King's collection *All My Relations...* in which Native people aren't caught up in the romantic vision of the Native...

Those books are more useful and accurate and beautiful than a falsified view from a non-Native person, which is not to say that those cannot be written as pieces of fiction, but what needs to be understood is that Native people have the right to say those books are false and don't reflect Native values. Those stories are not about Native people; they are about fictitious characters who have Indian names and Indian identities and may be set in a real place but those are fictions. They're not real. They're not Indians— they're somebody's ideas of Indians, but they're not us. We need to say that clearly and be understood. We need to be heard by librarians, by book buyers who sell to schools and integrate those materials into curricula that Indian children and non-Indian children are reading and being exposed to and influenced by.

Non-Native writers need to be told those things without being told they're racist because its not about racism, it's about truth— truth in relation to our reality. Native people themselves don't need to be saying "you can't write about those things..." They need to be saying: "Those aren't Indians, it's not truthful, it's a pile of shit as far as Indian reality is concerned."

FREEMAN ¶ Saying you can't write about something seems to wave a red flag in front of a lot of writers' faces... and they miss the other 99% of what the appropriation issue is all about.

ARMSTRONG § Censorship is not the issue. It's been used as an excuse. The non-Native writers will say: "We can write what we want." And I'm sure that it's going to continue to be done. In my mind my responsibility is to clearly articulate the reasons for criticizing those pieces. Criticism is not against the law in this country. Criticism is one of the ways by which we can identify clearly what our perspectives are, what our concerns are, and where we believe the writer may have gone wrong, and expose for the public the wrongness of doing that.

FREEMAN ¶ For any of us writing about contemporary Canada, we have situations where we have characters of many different backgrounds. Do you have any thoughts about ways to approach that?

ARMSTRONG § I've admired Paul St. Pierre's methods of approaching it. He is a BC writer who writes about Caribou country, where obviously there are a lot of Indians. In his preface, he says that these stories are not about Native people or an attempt to tell their stories because they need to tell their own stories, but they move around in this world, around his characters. The stories are an account of the white settlers and the ranchers and their perceptions of Native people, the things about them that they encounter and interact with. He doesn't attempt to speak for the Native people; all he does is recount the interaction with them and how the characters perceive them. From my point of view that's very valuable. I would like to know non-Native people's thinking and interaction with us from their perspective, what they really feel. It would be very instructive and informative to each other to talk about that.

Non-Native people don't talk about that, they don't write about the history, what the pioneers felt toward Native people. There's some romanticizing about [Native-non-Native interaction], but I haven't seen anything written, for example, about the residential schools. Let's have a few imaginative people put themselves in the place of those nuns and those priests and how they saw Native children and how they interacted. Let's see some truth.

FREEMAN ¶ You are saying that instead of just focusing on the "plight" of Native people or that sort of thing, looking at the attitudes of the white people in their interactions with Native people, so that Native people would be present in that story but the focus would be on...

ARMSTRONG § ...how the non-Natives themselves think and interact with Native people. Non-Native writers refuse to look at that in any serious sense. They attempt to put themselves in the head of the Indian person and talk for an Indian person and that is to me one of the greatest pieces of racism... that's avoiding the real issue. Racism in the deepest and most horrible sense has occurred on this continent and continues to occur and writers are not writing about those things in a truthful, courageous way. I don't mean those writers have to believe what those nuns and priests believed, what those people on the street believe, but they have to look at it. Those interactions are important to examine. *We* need to understand the dynamics of that. We need to know where that racism comes from. We need to know why those people find it necessary to believe that the white man is superior. We need to know where that generates and where it ends up. We can't put ourselves into the white person's mind and understand that.

FREEMAN ¶ Do non-Native writers ever write accurately about Native people?

ARMSTRONG § [laughs] Oh, I imagine they do. I haven't read a lot of non-Native writers writing about Native people. I imagine it's a question of the purpose of the writer.

FREEMAN ¶ What about the question of voice? What about a white writer writing something in the first person as if they were a Native person?

ARMSTRONG § I would say to that person that while I can't censor them doing that, it's not ethical from my point of view. Whether they write in the first person or the third person, they are saying: "This is how a Native person is or thinks or understands the world," and obviously a non-Native person has some insights about that and may want to expose their own people to some of the thinking of Native people, but that can be done in ways that don't put the person in the paternalistic, imperialistic and racist context of saying, "I can interpret for them, I give those cultures credibility by recognizing them." It's perpetuating cultural imperialism and racism, because it's saying, "A Native person can't say it well enough that my people will understand it. I have to reinterpret, reform the words. I have to speak the words for that Native person in order for my people to understand their thinking or what's valuable about their culture." That's very racist and I feel really insulted by it. There are other ways of doing it so that the Native person is allowed to speak, which the writer can do with integrity...

FREEMAN ¶ That would be a story.

ARMSTRONG § Absolutely. Let's have some courage here. That's the challenge that I put out. Let's talk about it. Let's talk about the encounters. Put yourself in the position of the person who can kick the Indian in the balls when he's lying down on a park bench. Put yourself in that person's mind and let's imagine what that person thinks and feels and maybe we'll have some clear understanding of that thinking. Let's see some imagination. I think there are ways of writing about our interaction with integrity.

Power and Non-power

MARGARET ATWOOD
by Marilyn Snell

MARGARET ATWOOD has published works of fiction, poetry, social history, criticism— including the seminal *Survival* (1972)— and children's books. Her novels include *The Edible Woman* (1970), *Surfacing* (1972), *The Handmaid's Tale* (1985), *Cat's Eye* (1988), and *The Robber Bride* (1993). Her latest novel is *Alias Grace* (1997).

MARILYN SNELL ¶ How does your political involvement inform your creative process?

MARGARET ATWOOD § I have no idea. People talking about politics usually start from the ass end backwards, in that they think you have a political agenda and then you make your work fit that cookie cutter. It's the other way around. One works by simple observation, looking into things. It's usually called insight, and out of that comes your view— it's not that you have the view first and then squash everything to make it fit. I'm talking about staying out of the Procrustean bed. You know the myth: everybody had to fit into Procrustes' bed, and if they didn't, he either stretched them or cut off their feet. I'm not interested in cutting the feet off my characters or stretching them to make them fit my certain political view.

SNELL ¶ So, do your political self and your creative self communicate at all?

ATWOOD § As an artist your first loyalty is to your art. Unless this is the case, you're going to be a second-rate artist. I don't mean there's never any overlap. You learn things in one area and bring them into another area. But giving a speech against racism is not the same as writing a novel. The object is very clear in the fight against racism; you have reasons why you're opposed to it. But when you're writing a novel, you don't want the reader to come out of it voting yes or no to some question. Life is more complicated than that. Reality simply consists of different points of view.

When I was young, I believed that "non-fiction" meant "true." But you read a history written in, say, 1920, and a history of the same events written in 1995, and they're very different. There may not be one Truth— there may be several truths— but saying that is not to say that reality doesn't exist.

When I wrote *Alias Grace*, for example, about Canada's famous nineteenth-century convicted murderer, Grace Marks, I knew there were some things that weren't true about this historical figure. After all my research, I still do not know who killed Thomas Kinnear and his house-keeper, Nancy Montgomery. Someone killed them. To say that we don't know exactly who did it is not to say that nobody killed them. There is a truth in their deaths, but some other truths— such as who really did the killing— are not knowable.

SNELL ¶ But are there certain discrete truths that you explore in your work? So often people on the left seem afraid to talk about transcendent truths, values, the ethics involved in even the smallest human interactions.

ATWOOD § I'm probably not exactly on the left in the way that you understand it.

SNELL ¶ How would you define yourself, then?

ATWOOD § I'm a Red Tory. To get a fix on this category, you have to go back to the nineteenth century. The Tories were the ones who believed that those in power had a responsibility to the community, that money should not be the measure of all things.

SNELL ¶ Would this be your discrete truth— that money is not the measure of all things?

ATWOOD § Everybody knows it isn't. Within one's own family, money is not the measure of things, unless the person is an absolute Scrooge. Only the most extreme kind of monster would put a price on everything. There are all kinds of other things that we are not supposed to sell— political influence being one of them. We too rarely have public conversations about the common sense of money. We too rarely talk about the human cost of putting some of these economic measures into effect.

SNELL ¶ What you're saying sounds great, but we live in a consumerist culture where money is the measure of who you are.

ATWOOD § Well, it used to be that your bloodlines dictated who you were. But the US became the land of the self-made man, in which not only did you make a fortune, but you could make up everything else about yourself as well. You move into a new town with a spurious pedigreed background and you just make yourself up.

I collect con artist stories. One of my favourites is that of a Portuguese woman who had been passing herself off, not only as a man, but in the military establishment as a general. Then there was the jazz musician who was married and had three adopted children and turned out to have been a woman all along.

SNELL ¶ Why do you think these women do it? For the power they gain by being men?

ATWOOD § Sometimes it's not even power so much as the absence of non-power, which is different. One actively exercises power. The absence of non-power is just that people don't bother you. You don't suffer the consequences of not being powerful.

SNELL ¶ In much of your writing, you explore the state of the— I don't want to say "victim"— of the person who is "not yet," and mostly these are women.

ATWOOD § You know why? Unless something has gone disastrously wrong, other people aren't that interesting to write about. Let me tell you a story: when my daughter was little, she and a friend decided to put on a play. It opened with two characters having breakfast. They had some orange juice and cornflakes and they poured milk on the cornflakes and they had some tea and they had some coffee and they had some more orange juice and cornflakes and toast and they put jam on the toast. Finally we said, is anything else going to happen in this play other than having breakfast, and they said no, and we said, well then, it's time to go.

This is lesson number one in narrative: something has to happen. It can be good people to whom bad things happen, a nice person getting bitten in two by a shark or crushed by an earthquake, or their husbands run off on them.

Or, then, it can be people of devious or shallow character getting into trouble or making trouble. But if you want to read a novel in which nice people do nothing but good things, I recommend Samuel Richardson's *The History of Sir Charles Grandison*. It goes on and on. I think I'm the only person who's ever actually finished the book.

SNELL ¶ I wasn't arguing for the crushingly boring novel. My question was about victimhood. Does this mean all your books need female victims?

ATWOOD § Let us change it from victimhood to people in circumstances that put some pressure on them, which is not quite the same thing. Some people tell me that Grace Marks is a victim, and I say, "Hey, just hang on a minute. What about Nancy and Thomas? They're the ones who ended up dead in the cellar." I don't think it's quite as simple as "These people over here are always the oppressors, and these people over here are always victims."

SNELL ¶ You turn the traditional victim into victimizer to chilling effect in *Cat's Eye*, where little girls are anything but sugar and spice and everything nice.

ATWOOD § Of course, I wasn't supposed to say that, because sisterhood is powerful and women are always supposed to get along with one another. It's not true any more than it is for men— and why should it be?

Women are human beings, and human beings are a very mixed lot. I've always been against the idea that women were Victorian angels, that they could do no wrong. I've always thought it was horseshit and does nobody any good. Remember, Lizzie Borden got off largely because the cultural agenda had convinced people that women were morally superior to men, so Lizzie Borden was "incapable" of taking the ax and giving her mother forty whacks.

In the early fight for women's rights, the point was not that women were morally superior or better. The conversation was about the difference between men and women— power, privilege, voting rights, etc. Unfortunately, it quickly moved to the "women are better" argument. If this were true in life or in fiction, we wouldn't have any dark or deep characters. We wouldn't have any Salomes, Carmens, Ophelias. We wouldn't have any jealousy or passion.

Tendencies and Philosophies

MARIE-CLAIRE BLAIS
by Janieta Eyre

MARIE-CLAIRE BLAIS has published many novels and plays since her first book, *Mad Shadows* (1959), including *A Season in the Life of Emmanuel* (1965) and *Deaf to the City* (1979). She has been awarded the Prix France-Québec and the Prix Médicis, as well as the Governor General's award (twice) and the Prix Académie Française.

EYRE ¶ I'm curious to know what your feelings are about Quebec–Canada relations. Do you consider yourself a separatist?

BLAIS § As an artist, I'm wary of any kind of fanaticism. I think we have to be careful not to become too nationalistic, as this is often our problem. If independence is the democratic wish, it will have to be so. My real concern, however, is the fate of our artists. Will we take care of them? This worries me a great deal because at the moment much-needed funds for all kinds of cultural activities are being cut. And as a writer, I think we need writers, painters, and musicians in the same way we need food. I think it's important to recognize that it is artists who are making the future, although the only people we talk about are our politicians. Politicians are not that interesting. They make too much money, they don't care about the poor or about the ethnic preoccupations of this country. Which is why it would be tragic if artists were stripped of their voices. In the time of Mr. Lévesque, we had a voice. He thought we were interesting. In the time of Mr. Trudeau, we had a voice. He thought that artists were important to this country. But now there is this indifference being shown towards the culture of our country.

EYRE ¶ But hasn't this disinterest in culture always been true of Canada? Culture has never been important to Canadians and their sense of identity.

BLAIS § I was at a Canadian Studies conference in Italy a few weeks ago with some other writers from Quebec and Canada. Many Canadian artists were thinking as I do, that we are in the background. But they thought also that it has always been like that. It is often when we go abroad that we really complain about this. In Venice, it was interesting to see that the Italian public was very interested in Timothy Findley, Susan Swan, and the rest of us. Many people came to our readings, listened to us and indicated they wanted to translate our work. It's all around that we see this interest in our culture, and I think it's important to take pride in it. A writer is a kind of ambassador, a poor one but one with a great vision, great insight. It's strange that in Europe they understand this, but we don't here yet.

EYRE ¶ What kind of pressure is there in Quebec to be politically correct? Is the question of whose right it is to tell what story an issue?

BLAIS § Yes, it's an issue in Quebec, too. I myself am terrified of being confined in this way. I think we have the right to speak about whatever. I mean, let's think in terms of other writers. If Dostoevsky only wrote about his particular experience in the world, we wouldn't have all those women he describes so beautifully. He shows us the female heart, and he speaks about it like a woman.

EYRE ¶ What kind of differences do you perceive between English- and French-Canadian literature?

BLAIS § Well, the French language is very different. We have certain tendencies and philosophies because of the French language. Maybe we are a little more sentimental, closer to our emotions, passionate. But English writers have other qualities, like coolness and humour.

EYRE ¶ When you began writing more than thirty years ago, the gay community was much less visible than it is today. Do you feel that the progress that's been made has influenced your writing in any way?

BLAIS § I think all these great changes have to be constantly worked on. People shouldn't assume they can acquire something and it will be there forever, because it's not true. We are very far from being open-minded, not only with respect to the gay community, but many other communities.

EYRE ¶ Do you feel part of the gay community?

BLAIS § I wrote a lot about the gay community in the beginning, with *The Wolf, David Sterne, Nights of the Underground* and *The Angel of Solitude*. My feeling is that gay people should not be noticed more than a black person, that everyone should be noticed equally. At the Canadian Studies conference in Italy, Timothy Findley said that he was very worried about ghettos. But people get close together in ghettos because they think they will be more protected, as I try to show in *The Angel of Solitude*. But there is a weakness in that, because we are all part of the world, whatever we are. We have to live with each other. It's very difficult, but we have to. I think that a writer has to be universal. I don't like to limit myself to any particular themes. If you think of a writer like Nicole Brossard, she is not only a poet, a feminist— some people may call her a gay writer— but she is also a universal writer who is writing about all kinds of preoccupations.

EYRE ¶ What kind of political responsibility do you feel is incurred by being a writer? Your two most recently translated books, *Pierre*, and *The Angel of Solitude*, are quite bleak in terms of a comment on the social and political situation for young people today.

BLAIS § The political landscape I depicted in *The Angel of Solitude* is exactly as it was then. Today there is a little more hope; what is happening in South Africa is hopeful and some people of conscience seem to be rising above this terrible inferno. As we get older we forget about Hiroshima, we forget about so many things. That's why I took these young women, because they don't forget, they care and don't want to grow up in such a terrible world. They want to make it better. But you can't do much when you're that young, and if nobody gives you any hope, it looks bleak. Even as we speak, a great deal of destruction is occurring; people watch it every day on their TV and feel it in their bones. We feel it too much, but I think the consciousness of very young souls is more open-minded, more subtle.

EYRE ¶ I know you come from a Catholic background. Do you still feel close to Catholicism?

BLAIS § I'm not feeling very close, like many of us, to any religion. I think it creates fanatics and people without vision. But I think it's possible to be spiritual or a humanist, like Simone Weil or Martin Buber. I am a humanist, I guess.

EYRE ¶ What kind of research do you do for your novels?

BLAIS § I speak with a lot of people and get close to them. I meet people all over the place. Some become friends, some are just acquaintances that I never see again. In *Soif*, the novel I'm currently working on, the characters are all people I knew very very well. I take real people and cocktail them; I mean, some of my characters are two people in one, or three people in one, but many people in *Soif* are real Americans or real North Americans or real Spanish or real black people, but all changed to suit my own vision.

EYRE ¶ Which of the novels you have written is your favourite?

BLAIS § The one I'm working on. It is called *Soif*, which means "thirst"— but I'm not sure it will be translated as such, because in French, "soif" can be plural and imply many thirsts. I've been working hard on it for three years. I also wrote two other books during the same period. A book of short stories that hasn't been translated yet and a book called *American Notebooks* that has recently been published in French and should be translated and published by Talonbooks in a few months. *American Notebooks* is a personal memoir, not exactly autobiography, but about the political events in the sixties in the US. In 1963, I was living in Cambridge, Massachusetts, because I had received a Guggenheim. I was in the midst of every important thing that was going on for young people then. The civil rights movement, the feminist movement, the assassinations of President Kennedy, Martin Luther King, and Robert Kennedy. *Soif* is also about the United States and is very close to my heart, which is why it gives me so much trouble. Really, the first book a writer produces is just the first step in an everlasting process. A writer looking back into his or her own writing past can often find the roots of current work. Over time you re-work the original idea again and again in order to perfect it and make it still closer to your vision. But it takes a lifetime to do this.

EYRE ¶ What is *Soif* about?

BLAIS § *Soif* is an impressionist novel with all kinds of people in it, many generations, races and a constantly shifting landscape. Stylistically, it is similar to *Deaf to the City*, but more luminous because of the presence of the sea. It's a work I have been planning for many years. I have been visiting Key West and studying the moods, the atmosphere, the moral climate there. Others of my novels have been inspired by Key West, such as *Pierre, Anna's World*, and maybe a little of *The Angel of Solitude*. For me Key West is a wonderful setting for a novel because it is a microcosm of the world. It has everything humanity has, people of different social classes and backgrounds: artists, bohemians, poor people, rich people, people from different cultures. I think it's a wonderful place to study people and also a good example of our contemporary landscape. Seventeen years ago, Key West wasn't much but I loved it because it was full of wild characters and because it was hippie and simple. I originally went because I often had problems with my lungs and asthma, and living there a few months a year helped. I liked it, too, because there was a certain loneliness and solitude there that I appreciated.

EYRE ¶ You seem to have escaped the influence of minimalism and the nouveau roman in your work. Has this been a conscious rejection?

BLAIS § Well, we are all exploring different things in our work. I think that for many North American writers a more intellectual way of writing is not as moving to us as the psychological portrait of a character or a tragedy and so on. I think the nouveau roman is very interesting, but the problem in France today is that there are a lot of bad novelists. These novelists have no depth and are bad writers but are making a lot of money. They're crushing the people who write beautifully. Thank God there are writers who continue to work like Beckett used to, or Kafka. I think this is what art is: a vocation. It's a very hard thing, too, to keep one's faith while knowing that during your lifetime you will not really touch as many people as you should. Just the fact that you have an ideal isolates you and makes it harder for you to get publicity. It's not only my case I'm talking about, it's the case of many writers all over the world. At least if one has faith in one's work, it's less damaging for the spirit.

EYRE ¶ What do you like to read?

BLAIS § I try to be in contact with English literature as much as I can. I think there's an unfortunate lack of communication between French and English writers because of few translations. I read a lot of French writers. I'm a passionate admirer of Jean Genet, a writer who's fallen out of favour in France. With a few exceptions France doesn't have as many prolific writers as we do in Canada or in the United States. There's a kind of dry spirit there at the moment. While there are wonderful writers, they are mostly people who study writing and are too intellectual.

Writing It

DIONNE BRAND
by Beverley Daurio

DIONNE BRAND is the author of several books of poetry, including *Chronicles of the Hostile Sun* and *Winter Epigrams and Epigrams to Ernesto Cardenal in Defense of Caudia*, as well as a collection of short fiction, *Sans Souci and Other Stories*; she is also the author of a book of essays, *Bread Out of Stone* (1994). A community activist, scholar, and writer, she has also worked with Studio D of the National Film Board as a writer and director. Her long poem, *No Language Is Neutral* (1990), was nominated for the Governor General's award. Her novel, *In Another Place, Not Here* (1996), was published by Knopf Canada.

BEVERLEY DAURIO ¶ How do you see your scholarly work interrelating with your art?

DIONNE BRAND § Well, during the years I've had about three lives; one doing community work in the women's movement and the Black movement, then a kind of academic life, and then my sort of literary life. I'm really cautious about the academic one. I always think it's dangerous just to stay in academia—it is only relevant if you can put it to some good use in the communities you work in and struggle for.

DAURIO ¶ You've now lived about half your life in Trinidad and half your life in Canada. That place split and that time split seems to be a main source of imagery in your work: the snow versus the ocean... I wondered if you could talk a bit about that, about how you ended up in Canada and how it affected you, particularly as a writer.

BRAND § Why I came... I think I was part of the social relations happening at the time; I got exported like a whole bunch of other people. I came to Canada on the wings of international capital. I came here to go to university and to go back, ended up doing more than that, and never really going back.

Where I come from is incredibly physically beautiful; posed against that is incredible hardship in the ways that people live and eke out a living. I was born in a country town, near an ocean; the imagery in the early part of your life is more sensual, less intellectualized, than later. Those are the things that stay with you; the landscape that you build on. I was lucky to know that you could sit beside the ocean and something was explained.

I also come out of a history of a people who were enslaved, and that struggle toward freedom was central to the whole ethos of that people. It was also infused in me in looking at that landscape. I guess if you were born in northern Ontario or something, the inevitability of the earth, the greatness of it, would strike you in the same way. But these things, posed as opposites in the beginning in my work, are somehow figuring themselves into each other.

DAURIO ¶ How old were you when you knew that you were going to become a writer? Did your impulse to write originally come out of politics?

BRAND § I think the first time I said I would do that I was thirteen. You know how obnoxious you are when you're thirteen; you pick up some industry and you're really self-righteous about it for a week.

All through my schooling in Trinidad, what I read as English literature never had me in it. I always felt the need to put me in it, and by me I mean Black people. When it did have them in it, they were awfully misrepresented, stereotyped, so flat and thin, and always at service of white characters. If countries of Black people were talked about, they were presented in colonial and derogatory terms. People need their lives to be elucidated, spoken about, and it struck me that that life that I had known was pretty beautiful, so why couldn't I write it down?

DAURIO ¶ Did that make it hard to see yourself as a writer? When I was a kid growing up in Canada, there seemed to be no Canadian writers, and it made it difficult somehow to believe writing was possible here.

BRAND § At that early stage of recognizing that I was not in the literature, it did strike me that it could be written. I became aware of certain Black writing in the Caribbean and in the States, and we were in it. Suddenly you get startled— it hadn't been written, and you could be part of doing that.

DAURIO ¶ You co-authored a book on racism, *Rivers Have Sources, Trees Have Roots*. How did that book come about?

BRAND § I'd always been involved in Black community action against racism in the city [Toronto], and there was a real dearth of information about racism in this country and about peoples of colour. It was important to document those experiences. I was asked to write the book, which was supposed to be about personal experiences with racism— but racism is a collective experience, it's a social experience. The word "personal" irritated me; it gave the sense that it might be like paranoia, or something quite individual. We interviewed about a hundred people, Black, South Asian, Native, and Chinese; we asked them, *what is it like in your daily life here?, when do you encounter it?, how do you cope?,* and *where is it most virulent, where is it most painful?* So the book talks about the randomness of racism, the way it permeates this society, the way it's just ordinary, or how it's institutional, where there are practices that you can see.

DAURIO ¶ All of your work is informed by politics, by philosophy, by history; it never rests on the beautiful phrase, the lovely story, though those things are equally and compellingly present in your writing. Do you believe there can be such a thing as pure aesthetics?

BRAND § No, I don't. In really vulgar terms, pure aesthetics means *who's in control to make that what that is?* We name the worlds we're in, and no one culture can define that, living in the incredible culture we live in.

DAURIO ¶ Would you agree that a basic tenet of writing is responsibility rather than just self-fulfilment? That it involves a responsibility toward a community?

BRAND § That's true of my work. I clearly have a purpose. Every relationship is social, and you don't exist outside of that. Even if you think you're not writing politically, you are in some way contributing to the making of the culture that we're in. Those who think writing can be done without responsibility are choosing that, too. Well, what does that align itself with?

But I'm not a social worker; I'm not an advocate for something that I'm not a part of. I believe that history, and the history of the people that I come from, is important, and that it is important to rewrite that history in a way that saves our humanity. Black people and women have to make their humanity every goddamned day, because every day we are faced with the unmaking of us. Sometimes any words I throw at this feel like pebbles, but the purpose in throwing them is to keep, to save, my humanity, and that is my responsibility. I mean to see Black people free from the kinds of hindrances we have hitherto encountered that have tried to and have killed us at various points in time. As a woman, as a lesbian, I have to redeem my life every day, in a society that thinks I should lead an existence that's second class; and every day I get to say, no way. I do feel that responsibility and I take it on. It doesn't feel like a burden because at the end of it is something wonderful, the day when I can be free of those things. Putting my skills toward doing that is the best thing I can do.

DAURIO ¶ A debate has been raging about the question of appropriation of voice. Lenore Keeshig-Tobias, for instance, has said that white writers telling Native stories is a kind of theft, and that it robs the stories of their power.

BRAND § Lenore Keeshig-Tobias is right about what happens to those stories; they become consumer items. This culture has always taught people they can take, buy, other people's things, consume everything— *so why can't we take your stories?* They don't realize they are really responding to commercials that tell you, *if you buy this car, you can eat a woman, too.* They are taking up the destiny of the culture that conquered and took Canada away from Native people and finds Native life dispensable. That's going on in that discussion; that's refused to be talked about by white writers who simply yell *this is censorship.* That's a deeper discussion than saying, *I can write what I want.*

I think white writers have to take on the responsibility of dealing with racism. Racism didn't just happen to Black people and Native people, it happened to white people. It was a relationship in which we were involved. White people cannot simply say racism was something that happened to other people. What was their role in it?

DAURIO ¶ Is access to reviewing and critical writing part of the problem?

BRAND § Reviews are equally racist, when you are reviewed. Work by peoples of colour has to prove universality; a white writer is never asked to prove that. The other things you look for in a review are words like "anger." Reviewers always talk about the anger of Black writers. Anger is not the only word that can be used; the experience is far more complex: it is remorse, it is sadness, it is absolute joy, it is beauty, it is all those things.

DAURIO ¶ So the mistake is in making the description a kind of containment, not opening up to what is actually there in the work?

BRAND § Exactly. What some white reviewers lack is a sense of what the literature that is made by Black people and other people of colour is about. If you read my work, you have to read Toni Morrison's work, you have to read Derek Walcott's work, Rosa Guy, Jean Rhys, Paule Marshall, Michael Anthony, Eddie Braithwaite, and African writers and poets... Bessie Head. I don't consider myself on any margin; I'm sitting right in the middle of Black literature, because that's who I read, that's who I respond to— I'm not on the margin of Canadian literature.

DAURIO ¶ In your book of short stories, *Sans Souci*, the women keep trying to solve Canada, even though it seems desolate and oppressive, racist and patriarchal.

BRAND § Survival is one of the running themes in our lives as Black women; when you get faced with the possibility of not existing, then you really want to. You just don't give in. That's what I've learned from the women in my community, and I have a feeling that's women's lives in general, that we know how to make do, how to survive.

DAURIO ¶ When you were writing *Sans Souci*, how much of a struggle was it not to become didactic?

BRAND § To be didactic is to be outside of it, to think of it as an object, rather than from the point of view of the subject. When you are inside it, it is complex, and each decision you make is important and dependent on a lot. To survive and not to go crazy, you must distinguish how much of what you are going to take today, but not tomorrow.

Because I was struck by the Little Black Sambo and god knows what other derogatory stereotypes I had to handle when I was growing up, I always thought that the way I would present and represent and articulate when I wrote, Black senses, if you like, would be in all their variousness. We had been struck as a piece of cardboard, just flat; my job as a writer was to express all of it, as complex and contradictory as it comes and goes, to address how I knew I lived, how I knew my grandmother lived, address the motivations, because Black characters in those things never had any motivations. In Tarzan movies there's no motivation, you just see all these Black people running after Tarzan. What for? In order to dehumanize people, you strip them of reason, of motivation. I wanted to draw us as we were.

DAURIO ¶ The stories have such different voices...

BRAND § I listen well and I try not to impose myself on the story so much. My imagination is not only my own and out of no place, it is what I know and saw and heard and felt. What I'm hoping and striving for is that each of the people that I'm writing about has an integrity— they wouldn't do weird things that are not part of that integrity, are not part of who they are.

DAURIO ¶ Were you consciously representing a whole range of different people?

BRAND § That probably chose me more than I chose it. I marvel at how people live. As somebody who has always been very cautious, and a watcher, since I was a kid, I'm just struck by the incredibleness of what they just told me... or lived.

DAURIO ¶ Your new book of poetry is called *No Language Is Neutral*. Why did you call it that?

BRAND § It's based on a line from Derek Walcott's *Midsummer.* "no language is neutral/ the green oak of English is a murmurous cathedral/ where some take umbrage and some take peace/ but all help to widen its shade." Walcott and I come from different generations and different genders; that English language that he wants to claim is not the same one that I want to claim. The one that I want contains the resistances to how that language was made, because that language was made through imperialism, through the oppression of women. As women and as peoples of colour we write against that language. The more power we acquire to speak and act and so on, the more we change that language. I write to say something about the world. That language that I encounter as a response to me in the world is no more neutral than mine to it.

DAURIO ¶ The book really reads, not as a collection of separate poems, but as a unified structure. Did you set out to write it as one piece?

BRAND § The poem "No Language Is Neutral" I set out to write as one piece, and it kept getting bigger and bigger. Then some other piece would come up in something else that I was writing, and I'd say, oh, that piece doesn't belong here, it belongs somewhere else, and so on.

It's difficult to talk about poetry, because what I'm asking myself to do now is to summarize perfect speech, and it's not possible.

DAURIO ¶ It's hard asking specific questions about the book, too; you can't take a little piece, because the elements of it are so interwoven.

BRAND § *No Language Is Neutral* was like a journey. It was like a memory of when language became possible, changed, through that experience of colonization. So the poem starts somewhere back then— about how a people, if they got transported to an incredibly distant place, where they no longer had names for things, how they began to name anything, how they began to say anything, and how, faced with incredible brutality, how did they not refuse to say, and what did they say of it, and so there's an image somewhere in the poem of standing near the sea and looking out into great possibility, but endless hopelessness, too.

What did they send down to me? All of the words that we learn from them contain escape and freedom and things like that. "A morphology of rolling chain and copper gong" refers to enslavement; those things now shape our talk. And that's what I mean in a sense by the whole poem, that "falsettos of whip and air/ rudiment this grammar"; this grammar; there's a new talk, a new grammar, a new language, being made in this.

There was no other way of saying it, but falling into dialect and showing how the relations of slavery, of brutality, but also of silence, of distance, of loss, begin to shape the language that I speak. My great-great-great-great-great-grandmother and -grandfather made that language, they passed it and passed it, and I've been making it. Within that language, it's not just questions of race for me, but questions of gender. What was there for my great-great-grandmother between the ocean and the sink? How did that shape what she said? And how did what she didn't say about being a woman shape it, too?

DAURIO ¶ In the first part of "Hard Against the Soul," you say: "this is you girl... this is where you make sense... and to be awake is more lovely than dreams..." which implies that being asleep sure as hell isn't...

BRAND § Ordinarily, people think fantasy is more interesting. I guess I find reality more interesting. That poem is about more than my first lover, but it is about recognizing I was a lesbian, and *why*, somehow. I looked at ocean and earth, and I thought, that's right, I love *that*, and that's why I love *that*. There's something about the fecundity of it, the richness, that somehow verified my love for women. To know this was really startling, and also to come to a kind of completion. We live in a world that doesn't love women, a world that doesn't like women, and I suddenly faced the possibility of having to live that out.

As women loving each other we didn't need to lie to each other, because we couldn't, and there could be no heterosexual fantasy, not for us, and there is no lesbian fantasy; you've got to make whatever you're going to have. The real was more wonderful than anything. It was great to be awake, to be walking up and down the street, to be suddenly solid. For me, it just was.

DAURIO ¶ The first section is followed by a section called "Return," which contains poems about particular women, political women. How are they related to the rest of the poem?

BRAND § At one time I admired those two women greatly, and still do at certain levels. Phyllis Coarde was the Minister of Women's Affairs in Grenada. She had been part of the coup, and is in jail now. I looked at them in that revolution, in that struggle, as very strong and capable women who were finally realizing the dreams of women, in a way.

DAURIO ¶ Aging, for women, is also a political issue, which you address, among other places, in the poem about Mammy Prater.

BRAND § I've always liked old ladies, because they lasted. It must take a hell of a lot for a woman to grow old in this society, with all the discrimination against women, all the taking care of the world that you do. That's part of my culture, too, that when you grow old you gain respect.

When I was about eight years old I saw this woman sitting on the beach naked, throwing water over her head and bathing herself, and I remember at first going by her, and suddenly looking back and thinking, she's naked, you know, and smiling to myself. And later, I thought, what freedom, she finally made it. She had earned the right not to be looked at in a certain way. It was in my mind, earning that right some day. The poem did come out of looking at a photograph of a woman one hundred and fifteen years old, and thinking of all that was in her shape, all the days and days and days and days of waiting to sit there, for the photograph... and while being enslaved, never allowing that slavery make her not wait for the day when it was over. That old woman had endured.

DAURIO ¶ The general structure of the book is very interesting. "Hard Against the Soul" begins before the section called "No Language Is Neutral," and ends after it, but it does more than begin and end the book; it wraps around it.

BRAND § I wanted to come back to "Hard Against the Soul," because there was something I had begun to say that didn't work itself out. I usually write in blocks, and I needed to say the rest. I needed to fully come out as a lesbian; I needed to say what that did in terms of how I was going to speak now as a poet. Much of my work before didn't deal with sexuality as politics; somehow I've gotten a deeper, more honest sense of myself since coming out. The other thing is, I never write until it is time to write. I suppose I could have dashed off a few love poems here and there, but until the thing can be said properly, and I hope it is said properly, I don't think it should be said.

DAURIO ¶ You are not of the school that says write reams and reams no matter what...

BRAND § No. I write purposefully. I really plod. It was time to say those things, and I became free when I said them, suddenly thinking that revelation is not bad, that in fact it's kind of freeing.

DAURIO ¶ *No Language Is Neutral* talks about language, race, women, the ocean, slavery, freedom; it creates an incredible synthesis, and at the same time, makes the reader trust in words to make a difference...

BRAND § In each piece of work that I write, I really want to own the world. Not as an imperialist, but as somebody who can speak of it and through it and for it. The poem tries to reveal all the parts of me, whether it's the Black me or the lesbian me or the woman me or the... and to say that it is possible for us to live this way, to talk in this way.

DAURIO ¶ The woman that you address in the poem, the "you," is also a complex/simple construction: it's you in the past and you in the future, it's the reader, it's history, it's even the future.

BRAND § When I was writing this, as when I first read *One Hundred Years of Solitude*, I realized you could write anything. There's a moment for lots of writers when you realize: *I can put anything into words.* The "you" that I talk to all the time is a way of coming immediately to your chest; it says it is you that I am talking to, it jumps across the possibility of being ignored, across the possibility of your saying that we do not know each other.

And the you is sort of historical. One of the poems is about going to the Museum of the Revolution in Cuba. Suddenly I was looking at this goddamned coffle, this iron cuff that was used in slavery. It was maybe two hundred years old, and yet it looked so dangerous, and I was scared, as if it was that day. I thought I should run from the room, or stand watching it, I didn't know which one to do. That's the history I address personally.

DAURIO ¶ In its rhythm of mood, emotion, and place, *No Language Is Neutral* has the time feeling, the structure of a novel.

BRAND § Writing it, I knew there was a tension I had to sustain, so that you'd be with me through it. I hope there's not a wasted word. Whatever emotions I moved to in it had to be precise, tight; taking the exact amount of time and the exact pitch, so that from the beginning to the end you're still there.

DAURIO ¶ What is your next project?

BRAND § *The Lives of Black Working Women in Ontario*, the oral history, that's going to be a book. And I have a long story I want to write, about a woman who lives here illegally and has about twelve lives...

Patriarchal Mothers

NICOLE BROSSARD
by Beverley Daurio

NICOLE BROSSARD has published more than twenty books of poetry, fiction, and theoretical writing, and has been translated widely. Her books include *Picture Theory, Surfaces of Sense, These Our Mothers*, and *Lovhers*. A founding editor of the seminal Quebec literary magazines *Barre du Jour* and *Nouvelle Barre du Jour*, she has twice won the Governor General's award for poetry. Nicole Brossard is a leading theorist in feminist literature, and released *She Would Be the First Sentence of My Next Novel* in 1998. Her most recent novels are *Mauve Desert* and *Baroque at Dawn* (both McClelland and Stewart).

DAURIO ¶ Among others, you have often referred to Djuna Barnes and Gertrude Stein in your work. Who else has influenced your writing, and who do you think people should be reading?

BROSSARD § I make a distinction between people who have influenced you and people who are accompanying you in the writing. In the beginning when you are writing, you are much more impressed by other texts. For me, the main influences were Mallarmé, Maurice Blanchot, and then, in terms of women's writing, when I was much older: Adrienne Rich in her feminist essays; Mary Daly; Ti-Grace Atkinson and Kate Millet were important to me at the time that I read them; Clarice Lispector, a Brazilian writer who is stimulating and exciting.

DAURIO ¶ It has been twenty-five years since your first book of poetry, *Aube à la saison*, came out. What have been the major changes in your approach to writing during that time?

BROSSARD § You can see Nicole Brossard in my first two books, but as with most first books, especially if the writer is twenty or twenty-one when they are written, you don't know exactly who you are, and therefore you assimilate influences, sometimes quite well; you are only beginning to design your own individuality or style. With the third book I tried to be more Nicole Brossard the way people have read me for a long time, until 1973-74, when, with *These Our Mothers*, there was a shift in the writing because of a shift in feminist consciousness and the lesbian experience. After *Picture Theory* came a novel like *Mauve Desert*, which is again very different. If I try to be objective, I think that my writing has become more lyrical. In my new book of poetry, *Installations*, the poems have many layers of meaning, but you can understand them on first reading. Superficially, the writing seems more linear, but the questioning remains: about writing, value, philosophical questions.

DAURIO ¶ In her introduction to *Lovhers*, Barbara Godard said the subtitle of *These Our Mothers*, "The Disintegrating Chapter," "points to the effect this feminist fiction has in dissolving the authority of the male tradition of the book." How large a part of your writing project is that dissolution? Or are you more interested in building a new vision?

BROSSARD § In feminist writing, it has to be both. You have to write two kinds of pages almost at the same time: one on which you try to understand and uncover the patriarchal lies; and another on which you try to give your new values, your utopias, and everything you find positive about yourself and about women. You have to write an unedited version, something that is totally new, to shape it. You bring in thoughts that have never been thought, use words in ways they have never been used. You want to bring your anger but also your utopia and your connection and solidarity with other women.

DAURIO ¶ For me, reading *Le Sens apparent* was like having my skin removed and entering another woman's body, seeing and experiencing without those usual signposts of narrative. You have spoken elsewhere about the lack of outer reality which confirms women in their experiences; was part of the intention in writing this book the desire to chart an inner and recognizable reality for women?

BROSSARD § I don't know if there was any specific project when I wrote *Le Sens apparent*, as you would find in *Picture Theory* or even *Mauve Desert*. I wanted to fall in love and so I had to write a book. In society we think that things have clear meanings, but things aren't clear for women, because we haven't produced that reality; it is only an appearance. The work of the writer is to dig at those appearances and into the real meaning of what we experience in a strong and sometimes frustrating way.

DAURIO ¶ One of the most profoundly interesting aspects of your work is the way in which theory and emotion, wildness and discipline, randomness and intellectual concentration intersect in it. In part, this has meant vast violence to the distinctions between poetry, fiction, and theory. Was this intentional or is this just the way it worked out?

BROSSARD § I cannot think properly or deeply if emotion is not there in the thought itself. At the same time, I wouldn't want to just express emotion, because I know that I wouldn't be able to visualize and envision things I am writing about. I don't think it's an intention; it's a necessity. There are two sides here: I have always loved science, discipline, order, but also the imagination, ecstasy.

DAURIO ¶ Do you think theory has become more important in feminist and lesbian writing because of the whole project of making new visions?

BROSSARD § It is the theory that I make which interests me; of outside theory, I will only take the parts that stimulate me. I do not follow any theory; there would be no point in writing fiction if you were just a civil servant. For me, theory is a way of being able to mentally visualize and to read the patterns of the way people relate in life, patterns in creative work, patterns of rain or snow. Theory has true value when it comes from the subjectivity of someone who values awareness in movement.

DAURIO ¶ In *The Aerial Letter*, you wrote: "Reality has been for most women a fiction, and women's reality has been perceived as fiction." This seems to pose an incredible paradox for writing for women.

BROSSARD § The reality we live in is fictional for women because it is only the fantasy of men throughout history who have transformed their subjectivity into laws, religion, culture, and so on. Nobody believes what women live in their reality, whether it is about motherhood or rape or incest, good *or* bad things. What women were experiencing or saying was always understood as a result of "she fantasizes," whereas men's fantasies are there and are supposed to be the reality, in architecture and everywhere. Women's perspective is a territory which has not yet been mapped. We are the only ones who can do it, but sometimes we don't have the appropriate words. The words which were available would always push us back into madness or fantasy. The way we think when no-one knows about it is called "fiction," but when everybody agrees, it is called reality. In terms of women's texts, all the doors are open. Memory is one of the things we have to use, and it explains a lot about the way we go from narrative to prose to poetry. Women's memory is very loaded with narratives which have not been told, and it is important to tell those stories no-one wanted to tell or hear. Poetry is inner certitude, but without narrative yet, before narrative. Out of each verse you could start a novel.

DAURIO ¶ You have said: "The origin is not the mother, but the sense I make of words." What did you mean by that?

BROSSARD § That relates to the virtuality of the creative potential in each of us. It's too late to go to mythology. I can't believe in god so I can't believe in a goddess, either. Most of our mothers were very traditional, patriarchal mothers, so we cannot go to that concrete origin in real life. Maybe this generation of writers can become symbolic mothers to another generation; and if we are not patriarchal mothers, maybe we can have a continuity.

DAURIO ¶ Does that mean you are disappointed in the women of the past?

BROSSARD § I don't know what to do with the word "disappointed." We all know the pressure that the women of the past were under, the intimidation, the fact that they were deprived of many things. The process of fictionalizing the heroine, that is where you can envision a process of validation of women, whoever they are. One of the problems of feminism is that we are moral: we don't belittle men, and we don't overestimate women. So it's hard to create a validating mythology.

DAURIO ¶ Your novel *Mauve Desert* is set in Arizona. Have you ever spent time in the desert?

BROSSARD § I wanted the book to take place in a North American desert, and that is the desert where they exploded the first nuclear bomb. It is a place where you can find high technology and also the greatest decadence: extremely rich people and extremely poor people. The desert is important as a symbol of highly spiritual life; and it is also a place of death, where everything can be dangerous. It is a place where life has to find very tricky ways to survive, and it's very beautiful how nature finds ways to remain alive. The horizon has always been important for me. I like open spaces, and the horizon is always open. It can be frightening, because we don't know where it ends, but you can project on it whatever you want.

DAURIO ¶ *Mauve Desert* is a mystery, in some senses, and it is written in three parts: first, "Mauve Desert," the short novel by Laure Angstelle about fifteen-year-old Mélanie Kerouac; second, a section written through the eyes of the older Maude Laures, who is obsessed with Laure's text; and the third, which is Maude's homolinguistic translation of "Mauve Desert," "Mauve Horizon." This structure gives the feeling of a book that has been expertly taken apart and surgically reassembled, so that all the parts can be examined. Do you think that's a valid way of looking at it?

BROSSARD § I knew that I would be writing a novel set in a very hot place. I knew that I would like to have that challenge of translating myself from French to French. I wrote the first section, Laure's novel, and then I asked myself, as the fictional translator of "Mauve Desert," *what do you find in a novel?* You find characters, you find objects, you find ideas, you find dialogue. And so I wrote those things, but in a different order. I liked the way the translator started to imagine those characters, to try to visualize the faces, the bodies, how they moved, the places and the people; and, in fact, Maude, as translator, does what we normally do as readers. I also enjoyed imagining the dialogue. I didn't know I could write dialogue. I didn't talk about anecdotal things, I went to the heart of the relationship between the daughter and the mother, between the two women lovers, between the the translator and the author. In Maude's conversation with Angela Parkins, Angela wants to know why the author is killing her. The author replies, *I'm not killing you, he's killing you.* The ending seems very surprising, even gratuitous, but it's exactly what happened at the École Polytechnique, it's exactly the same kind of hatred. So I haven't imagined anything, I have only decoded a pattern which does not explode all the time, but which is there all the time. In the book, the act comes from a physicist, a man of knowledge, who's got everything; in our society he's "the perfect guy."

DAURIO ¶ Is it possible now to write a more traditional book, as in *Mauve Desert*, and have it carry the weight of feminist and lesbian ideas, without it having to be so radical in the way the language works?

BROSSARD § Writing *Mauve Desert*, sometimes I would pretend I didn't have the kind of knowledge that I have, because I needed that kind of innocence to go on with the characters and make them alive. If I, as the writer, knew everything, then I could not have created the characters. There are many things that I know because of the difficult work of *These Our Mothers*, of *Picture Theory*, and of *The Aerial Letter*, difficult work that you pay for. If you look at things from a lesbian and feminist point of view, reality has no more meaning, because we are not part of that meaning in the symbolic. It's as if you have to do the whole world again. So you have to be careful. There's a limit where you don't know if you are making sense.

DAURIO ¶ What do you mean by "pay for?"

BROSSARD § Some books that you write cost you more than others. Some books I have written in cold blood, some books I have written with tears in my eyes... but the result is not that one book is better than another. The price you pay is in terms of psychological energy, emotive energy, mental energy, intellectual energy. The more difficult questions call for more energy at all levels.

DAURIO ¶ Laure Angstelle's version of "Mauve Desert" seems younger and more fiery than Maude's, which is more fine-tuned and optimistic. Is the second version of that text there only because of Maude's obsession with it, or is it also there in order to provide a more mature version of the first text?

BROSSARD § The second version, the translation, is the result of the crafting of the first text. In the first version I found myself being very passionate; in the second version I had to craft very carefully. It was a different rapport with words; I could not choose or let myself go because I had to check on the sentences in the first version. In the middle section, where Maude Laures is re-imagining the characters and so on, I had a lot of freedom, because I was still inventing through the information I got in the first book, where very little had been said about the characters and spaces. That explains why the third part is less fiery but more precise, because I was also considering the structure of the whole book. I had to be very properly attuned to everything that was going on, each word and each sentence. Writing the third section— because I was not learning more, though I was learning the pleasure of crafting new sentences— I remember, I said, Nicole, you'd better go along and go through that whole project; otherwise, I'm not talking to you any more.

A Narrative of Echoes

CAROLE CORBEIL
by Barbara Carey

CAROLE CORBEIL is a Toronto writer who was born and raised in Montreal. As a journalist, she has written extensively on the arts for the *Globe and Mail*, where she was a staff writer and columnist, and for *Saturday Night, This Magazine, Toronto Life* and *Canadian Art*, among others. Her short fiction has appeared in the anthologies *Cold City Fiction* and *Frictions*. Her first novel was *Voice-over*, and she has since published *In the Wings*, a novel that explores theatre.

BARBARA CAREY ¶ Your first novel, *Voice-over*, is a bestseller, and has enjoyed widespread critical acclaim, so in a way it's become a very public book. But on an emotional level, it feels like a very private book, which is why I think a lot of readers are drawn to it. Is there a sense in which you've had to let go of what it means to you personally? Do you look at it differently in the light of other people's reactions?

CAROLE CORBEIL § I would say that my relationship with the book has been quite transformed by the positive reception it's received. It's the fact of being understood— some of the reviews have been so perceptive and insightful— that's so surprising and wonderful. I had a lot of fear about it going out into the world. But because the experience didn't turn out to be fearful at all means that I can let the book go.

CAREY ¶ How does that prepare you in terms of what you're working on now?

CORBEIL § There are two sides to it. One that I find very hopeful, and has been part of what women have been doing in literature, is that when you throw light on something or illuminate dark corners, things actually do get better. So to have that experience confirmed— that this is an okay thing to do— is really encouraging. Another good thing is to be recognized as the writer of a novel, because coming from a journalistic background, I felt insecure about whether I could do it. So that validation is important to me. At first I thought I wouldn't be able to write in this vein again, but actually I'm discovering that there are a lot more dark corners in me...[laughter]

CAREY ¶ Don't you think it's the dark corners that are the most intense and the ones writers most want to explore? Also the ones that readers connect with.

CORBEIL § I've always felt that if I was going to write fiction, I wanted to write the kind of fiction that would relieve people of their loneliness. That's why I read fiction from an early age. I felt that I was surrounded by lies, and here was a place where I could find truth. Here was a place where some of what I felt and thought was actually set down, so I wasn't alone.

CAREY ¶ Structurally, *Voice-over* goes back and forth in time, and switches in focus from the story of the mother, Odette, to the daughters, Claudine and Janine. This allows the reader to pick up on patterns in how the central characters relate; as one reviewer put it, "how pain is transferred from one generation to the next" in the family. Did you actually write it that way, or did you chronologically follow the path of each character separately? How did it unfold?

CORBEIL § That's really a two-part question, because there's the actual process of writing and then what the book becomes through editing. When I first started, it was with little bits and snippets of memories.

CAREY ¶ So it wasn't associated with character at all?

CORBEIL § No, not initially. Then I started to write present-day material from Claudine's point of view. Well, not present-day, exactly; I set the contemporary sections in the summer of 1984, the summer before Brian Mulroney got elected. Anyway, the moment I started writing from Claudine's point of view I got all wound up in a ball about it, because I also wanted to write from the point of view of the other women— the mother, Odette, and the sister, Janine. And I just did. But I berated myself throughout this process, because I had in mind that it would never work, that the book had to be from a single point of view and it had to have a conventional narrative arc of moving forward. But everything wanted to go *backwards*, and it was impossible for me to privilege just one character. I had a lot of critical voices in my head about this, many of which I projected onto what I imagined as male literary conventions; you know, a fictional journey from one point of view with a major conflict and resolution at the end. I had trouble inventing a model for myself. And I was always fighting my own organic structure for the book. I think that's why I made the character of Colin a writer— I had to give voice to the conventions that were bothering me. I came to the title *Voice-over* after discarding many things, but the idea that we carry critical, judgemental voices inside us and that we have to look at where they come from is important to me.

CAREY ¶ Were there voices or characters you found easier to write than others?

CORBEIL § There were scenes that I would say came straight from the unconscious, that really did just flow out. The writing about language came out like that— practically nothing changed in that passage, which I wrote in a gush. But I was always struggling with the tension between those "gushes," which were unconscious, so to speak, and creating for the reader a concrete world. I would say that I wrote with a sense of discovery— I didn't know where I was going. In a way it mimics the therapeutic process. Once I became conscious of the direction, then I could create a structure that reflected how things were like boxes within boxes. So I could play around consciously with what I had brought forth unconsciously. In terms of the process, I wrote a lot of stuff in between, probably one or two thousand pages of material, most of it poems, some of it dreams, some of it more memories, some of it complete flights of fancy. But they were always written to get to something else in the book.

CAREY ¶ What you're describing reminds me of Virginia Woolf's comment that she wrote *The Waves* "to a rhythm, not to a plot."

CORBEIL § Yes, that's it exactly, to a rhythm, but I was also conscious of linking sections through sensual and visual details so that the past and present are experienced as layers, not as a linear progression. So the narrative, such as it is, is a narrative of echoes, of links between past and present, and of the unconscious links between mothers and daughters.

CAREY ¶ Do you find that what you're working on now is following the same process?

CORBEIL § Yes. I have an idea of what the overall structure is going to be and the time periods that it's going to cover, but I'm not writing beginning to end. I've just now written the beginning, and I've already written many, many scenes that I know will occur later on. But it's the material itself that has dictated what the structure is going to be. I said to myself after writing *Voice-over* that I would never do that again. There are novelists who dream up an entire novel in a year or two and then just write it. And I thought, oh, that's a really good way. [laughter] But if I know where I'm going, I'm bored. It's got to be about discovery, at least for me.

CAREY ¶ One reason the book has hit home with a lot of readers is that it deals so vividly with French-English cultural conflict. When Odette remarries, to a wealthy Westmount executive, there's a struggle that takes place at the level of language. For Claudine, French is the language of emotion, while English is "a steamroller of a language." In effect, she experiences the "voice-over" of English dominating the French. Did you feel that, too, when you were growing up?

CORBEIL § When I was learning English, I was desperate to learn it as a way of defending myself. It was a mode of defence because I went to an English school when I was fourteen, so I was very vulnerable, as all teenagers are, to the opinion of peers. To not get the language and the pronunciation right was a source of shame to me. So there was a real drive to get it right. As I got older— I went to schools in England, to English university— it lingered in me, and it still lingers in me now, as I speak to you, that I'm not speaking properly.

CAREY ¶ So in other words you're not at home in English. Are you at home in French?

CORBEIL § No, I'm not as sophisticated in French as I am in English now, in terms of expressing ideas. But I think over the years I developed a myth that not everything was available to me, in terms of feelings and colours and memories, because they were locked in another language. That has been a really big operative myth in my life. It's almost a myth of loss— you're never going to have what you had, it's not possible. Because of that myth, I had quite a lot of despair about whether I could write fiction, because to me fiction is not really the province of the intellect but of feelings and the sensual world. So writing the book was disproving that myth, in the sense that I could write in English, with some French touchstones, about all kinds of strong, vivid, intense things.

CAREY ¶ I grew up in English, but I still strongly feel the inadequacy of language. I wonder if everybody has that sense of loss?

CORBEIL § Yes, I think that everyone has a sense of paradise lost, the question of language aside. You know, some of the material I wrote, out of those thousands of pages, were actually in baby language, nonsensical. And I did exercises, writing on huge pieces of paper in huge letters, and doing that brought back memories of having to constrict the movement of my hand to write between lines in school copybooks. It was very interesting— and physically liberating— to play around with that.

CAREY ¶ There's a sense in which we've forgotten that writing is a *physical* act. It's not as physical as, say, painting, which I know you do, but it's still an act of the body.

CORBEIL § Yes, it's making a real mark. And in school, when I was growing up, it was about the way the writing looked, and the frustration of not having the motor skills to do it right. In school I also experienced writing as a mode of expression that's all about getting approval from others. It became associated with getting the right answers. But we're always dealing with these constrictions. Dancers, for instance, explore the ways in which the space around them has been constricted; and I think that for women, many of those space constrictions— the amount of room we're supposed to take up— have to do with gender expectations. There are a lot of things in our society that conspire to make us smaller than we are.

CAREY ¶ What about visuals— did you do drawings in the process of writing the book?

CORBEIL § I did a lot of drawing, in charcoal and pastels, and I'd mix words up in the drawings. And I did self-portraits and a lot of abstract compositions. The most wonderful thing about doing that kind of work is that you're doing it completely for yourself. It's about discovering and just letting go, and trusting what wants to come out. I needed to do that. I think that years of working as a journalist, and using writing in a particular way, had formed certain habits that I needed to break, because to me they were about controlling words, controlling personae, controlling an argument...which I really wanted to break out of.

CAREY ¶ Most reviewers have picked up on the theme of how important language is in giving people a sense of identity. But one of the things I found most affecting was the way that images played a role in that, too. Odette, in particular, always relates to some kind of model of feminine behaviour— the self-sacrificing mother, say, or the romantic ideal of film stars such as Marilyn Monroe or Joan Crawford. And of course the adult Claudine is a filmmaker, so she's manipulating images, too. The book seems to be suggesting that women have to struggle against images that are essentially male fantasies.

CORBEIL § Definitely. Unfortunately, it's a huge task in our society, because when you're born a woman, you're dealing with projections of what is female all over the place. And I'm not talking just about sexual projections, but all the other fantasies that have to do with ideals in terms of looks and behaviour. And they cause women tremendous distress, because we end up internalizing them and measuring ourselves against impossible ideals. But there are reasons why someone like Odette is more vulnerable to those free-floating cultural fantasies, reasons quite apart from the time period in which she lived. She's susceptible to fantasy because her sense of self is seriously damaged. And I think people whose sense of self has been damaged are very vulnerable to fantasies. It's a way of escaping, of self-aggrandizing, of existing outside yourself.

CAREY ¶ It's doubly ironic in Odette's case because here's this woman who's French, and yet she's dominated by Hollywood ideals.

CORBEIL § Yes, that was very important to me because the American influence in Quebec was so strong when I was growing up. It's always struck me— you're borrowing fantasies that aren't even from your own culture. Which is very Canadian, in a way, but which happens to every culture living in the shadow of Hollywood. I remember reading an interview with the Filipino filmmaker Lino Broca, who said that when he watched Esther Williams movies when he was young, he thought all Americans could breathe underwater!

In terms of Claudine, Odette's daughter, I always saw her drive as a documentary film-maker as the drive to make conscious what was unconscious in her mother. That's why Claudine is obsessed with the kind of subjects she's obsessed with.

CAREY ¶ Yes, but when you're the one behind the camera, you have a detachment. So it seemed to me, though she was acknowledging this pain by focusing on it, she was denying it at the same time by stepping back from it.

CORBEIL § Yes, it's two sides of the same coin. The mother, as a model, lived in front of the camera, and the daughter ends up behind the camera. And part of what I was thinking about was that it's not enough to have control of the camera, as the daughter does. At one point Claudine says she wants to be equal with Colin, "equal meaning the same." There was a time period in my life, and I think in many women's lives, maybe in your late twenties, early thirties, when you have some kind of power, and you want to do exactly what men are doing and do it better or whatever. This is a time when you can "pass" as a man. Having a child, getting older, tips the balance, somehow, and that's why women get more radical— and not less so— as they get older. Anyway, this time period interests me as a kind of putative stage, when you can take the means of production, so to speak, but not go that much further with it.

CAREY ¶ So that's why Claudine has reached an impasse with her filmmaking? She realizes that it isn't enough?

CORBEIL § Yes. That summer, all the characters are at the point in their lives when they've exhausted their old ways of being. But Claudine also ended up doing that kind of work because she had witnessed very intense things in her life. She was obviously in the habit of being the voyeur in a situation. I think of her very much as the kind of person who watches, has reactions, then discounts those reactions so she can keep watching, because that's the mode of being that she's comfortable with. Her relationship with Colin was very much like that— she's a voyeur of her own relationship.

CAREY ¶ One reviewer commented in passing that the book doesn't resolve the problems it sets up. But it seems to me that to expect a tidy wrap-up of such complex issues is a bit unfair. It's like wanting a contrived resolution.

CORBEIL § If I remember the context of that right, it was something about the French-English question. I really thought the comment was sort of a rhetorical flourish. We've spent years, there are still constitutional debates going on, and who's at the table and who's under the table and who's distinct and who's not... It's an endless thing. I couldn't possibly resolve that.

CAREY ¶ I think the underlying implication is that we read fiction that speaks to things we care about, and expect it to give answers. But that doesn't seem like a realistic expectation to me.

CORBEIL § It's not a realistic expectation of how life works, never mind fiction. [laughter] There are things that can be resolved, but it's a very long process. In fiction you can shorten that, but it's never "the end." Margaret Atwood said to me about the ending of a book that you can't have resolution, but you can have insight. I get really resentful when I read a book that leads me to a too-easy resolution— I feel that's part of the lie, that's part of the fantasy. Especially in this case, when I'm dealing with, for instance, the issue of sexual abuse. The remembering of it is only the beginning of the healing process. And it would be such a horrible thing to indicate to thousands of women who have been sexually abused that overnight, because you remember it, you're fine.

CAREY ¶ Bronwen Wallace wrote in a story that, "You never really get over anything, you just learn to carry it more gently."

CORBEIL § I think you don't get over it, but you can come to terms with it to the extent that it no longer dominates your life. But it will always be a part of your history. And there is a down side and an up side to that. If it no longer dominates, then you can experience the up side, which is that history has given you certain things, *if* you've survived it: certain understandings, certain depths of feeling and compassion. In terms of resolution, what surfaces in the last scene of the book is a bit of truth between the sisters. Again, to me, that's a beginning. When truths are spoken, as opposed to being masked, something can move forward. But it's not the end of the story. To me the whole book is about struggling to become conscious, and the characters are just beginning when the novel ends.

CAREY ¶ Is there anything that reviewers haven't picked up on yet that you feel is important?

CORBEIL § Something that I feel strongly about, though I don't mind that it hasn't been picked up on, is that between women who have shared families— mothers and sisters— there are incredible psychic connections, and when one person becomes aware of certain things I think it has an effect on the others, whether this awareness is spoken or not. And one of the things I've felt, almost as a task that we all have, is to be able to see our mothers as human beings and how very, very difficult that can be. To see them not just in terms of ourselves, but as having had lives with pressures and conditions and conditioning, and dramas and stresses that have nothing to do with us, but have had an impact on us.

CAREY ¶ I know people have reacted personally to the book. Has there been any particular incident that's had an effect on you?

CORBEIL § What I'm really surprised at— because to me it was such a painful book to write and there's so much pain in it— is how people connect with it. The response I expected to get was, *these people are really fucked up*, and *who wants to hear about it?*

CAREY ¶ I think there's an emotional honesty to the book that appeals to readers; they identify with the struggle of the characters.

CORBEIL § That's the thing. To me, they're really struggling and they're really brave, in an odd way. They're not numb or shut down completely. I think you find that in everybody's story— how amazing it is that they survived certain things and have been able to create a life.

CAREY ¶ Do you feel you've learned anything from writing this book?

CORBEIL § I've learned a lot. One thing that fiction taught me was the necessity to love; that it's impossible to sustain a book with anger or revenge or hatred. And that if you want your characters to live, you have to learn to love them. When you're dealing with very personal material, the act of writing fiction is a gift in itself, because it shows you that when something isn't working it's because you haven't embraced it totally, you're judging it or putting yourself above it. For me, it only works when I'm fully compassionate and open and kind of in love with foibles rather than being impatient. That comes through in the process of writing and rewriting and rewriting. You get very intimate with your characters, but they're also part of yourself, so you're getting more accepting of parts of yourself. That meant a lot to me.

The Whole Lake Beneath

TIMOTHY FINDLEY
by Jeffrey Canton

TIMOTHY FINDLEY is the author of seven novels: *The Last of the Crazy People, The Butterfly Plague, The Wars,* which won the Governor General's award for fiction in 1977, *Famous Last Words, Not Wanted on the Voyage,* and *The Telling of Lies,* and *Headhunter.* He has also published two collections of short fiction, *Dinner Along the Amazon* (1984), and *Stones* (1988), and the memoir, *Inside Memory* (1990). He has performed and written for radio, television, and the stage. Timothy Findley shares Stone Orchard (near Cannington, Ontario) with his long-time companion, Bill Whitehead.

JEFFREY CANTON ¶ I first heard you reading from *Headhunter* in the summer of 1991 at a benefit for *Out* magazine. You read a passage where a middle-aged man watches his three nieces swimming, from a window in the family cottage. But he's not just looking at them— he's raping them in his imagination. It's a difficult and disturbing book to read. Was it difficult to write?

TIMOTHY FINDLEY § I'm glad you used the word "disturbing" because, yes, it was very disturbing to write *Headhunter.* I've had to resist saying "No"— which may sound like a double negative— but I've had to literally say, "You must do this. This is how this must be." The section I read at Buddies in Bad Times in 1991 was an early foray— the first foray, incidentally, for me— into this kind of child abuse where you realize it isn't just sexual. It is the using of children utterly. It's like cannibalism.

I called this piece "The Lake of Manly Dreams," because it ends with the image that Benedict Webster, this middle-aged voyeur, has of these three girls, his young nieces, swimming— and wondering if they realize that the whole lake beneath them is full of men and boys yearning upwards towards them.

That reading that we did at Buddies— what an evening! I'm so admiring of what that place stands for and has done for all of us— it gave me the chance to take a chance. And afterwards I decided that it would go in the book, horrifying as it was. I began by writing some odd pieces here and there to see if I was capable of handling it. Because it isn't just that you are capable of writing it— but can you handle it?

CANTON ¶ This is a novel that begins with a fictional character, Kurtz from Conrad's *Heart of Darkness*, being conjured up in Toronto's Metropolitan Reference Library. Was there a specific impetus that got *Headhunter* going?

FINDLEY § As long ago as five years, I had been telling people that I wanted to explore the idea of *Heart of Darkness* set in Rosedale. And whoever I told would laugh and ask me what I meant. It might have sounded like a joke, but I was serious. I meant that I'd discovered a similar situation. I wanted to reverse the process. This was my early thinking.

If Marlow and Kurtz, in Conrad's *Heart of Darkness*, go into the darkness at the end of the last century, they go into the unexplored, into the true wilderness of whatever is going to be there— in the darkness that was then Africa, as far as European civilization was concerned. Because it was utterly unknown. But it had this other exotic quality that there was something there to be had. And of course, what we did, by taking civilization into that place, was reveal civilization for what, alas, it really is— a rapist, a headhunter.

And I wanted to reverse that. I wanted to have the river deliver Kurtz, and therefore Marlow, into the middle of what's become of that civilization— which for us is a place like Rosedale, with all its highfalutin' standards and ideals and pretensions. But pretensions founded on the basics of what truly civilized behaviour is. Griffin Price, in the novel, describes that Rosedale attitude— "More Torontonian than Torontonian."

Now I didn't know who Kurtz would be. I didn't know he'd be a psychiatrist. I just thought that this would be the basis for starting my exploration.

And in exactly the same way that hearing Phyllis Webb reading "Leaning" brought me Mottyl and the ark in *Not Wanted on the Voyage*, or Robert Ross in *The Wars* riding through the fog and into my hotel room— I had this revelation. That's the only way to describe it. Because all it is is just a sort of bang— and there's the image that captures you and pulls you in.

It was this odd little woman with her wisps of crazy hair, Lilah Kemp, and I knew she'd be schizophrenic. And I thought, Jesus Christ, she's a medium! A spiritualist. And she can raise the dead, and this is the unique aspect of her talent. She raises Kurtz out of the book without meaning to. And that was when the shivers ran down my back, and— kaboom!— the whole book was in place.

CANTON ¶ Who in this book would best represent what civilization should mean to us?

FINDLEY § Amy Wylie is truly civilized— if we have an ideal. I'm not sure that I love the word "civilization" any longer, but, in the sense of what it might have been, that's what Amy is. Marlow is forced to decide that Amy has to live with her demons in order to be who she is— a poet, an activist, and a paranoid schizophrenic.

This comes out of Jung. I've always worshipped his ideas a little. He was so open to having anything present itself as a possibility of what the human mind might contain and where it might go.

In the early part of this century, when he was still making his explorations— those explorations that drove the wedge between himself and Freud, and which got him into a lot of trouble but which were immensely courageous, he said— "Here is a patient who will perish if we bring her back, and the only way to give her back her life is to let her go into the magic of the disease, and that's what will sustain her and keep her alive." I'm paraphrasing, of course. But that's Amy Wylie. And more of us should go into the magic of our disease.

CANTON ¶ We are all a little mad, aren't we?

FINDLEY § I believe that madness and the imagination walk a fine line. Lilah describes it in the book as, "Like a journey made on a long narrow bridge—that's what it was. Tightrope walking. A high-wire balancing act, with your sanity perched on top of your head." I believe this. It's not something I can explain intellectually— it's like being a witness and you know this is true but maybe you cannot explain it to other people.

Take a figure like Hemingway, who ended his life in a state of mental collapse which led to his death. His death was a very deliberate and brave thing that he did, though "brave" does not adequately cover it. He was not, by the way, a man I admired, because of the destructive and macho elements of his personality. But it occurred to me, in one of those moments lying in bed when you can't sleep and drift into these areas— watching him in my mind— that he'd come to a moment where the artist had died inside him. Perhaps it was the drugging of his being, which was what the power trips were about— masking the fears that led to him staving off and driving people away. But when his art failed, his great creative gift, then he fell all the way into the darkness.

And then I made the connection. We are all schizophrenic. Those of us who write and paint, dance and act, we're the lucky ones. As long as we're sustained and have that outlet, we can craft it, use it, and hand it over— to make and create order out of it. It is the single-line direction that only the mad have. That's absolutely true.

CANTON ¶ But madness in *Headhunter* also has a horrific and violent aspect.

FINDLEY § It's there in all of us— all of that's in everybody! I don't think the violence that we meet in this book is "madness" or "insanity," but it is what should be called madness. It's that aspect of humanity that civilization attempts to control.

In Conrad's *Heart of Darkness*, it is demonstrated by what becomes of Kurtz— that he can put those heads up around his compound on poles, "because I can." It really can happen. All you have to do is realize that something that was held in check has broken free. And that is not madness— that is the human appetite for power, for *me* first. This whole business that started in Montreal in the 1950s— which is part of *The Telling of Lies*— backed by the CIA, to wipe out the mind in order to establish a new human being living inside a "previously constructed" and once-occupied human body... Is it any wonder that Nicholas Fagan chooses Frankenstein as the "subtext for the twentieth century"? This is what we do!

We had a young lad who worked here at Stone Orchard, and when he left school, he went into the army. And this quite wonderful, wild, and free-spirited young man, with his flying blond hair, came back in uniform with all his hair cut off— and Bill and I sat at the table with a Nazi! He didn't even talk the same! He told us with pride that he and two other guys had driven someone mad and broken someone else's leg. And this was all approved of in order to discover the man who can go to war and kill.

And in *Headhunter*, we've got this new drug and that new system— all those people sleeping in those honeycomb-like rooms in the sub-basements of the Parkin Institute of Psychiatric Research— and it's all true. Every bit of it is true.

CANTON ¶ "Kurtz is everywhere," one of the characters of this novel tells us. What is it in particular that makes him the horror-meister, the headhunter, in your novel?

FINDLEY § That's what I wanted to explore— who was giving these people permission to do this or that? "It was part of his scheme, his plan. He wanted to see what could be accomplished by giving what he called *permissions*. Let a psychosis have its way with a client— and see what the client would do in return for permissions having been given." Kurtz is the man who controls their heads.

CANTON ¶ How did you feel using Kurtz and Marlow as characters in your novel?

FINDLEY § You feel as if you're trespassing, so you want to be very careful what the trespass is about. Is this illegal entry justifiable and therefore defensible— in the sense of Daniel Ellsberg's breaking into the Pentagon, which changed history? But I was aware all the time that I was their guardian. And the last thing I wanted was to damage any of the characters who are brought from other books— like Jay Gatsby, Emma Bovary, Peter Rabbit— but I did want to extend them by bringing them into our light.

One of the other things that motivated this book was to answer a question I have gnawing away at me: why do we have these great explorations of human beings? Why do we have great paintings, if all that happens in their presence is breakdown, subterfuge, mean-spiritedness, violence, and destruction? It's like saying, "Fuck Off! Don't bother me with your ideas that we could actually amount to anything. Who is that going to be any good for?" It still makes me very angry.

And as these characters came out I tried to keep them recognizable. Emma was generated by the fact that there is the famous prostitute who rolls around Toronto in her big, white limousine, and that is her bordello. Now, I remembered that there was a scene in *Madame Bovary* where, towards the end of Emma's life, she is desperate for money, and with one of her lovers she drives around Rouen in a carriage making love for twenty-four hours. And we have this other great dreamer, Jay Gatsby, who should have led us somewhere— and what happens if the two great dreamers end up in each other's arms? The ending is still ghastly, as it ever was. But the point is that they are the people but refocused.

CANTON ¶ But Emma doesn't kill herself, and that is one of the moments in *Headhunter* where the reader feels that Timothy Findley is saying "Yes" to life.

FINDLEY § And we must go on saying "Yes!"

CANTON ¶ Like in E.M. Forster's *A Room with a View*.

FINDLEY § And Forster, who is one of my gods, too, lays that on the line in that seemingly otherwise gentle, genteel book. That is also in Joyce. And Thornton Wilder. That roaring "Yes!"

CANTON ¶ And "Yes" is the spirit, I think, of Nicholas Fagan— critic and storyteller extraordinaire— who has appeared before in your work. What made you conjure him up in *Headhunter*?

FINDLEY § I have always used him as a point of reference. He could say things about Kurtz and Marlow that I, Timothy Findley, could not say, because they would be unacceptable. And given his academic standing, and given his mode of exploration, his passion for literature, he could say these things. Then, slowly he became whole, and I realized he belonged in this book. But the interesting thing about Fagan is that he rises out of schizophrenia.

When my aunt was in her mid-teens, at a point where her schizophrenia was not yet apparent but was beginning to emerge, she started writing secretly, and Nicholas Fagan was the name she called herself. It was not until her thirties that her schizophrenia fully manifested itself and she was declared a lunatic. But Nicholas Fagan was her great-grandfather who came to Canada in the 1840s from Dublin and was in many ways a kind of literary figure who wrote in journals and things. Well, in turn, I seized on him as a sort of tribute to her. That's how he came into being.

CANTON ¶ I particularly enjoyed his vision of what's become of Canada: "My journey up the river made me think about what it was those others who came before us had in mind. They might be greatly surprised by what they found here today. And greatly dismayed, I fear... There is nothing here of what anyone proposed. There is little beauty left— but much ugliness. Little wilderness— but much emptiness. No explorers— but many exploiters. There is no art— no music— no literature— but only entertainment. And there is no philosophy. This that once was a living place for humankind has become their killing ground."

FINDLEY § It could only have been said by someone coming up the river, so to speak— although Fagan does come up the St. Lawrence by boat. And that was the gift of that character— there was someone who could look at all and everything with absolute objectivity. And that was necessary.

CANTON ¶ But Fagan's journey up the river, which takes us back to the Conrad novel and the image of the headhunter which the title of the novel reflects, is, at the same time, another journey. A journey into the human mind. And you, Timothy Findley, are taking this journey, too. You are a character in your own novel!

FINDLEY § What I wanted to explore is what Fabiana Holbach, the owner of a prestigious gallery in the novel, explores herself in an essay she writes for Kurtz. She uses Findley, and, later, Modigliani, Julian Slade, a fictional artist in the novel, and Alex Colville to explore her identity, to define herself: "I have a friend. He writes. Novels. Stories. Plays. He pokes and prods and listens and describes. After we've talked, he waltzes off with bits and pieces— a person's voice— a person's eyes— a person's fear. This doesn't mean that he knows who you are. Do you see what I'm saying? No one knows who you are."

As I looked at Fabiana and put her on the page, I was looking from my moment. So the person dictating the character is also in a moment or a mode that influences my cycle as writer, artist, maker. And when she says, "Who do you think is writing this?"— I love that. Because it isn't that it spins back to me, but through: to *whom* was Findley writing? And to *whom* was the person writing Findley? Who is making this moment— the person who sees the moment or the person who thinks it?

CANTON ¶ So who controls whom? Do you control the characters or do they control you?

FINDLEY § I remember that when I was writing *The Wars*, I couldn't make Robert Ross swear. I tried to put "fuck" in his mouth and it wouldn't come out. It simply wouldn't come out. Robert Ross wasn't a prude but he didn't employ foul language.

I'm Lilah— I'm the medium and I try to let her out through me. But the other aspect of it is— and this is very dangerous, not as a thought, but because people refuse to understand what you mean when you say what I'm about to say— characters are themselves. And I don't know what that means, Jeff. I only know that, as you perceive them, they are them. You are using yourself and drawing on whatever is in there to draw on. Giving them access to as much as you possibly can. When the question is asked— who do you think is writing this?— the first person it spins back to is the character himself or herself. Fabiana put that question on the page. But the first person it elicits is Findley.

CANTON ¶ That seems to me the point that Fagan makes in his final comment on *Heart of Darkness*: "Every Kurtz must have his Marlow— and Marlow will always come to take Kurtz home. It is a mark of our respect for those who lead us into darkness that we bring them back for burial, pay their debts and console their loved ones with lies. This process is played out over and over— and with every journey up the river, we discover that Kurtz has penetrated just a little farther than his counterparts before him. Poor old Marlow! Every time he heads upstream, he is obliged to a longer journey through darker mysteries. Well, we might wonder, why does he always agree to go? For myself, I would guess it is because he is beholden to Kurtz for having provided him, after darkness, with a way to find new light."

Earlier you questioned the value of literature. Do you see literature as relevant to your own life? Can it help us, as individuals, order the world?

FINDLEY § My next novel is about a writer— not in the classic sense— but about a writer's life, and that is one of the questions. Your question has started speaking into the next book. It's about a guy at the end of his life— Who have I been?— and nothing comes of it. This is only the vaguest sketch of where I'm at. And it goes back to what I was saying about Hemingway, which is also about Virginia Woolf and Jane Austen— God knows what happened to her as she lay dying at that dreadfully early age— and Emily Brontë.

What was it all about? When you pass out of who you are, which is what you manifest, not what you do. And as you were asking that question, I was thinking about its implications: what does the literary imagination offer the future? I had a vision of people in the twenty-first century, who will have been who we were and they will be mad. We're shutting the imagination away. Which is just about all I know about that next novel so far.

The motive for being alive is to articulate what's wrong out there. And no one is interested. That's the excessively negative answer to your question. And it's in *Headhunter*, too. You want to pick up *Heart of Darkness* and say, "Pay attention!" Immediately after this was written, we went into this century and— holy shit!— you can't become more barbaric than we are right now, even though we think of ourselves as ultra-civilized.

As we sit talking here right now, President Bush is organizing the next Gulf War. And while America is trying to take a whole turn away from that, he's cramming it down their throats. He's their Kurtz, and we have one here, too. And this is panic speaking, not paranoia. They are going to do it all in! And as they do it in, people turn away from art, literature, music.

What's music got to do with saving the world? It re-engages you in wonder!

Essential Furniture of the World

DOUGLAS GLOVER
by Melissa Hardy

DOUGLAS GLOVER was born and raised on his family's tobacco farm near Waterford in southwestern Ontario. He studied philosophy at York University and the University of Edinburgh from 1966 to 1971, then taught for a year at the University of New Brunswick. Between 1972 and 1979, he worked as a reporter, sports editor, and copy editor on daily newspapers in Saint John, Peterborough, Montreal, and Saskatoon. Between jobs he lived in Edinburgh, Cedar Key, Florida, and Santa Fe, New Mexico. During this time, he wrote the stories which appeared in his first collection, *The Mad River*, and began work on his novel *Precious*. A second story collection, *Dog Attempts to Drown Man in Saskatoon*, appeared in 1985. He won the 1990 National Magazine Award for Fiction. He is also the author of the novel *The South Will Rise at Noon*, *A Guide to Animal Behaviour* (stories), and *The Life and Times of Captain N.*

MELISSA HARDY ¶ Have you ever given an interview before?

DOUGLAS GLOVER § No, and part of the process of being legitimized as a writer in this country is being interviewed and having those interviews published in literary magazines, so it's very important. I'm quite pleased, but also nervous. Actually, I had this dream.

HARDY ¶ What was it?

GLOVER § Well, we were sitting in a living room much like this, except I was in my bathrobe and there was a huge audience. The worst part was that the audience kept challenging me, and I had to start all over and explain things again and again.

HARDY ¶ Well, I dreamed my car crashed on the way here. I wonder what that means?

GLOVER § That an interview is an accidental encounter fraught with unexpected hazards.

HARDY ¶ You're from Waterford, and this is obviously the ancestral home...

GLOVER § My grandfather bought this farm in 1900. Both sides of my family were United Empire Loyalists. My mother's people came to the Long Point Settlement on Lake Erie after the American Revolution; my father's started at the Forty Mile Creek on Lake Ontario, then moved to Vanessa, a few miles from here, in the early eighteen-hundreds. In the nineteen-twenties, my mother's family moved inland from St. William's, and, a generation later, just after the war, my parents met at the Officers' Mess in Simcoe.

HARDY ¶ So it's been a slow creep toward the farm?

GLOVER § [laughing] A slow creep toward the centre, where I was born.

HARDY ¶ It seems to me, looking at this house and the fact that your family has been in this small community for so long, that you're carrying a heavier weight of tradition than most people nowadays.

GLOVER § That's probably true. Aside from the Indians and the French, few have been in this country longer. My ancestors fought two wars against the United States before Confederation. But, at best, it's a tradition that sends you a mixed message. It puts you in a classic double bind.

Over the course of the nineteenth century, the liberal Enlightenment ideas of the American Revolution took the moral high ground and completely absorbed the political centre of what we call white western civilization. The Loyalists— whether they were middle-of-the-road re-formers, Burkean romantics, prerogative men, or mercantilists— found themselves intellectually marginalized. Militarily and politically they held their ground here, but in terms of ideas the rest of the world simply left them behind. The Loyalists were forced into the unenviable mental bind of being against the future.

Hence our notorious stodginess, our self-deprecation, our pernicious anglophilia (there is a portrait of Queen Victoria hanging on the wall on the hall landing upstairs), our distorted suspicion of the United States, our ignorance of our own history, and until recently, our lack of a thriving cultural scene.

This can be a lethal mind-set, and we all make peace with it as we can, rejecting it or embracing it and becoming typical Canadian schizophrenics. My family has had more than its share of both— scapegraces and dotty family historians. A great-uncle of my mother's took the money meant for his McGill medical school tuition, ran away to Europe, and ended up a doctor in Argentina. Another relative abandoned his wife and children for the Klondike gold rush and never returned. My cousin died this year in suspicious circumstances in Berlin, where he had lived for almost a decade.

Clearly, I haven't made my own mind up yet. I stay out of the country for long periods, especially when I'm writing, yet I always come back. And I am obsessed with family and southwestern Ontario history. I'm writing a novel about the Loyalists to follow my book of stories coming out next year.

HARDY ¶ Actually, one of the things I'm struck with in your stories is men leaving women, or about to leave women. And it seems inadvertent. The time comes, and he has to go. The reason I'm picking up on that is that you talk about leaving this place and coming back to it, and leaving and coming back...

GLOVER § Canada, or the family farm, as the Eternal Female. I'll buy that, at least partly. I mean, if I had my Freudian or Deconstructionist hat on, I might say something like it.

Of course, when I'm writing the story I think nothing of the sort. Then it's simply a kind of game-playing— you have to have conflict, and you don't have conflict if the man and woman agree on everything. In fact, sometimes my couples do end up together, and then you have a romantic ending like the ending of "Red" or "Story Carved in Stone." But, all in all, when I put men and women on the page, I am thinking of strategies for generating plots rather than symbols. Symbols and image patterns develop in different mental space.

Beyond that, I am always interested in ideas about language, language being the essential furniture of the world we inhabit. And I do have a take on life and art which is more or less pessimistic, which views human relationships, fictional or otherwise, as illustrations of certain philosophical problems— the Problem of Other Minds, the Private Language Problem. So, for example, in *Precious*, the narrator says things like, "When I went out to get smashed with a friend, Rini had drinks with a colleague. In moments of drunken excess I am still liable to suggest the marriage died of incommensurate vocabularies."

HARDY ¶ I was wondering about that. In some of your stories— "Dog Attempts to Drown Man in Saskatoon," for example— the philosophical underpinnings are obvious.

GLOVER § It has a tendency to bleed into everything I do. I used to embed Wittgenstein quotations in my stories just for fun, often with truly disastrous results.

I always saw philosophy as a training for writing. In a sense I never stopped doing philosophy, and now everything has come full circle as I begin to write more critical non-fiction for which the philosophy is invaluable. Critical and aesthetic movements tend to run in tandem with philosophical debates. Nietzsche announced the Death of God just as the French invented Surrealism, Modernism, and the Death of Meaning. Husserl and Wittgenstein questioned the legitimacy of the great systematic philosophies of the last two centuries, and suddenly we are into postmodernism, with all its game-playing and lack of certainty.

These things permeate the cultural air we breathe, and we ought to bend every effort to make ourselves as conscious of them as possible.

HARDY ¶ That makes me want to ask you what you think of contemporary critical theory.

GLOVER § It's been vastly helpful to me. People like Todorov have led me back to Viktor Shklovsky and the Russian Formalists whose emphasis on technique over subject matter has completely altered the way I read, the way I think about writing, and the way I teach it. Ditto for Mikhail Bakhtin and his ideas about discourse and the dialogic imagination. The concept of inter-textuality (which the Europeans got from the American philosopher Pierce, who said the meaning of a sign is just another sign) has relieved all my anxieties about influence and borrowing. Derrida and Lyotard have put the element of play back squarely in the arena of serious thought and writing. (As Milan Kundera says, "A novel is a long piece of synthetic prose based on play with invented characters.") And finally, the so-called anti-legitimation philosophies of Foucault and again Lyotard have liberated me from spurious allegiances to particular literary movements which claim priority on the cultural scene. Literary realism, for example, has become an imperialistic product of the dying American Revolution; literary feminism is the last gasp of the eighteenth-century liberation philosophies.

All this is wonderfully invigorating; writing and thinking are suddenly fun, occasions for exuberance and joy. All of a sudden, the playing field is level and you can do whatever you want— no more of this moral fiction claptrap for me, though I don't mind if anybody else wants to do it.

HARDY ¶ Can you give me a more precise idea how your ways of reading, writing, and teaching have changed?

GLOVER § Well, I read now primarily for technical information. I see a piece of writing as a complex image with a certain process behind it. I look for the problems the author set himself and the techniques he used to solve them, for the decisions he or she made, even for the mistakes and fudges. I keep a running compilation of this technical data in a set of special notebooks for use in my own writing and teaching.

When I'm writing now, I always have Shklovsky's *ostranenie* ("making strange") in the back of my mind. And I am much more relaxed and playful than I used to be. My work is becoming increasingly picaresque as I learn to trust the writing itself to take me somewhere, while I use devices like image-patterns to control the meaning. In *The South Will Rise at Noon*, I spliced together elements of classical farce and a Christian Dark Night of the Soul and worked out Tully's redemption almost completely in terms of bird imagery and a climactic chapter that conflated everything, from the Tarot, to Norse mythology, to shamanism.

Likewise, when I'm teaching, I teach technique: what it looks like, how to find it, how to use it. Naturally, every writer brings his or her own content to the typewriter— I don't mess with that. But I try to demystify the process. I even invented goofy names for some of the techniques I teach: globs, globules, stuff, boss images, that sort of thing.

HARDY ¶ What in heaven's name is a glob?

GLOVER § Globs got invented because I could make no useful sense of Percy Lubbock's distinction between scene and summary. Lubbock, of course (as far as I know), was no writer of fiction. In the kind of writing I admired, summary was always mixed up inside scenes, and you could have scenes within scenes, etc.

A glob, then, is just a chunk of information that fits somewhere into a narrative. In operational terms, you can generally tell where globs begin and end by watching for places where the narrative switches from one time sequence to another. Globs can be scenes, descriptions, anything. They can be any length. And there can be embedded globs (globs within globs), nested globs, and running globs. This is fun, isn't it?

The value of thinking in terms of globs is that you begin to see writing as the process of ordering a series of chunks of information— nothing mysterious about that. The narrative becomes modular and malleable. This helps people learn to rewrite. You can vary rhythm and pace by splitting them up. And you can arrange emotional climaxes by modulating the emotional intensity of globs.

This probably doesn't make much sense without examples, but in the classes I teach my students seem to get the hang of it quite quickly. You see, writing is a game in the sense that contemporary thinkers, say Lyotard, see language as a game. And the interesting thing about games is that you learn them by playing. You don't learn to play a game by reading the rule book. So, when I teach, I use a mixed strategy that includes a series of graduated exercises, readings, potted lectures, and guided workshops, all focussed around a few selected technical devices.

HARDY ¶ I think if someone were to adopt a critical stance to what you're saying, I suppose he would say, if Douglas Glover is just playing games, he's not writing from the heart; he lacks sincerity.

GLOVER § It depends what you mean by sincerity, I guess. If you mean, *does Douglas Glover sincerely believe in the factual truth of his stories? is he sincerely advocating some political or ideological line?* then I'm not sincere. But if you mean, *is Glover sincerely trying to make the most beautiful piece of writing he can?,* then I'm sincere.

Also, when I speak of games, I don't mean a recreational activity. I mean any activity that has its own cohesive set of operational rules and goals. This can be playing hockey or it can be passing legislation in the House of Commons or it can be writing a novel. Contemporary philosophers tend to see the world as made up of a large number of these activities, without any over-arching, totalizing set of rules. As I mentioned at the beginning, one of the ways of becoming legitimate as a writer is to do interviews. It is a commonly understood sign of legitimacy (just as there are rules for scoring goals in hockey). To say this does not diminish the act of interviewing; it only helps to organize it in our minds. Likewise, recognizing the game-like aspects of what we are doing injects a note of humility into the process of legitimizing writers and writing, because it implies that ours is not the only game in town. For example, there is a whole other, equally cohesive, game for becoming and legitimizing Native storytellers.

Beyond that, your question is interesting because it lays bare one of the basic criticisms of the anti-legitimation philosophies, so-called postmodernism. When you talk about life and writing as a set of games, then there is a tendency to feel cut off from what one would like to think of, in that old nostalgic way, as substantive reality, a solid, simple, earthbound system of judgement about facts and actions. Suddenly, you're floating up there with the clouds. It makes you dizzy. You want to grab for the nearest solid-looking object. This is what happened to Kierkegaard. He argued himself completely out of religion, then had to invent the Leap of Faith to get back in. But the Leap of Faith isn't certainty either, because, of course, Kierkegaard had a lot of integrity as a thinker. The Leap of Faith is embracing uncertainty; it's saying, I believe in God though I have no earthly reason for doing so. You decide to love difference and contradiction because, simply put, that appears to be the nature of the world we live in.

Keats invented the idea of the Leap of Faith long before Kierkegaard came along, although he called it Negative Capability and applied it strictly to the act of writing. Negative Capability, he said, "is when a man is capable of being in uncertainties, mysteries, doubts, without any irritable reaching after fact and reason." This is the quality, he said, that "went to form a Man of Achievement, especially in Literature, and which Shakespeare possessed so enormously." Creative writing school teachers tell us, *write what you know.* But Keats is saying the exact opposite. He is saying that the greatest writers play some wonderful linguistic game above believing. He's saying you won't be a great writer unless you cut yourself off from the conventions of substantive reality and float above it, unless you are able to entertain every reality and every construction of reality. Unless you learn to play.

HARDY ¶ I wonder if this fits in. A while back you said, "No more of this moral fiction claptrap for me." But in many of your stories you seem to grapple with overtly religious or moral themes— I'm thinking of "The Travesty of Sleep" and what you call the Dark Night of the Soul aspect of *The South Will Rise at Noon*— or you make large statements about "Life." Aren't you contradicting yourself in some way?

GLOVER § Well, what a story might mean is part of the pattern a writer creates and is quite different from what a story does mean. And as for the meaning of life, I'm not interested in that— only the mystery of it, its insolubility, its resistance to meaningful explication.

My themes are religious, in a sense, but never moral. There's a difference. For me, it's too late to be moral. I'm not a good person— I am a patriot who wanders off, a wandering Canadian. I have no place on which to take a moral stand. Besides, morals are for small minds— that's what Nietzsche said. What I'm interested in is redemption, which is something else entirely— redemption, intoxication, and prophecy. "The Travesty of Sleep" is almost all a kind of prophecy; my new novel is called *The Redeemer.* In *The South Will Rise at Noon*, Tully is a bad man, a weak man, but, at the end of the novel, he mounts the Hill of Bones, ascends the Tree of Life and

Death, and flies. God— or whoever is in charge up there— is not interested in morals. Grace is mysterious. It doesn't necessarily come to the deserving. Even a bad man can go to Heaven. That's the mystery of life, that's Negative Capability.

Threads of Order

JANETTE TURNER HOSPITAL
by Kevin Connolly

Born in Australia in 1942, JANETTE TURNER HOSPITAL came to Canada in 1971. Her debut novel, *The Ivory Swing*, won the 1982 Seal First Novel Award, and was followed in 1983 by *The Tiger in the Tiger Pit*. *Borderlines* (1985), and *Charades* (1988), were both shortlisted for the Australian National Book Award, but it was *The Last Magician* (1992) which earned Hospital her widest international acclaim. The novel was a finalist for several awards, including the Trillium Award, and was hailed by critics in New York and London as one of the best novels of the year. Hospital is also the author of three collections of short fiction: *Dislocations* (1986), which won the Fellowship of Australian Writers' Fiction Award, *Isobars* (1990), and *Collected Stories* (1995). Hospital's most recent novel was *Oyster*, published by Knopf, Canada.

KEVIN CONNOLLY ¶ So thanks for a very twisted experience. *Oyster* is a quite disturbing and strange book.

JANETTE TURNER HOSPITAL § Yes, I actually spooked myself doing that scene down there in the tunnels with Oyster because when I'm writing I get into very intense states inside the material, you know. I have a very long germination period. I like the description of it that Rilke wrote in a letter to a friend: "I'm now settled down inside my work like a pit inside its fruit." I liked that description because that's how I feel when I'm writing. I just absorb all this data, then I kind of climb down inside the material and what comes out is as much news to me as to anyone else.

CONNOLLY ¶ It must have been a bit unnerving.

HOSPITAL § Yes, it was. I gave myself a few nightmares. A lot of that was based on Rock Theriault. He was a truly grotesque man. But there's a big artistic problem presenting someone like Oyster— any of these cult figures, Jim Jones, David Koresh. Because they're part buffoon— theatrical clown, you know— but they are sinister and they are dangerous and they do have enormous power. Trying to get the balance, to show the clownish aspects... well, it was quite an artistic dilemma really, just to make it work.

CONNOLLY ¶ At one point in the book, I think it's Jess who says, in the end it's not something these people possess, but a lack of something that makes them so powerful.

HOSPITAL § That is now what I feel about it, having read a great deal about these figures. It was not my hunch, starting out. My starting assumption was that these people began, probably, with burning idealism of some kind. And I particularly thought that, I guess, because of Jim Jones, working with the black and the dispossessed understrata of San Francisco society. I thought Oyster would be the core of the book, and that I would be presenting a classic Aristotelian figure in a way, who began with burning idealism but got corrupted by his own immense power over other people.

But the more I read about various cults, and the more I read accounts from escapees from cults and communes, the more I began to feel that this was not the case; that these people were mostly psychopaths from the start. All they had was a will to power and they just intuitively knew that this was good field to operate in.

CONNOLLY ¶ It's almost like they hold up a mirror to the people who are looking at them. There are a couple of occasions in the book where characters talk about feeling transparent in front of Oyster. Because there's nothing to echo off.

HOSPITAL § A lot of people have said that, who've been in cults. They've said that about the eyes. Oyster's eyes actually are Paul Bernardo's and Karla Homolka's as well, because that was going on at the time, and I came to feel that they were the same type. I think Bernardo could have been a very successful guru figure if he'd chosen that route instead. These eerie eyes that have nothing behind them, but very intense and spooky.

CONNOLLY ¶ Are there Australian models you could work from, or are they all North American?

HOSPITAL § No, not at the time. But the bizarre thing is, there is now. But I didn't know about him until I was well along in writing the book. Someone sent me an article from the Australian press and I realized that there *was* one, and he does go on Outback treks with his young people. I've always felt that fiction doesn't keep up with reality, but this time I felt I kind of blueprinted it.

It's quite a weird story. His name is Jeremy Griffith and he actually went to Geelong Grammar, where Prince Charles was sent, you know, the same way Andrew was sent to Lakefield, here. It's a similar kind of place, where they raise spartans, and do the outdoorsy kind of thing.

He didn't graduate, he was a very poor student— and that seems to be a constant with these types of people. But they are intelligent, and they become autodidacts. They're definitely intelligent people, highly intelligent, in fact. He repeated his final year, and he did matriculate, but then he went on to university and failed to graduate from there.

But what's disturbing about him is that his followers are the best and brightest of a number of elite private schools in Melbourne, and his right-hand man is a young Australian hero named Tim McCartney-Snape, who climbed Everest alone and has the Order of Australia. And he's the main recruiter and right-hand man of this guy. He comes across as a buffoon and yet these kids take him seriously. It's just so puzzling. I mean here's a man who has quite calmly announced on national television that he's the successor to Christ, and supersedes Christ, and so on. It's just so strange.

The other thing that his followers do, which seems to be typical of cults, is that there's considerable gender-role regression. The women have to wear kerchiefs and they totally wait on the men, that kind of thing.

CONNOLLY ¶ One thing that rang true, but I still wanted to ask you about, was that there were two characters in particular— and Mercy, too, to a certain extent— who resist Oyster. Charles and Susannah. And there seems to be a kind of intellect versus superstition thing going on there. But I was curious why would they be able see through him, and nobody else. Whereas Jess, for example, can't.

HOSPITAL § Well, Jess is also wary from the start. I certainly didn't mean for you to think that Jess was won over to Oyster, no.

CONNOLLY ¶ She admits to being enthralled, at one point.

HOSPITAL § Yes, she admits to being mesmerized by him, because he is very beautiful...

CONNOLLY ¶ There's a sexual connection...

HOSPITAL § Yes. At a fairly primitive level she is drawn to him, and she doesn't forgive him for that. But she never really succumbs. Because of incidents in her past she has kind of absolved herself from interfering in life. She's cast herself as the silent bystander.

With Susannah Rover and Charles Given, I didn't mean it so much to be one resisting for intellectual reasons and the other for faith reasons, but just that there are some people whose sense of integrity is so great that no matter what it costs— and they know it's going to cost— they simply can't do otherwise. It seems to me that kind of integrity, that sense of self, is no respecter of intellectual levels. People have it or they don't, it seems to me.

I wanted to have Charles Given as one of the resistors because I'm at pains to show that it's not an automatic progression from being a fundamentalist to being a sinister crazy.

CONNOLLY ¶ He even describes himself as being an autodidact, in a humble way, talking about his learning. He's very much the kind of self-taught person... maybe he understands the temptations someone like Oyster might have.

HOSPITAL § I have to admit that he's based fairly closely on my own father. Although I don't like talking about my private life, I grew up in a very fundamentalist family, against which I began rebelling extremely early. Like about when I was ten, or even earlier, I started asking what were considered improper questions, and the more I was dissuaded from asking them the more I became fascinated by them and wanted to have answers to them.

However, I have always remained close to my parents, who are still living and still in that faith, and I respect their integrity. The community that I grew up in consisted of very marginalized, lower working-class people. Faith was a form of consolation and validation when there really weren't any other forms. They were marginalized in every sense in society. There were aboriginals in the congregation, which was extremely rare in Brisbane when I was a kid. So I actually grew up almost automatically within that community with quite radical left-wing sympathies because of the nature of that congregation.

CONNOLLY ¶ But you reacted negatively to the fundamentalist religious aspect?

HOSPITAL § Well, I simply began rebelling against the strictures. I mean, I was twenty-one before I saw a movie. We didn't have radio or a television, and we were supposed to read only the bible. And my father himself was perceived as a rebel because he believed you should read books. He was also criticized by the congregation for "permitting" his daughter to go to university— I won a scholarship to go, he couldn't have afforded to send me. And the congregation felt I should be forbidden to go. So Mercy's childhood is, to some extent, mine.

CONNOLLY ¶ It's interesting, too, that there are the two father figures, Charles, and the false prophet character, who takes over the church and who Mercy rejects quite quickly.

HOSPITAL § There were people in the congregation I disliked profoundly because they were terribly dogmatic. But I always felt my father entered that faith as an adult in the years of the Depression and the war. I sort of feel he was an intellectual manqué who went in that direction because it was the only one available to him.

Actually, this has nothing to do with the book, but my dad... he'd never finished high school because of the Depression, but he had a tremendous reverence for books— he was terrified, but under my cajoling he presented himself to the University of Queensland in his seventies and got a BA and an MA.

CONNOLLY ¶ That's an amazingly brave thing to do.

HOSPITAL § Yes. All my life I've moved in university circles— I'm married to an academic at Queen's— and I get very annoyed at the glib putdown by intellectuals of fundamentalists. I also wanted to show that it crosses all faiths, it's not just a Christian Protestant tradition, it's also Jewish and Islamic and everything else. Although fundamentalism is too stifling, too restrictive as a way of life, and all too quickly turns into its own oppressive system. That's the tragedy. Look at Islam— it freed the Iranians from the Shah, and was a tremendous force— or in Poland, Catholicism freed them from Russian oppression, but it so quickly turns into its own system of oppression.

Partly the book is a plea against an us/them mentality and against the dynamics of polarization.

CONNOLLY ¶ There seem to real comparisons, too, between the anti-government, land-owning Australian cattlemen and miners there— a kind of right-wing libertarianism gone to an extreme— and what's going on recently in the United States, with the events in Waco, Texas, and the Montana Freemen.

HOSPITAL § It's amazingly close. I was on of these Outback journeys when word about Waco came out. And it hit me then, that this could happen here; it was just ripe to happen here. I originally had something in the novel, and I took it out because it was too clownish to be believable. But there are cattle farmers out there who buy tanks through army surplus and go careening around. They're incredibly racist— it just turns your stomach, and they've got tanks for when the government comes to take their land and give it to "the abbos." They've got tanks and caches of arms, it's quite scary.

But some of it is just too ludicrous to be believed. I had it in the first draft and Louise Dennys said, you know, this seems sort of "Mad Max." Mind you "Mad Max" was filmed out in opal country. I said: "Well, it's true, in fact, they do have tanks." But in the end I felt I couldn't get the balance between the ludicrousness and the truly alarming, sinister quality of these guys.

But there was a cattle property in the state of Queensland, that two years ago seceded from the country, like the one in Montana. And there was an armed standoff— no shots were actually fired— but there was an armed standoff that was eventually resolved peacefully.

CONNOLLY ¶ Are weapons relatively easy to get in Australia?

HOSPITAL § After the massacre in Tasmania last year, they were, yes. They were extremely easy to get. And it has become a *huge* issue with the Outback lobby, which is very powerful because they're very wealthy— you know it's the backbone of conservative party funding. The conservative party in Australia is called the Liberal Party, but they are the conservatives. But it's a powerful lobby, the cattle and sheep people. We call it the "squatocracy" in Australia.

CONNOLLY ¶ The book draws from all kinds of genres. There's Southern gothic in there, especially in the scenes with Mercy in the chapel, and then there's a weird kind of transplanted Western thing going on.

HOSPITAL § Yeah. I've felt for a long time that Queensland, which has produced a disproportionately high number of Australian writers that are well known— is very comparable to the Deep South in the US. I keep saying to friends who are academics that they should do a study of Deep South and Deep North. There are enormous similarities between them. That same racism and redneck politics. Queensland is notorious in Australia for the most corrupt and brutal police forces.

And fundamentalism. Even most Anglican and Catholic churches in Queensland have gone "charismatic." They are speaking tongues in Catholic churches. It really is like the Deep South.

CONNOLLY ¶ What is it that mixes with the religion that makes it go that way?

HOSPITAL § I just think it must be a climatic link. When you've got steamy tropic and sub-tropic surroundings...

CONNOLLY ¶ It makes people a little nuts...

HOSPITAL § I don't want to subscribe to the notion of it being "nuts," of course, because I'm from there. But in Melbourne and Sydney they talk this way about all Queenslanders— the expression in Australia is "gone troppo." It certainly makes for a kind of technicolour living, put it that way. It's a bit like Latin American magic realism, too. It's a great place to come from as a writer because life is larger than life there, all the time.

And with the Outback you also have the same kind of Western tradition, you have these little frontier towns.

CONNOLLY ¶ It's seems more extreme, even. I've been down in the American desert where it's got close to 50° and that was something...

HOSPITAL § Well it's regularly 50° and above in the Red Centre.

CONNOLLY ¶ Places where you can't function outside, at all...

HOSPITAL § If you're climbing Oolaroo, as it's now called again— Ayer's Rock. I've done it, but it probably won't be done for much longer because tribal people are reclaiming it and it's a sacred site and they're not going to allow people to climb it. I actually feel a bit guilty now that I have climbed it. But if you climb it you have to do it in the winter and you have to start about six in the morning, or you have to do it at dusk— but that would be very dangerous because you might not get down by nightfall. What's weird about the desert is that it's below zero at night. The extremes are quite amazing. It can get really really cold. So you have to bring a Canadian arctic type sleeping bag and lug it through the hot day.

CONNOLLY ¶ The structure of your book is quite interesting, and the only thing I could easily connect it to is the sequence in the prologue where you talk about the mirage. How it combines spatial issues with time issues. I think there's one example of a person looking out toward the sea and seeing a ship that passed two days ago...

HOSPITAL § Upside down. That's a frequent phenomenon. Mirages of ships upside down.

CONNOLLY ¶ I wonder if you could tell me a little bit about mirages and what you know about them. Are they physical phenomena, or psychological phenomena, or what?

HOSPITAL § No, no. It's an actual... well, I don't know if you can call it a physical phenomenon, exactly, because the mirage is nothing. But it's certainly not psychological. It's an optical effect, it's sort of like periscopes projecting images. It has to do with layers of air, and moisture in the air, and light being bounced around by the air.

CONNOLLY ¶ But is it actually possible to see something that was there two days ago?

HOSPITAL § Yes, because the person would be somewhere else on the track and the image can be bounced back and thrown around. When I was in school and we all read about the early Australian explorers who were all after this great inland sea. And they kept believing that they'd seen it. What we always thought in school was that they'd seen what they wanted to see, it was like El Dorado. But now that I've been in the Outback I can absolutely see what they thought they actually saw. I mean, I saw it a number of times. I mean you could swear that... there's the ocean and you can see the surf breaking on the shore. But it's a salt pan. It's dry, crusted salt— sometimes it's actually a slush of salt, an icy slush. And the light on it, the sun, it just shimmers. You can see waves and surfers. It's really something.

CONNOLLY ¶ Is the structure of the novel related to the image?

HOSPITAL § I did want to make clear that this is sort of why mad prophets come out of the desert. It's awe-inducing. You're sort of overwhelmed by this sense of immensity. Because I did find fossilized oysters, fossilized mussels, fossilized dinosaur shit, next to crushed coke cans. I did have that surreal sense of time collapsing on itself, of linear time not having meaning any more when you can get a crushed coke can alongside some ossified dinosaur shit. You know?

And space is certainly profoundly unreliable when you're never quite sure if what you're seeing is really there or it's some projection from somewhere God knows how far away. So I did want to give that sense of the unreliable quality of space and time. And I've always explored that in my novels.

CONNOLLY ¶ I found some of the book quite confusing in the first hundred pages, but I bore with it because there did seem to be a sense of order to all this. It was vertiginous, but it was sharp-edged and you somehow sort of knew things would come through in the end.

HOSPITAL § People always tell me they find my books difficult, especially with *The Last Magician*, that they had to read it a second time before they figured out what happened.

CONNOLLY ¶ I didn't find it "difficult," I just realized that patience was required before I found things out, and when you first get into a novel you're not sure what to expect. There are great portents of things which will happen right from the beginning, and I naturally wanted to know what had happened.

Did you actually plot it out in advance, or did it happen sort of organically? Because it seemed impossible to blueprint.

HOSPITAL § No. When I start my novels I don't know what will happen. I used to think that the best description I'd heard of novel writing was William Styron's. I heard him give it in an interview after *Sophie's Choice* came out. He said writing a novel was like travelling from Vladivostok to Rome on your knees. And I used to think, *oh yes, that's what it's like, it takes years to write*. But then I decided, no, that's way too linear and ordered— you know where you're going and it's just a long hard journey to get there. It's much more chaotic than that. I feel like I'm one particle of yeast in the middle of the dough, and it's all around me and I'm trying to pull it into order.

I simply plunge in, and it's very intense and obsessive and when I'm writing I work six days a week, about twelve hours a day. But then the thread of order begins to become apparent to me in the writing, and then I will go back and forth and change sequence. It's as though I find the thread.

When I was a kid we had a mulberry tree in the back yard and we used to keep silkworms every year in a box. I don't know if you've ever seen a silk cocoon? It's about the size and shape of an acorn and it's a golden fuzz. And you've got to keep pinching at it until you find a thread that keeps going, and then you can wind miles and miles of it. But it takes quite a long time to find the end of the thread. That's kind of like starting a novel, for me. I start at what I always think is the beginning but it never ends up as the beginning. I find the thread and follow it along and often pre-empt the beginning, sometimes several times.

CONNOLLY ¶ You have an amazing amount of geographical, cartographic, meteorological imagery in your work, and to be honest, in most other writers I wouldn't like it. Because in Canada it's become such a cultural imperative, a cliché, really. It's supposed to be a sign of true Canadian culture to be interested and obsessed with certain things, and landscape is one of them. But you use it to such a degree that it almost becomes less subtext and more an element of style.

HOSPITAL § I did a joint major in English and Geography as an undergraduate. So partly it's just I come equipped with this knowledge. But it's also the particular nature of the Australian consciousness. I was heavily influenced by a brilliant book by Paul Carter called *The Road to Botany Bay*. Paul has become a friend and we toured England together a few years ago doing readings. We sort of had this thing going about whether it would be possible to use maps to disguise the existence of places. Because Paul's feeling is that European Australia came and sort of imposed this map grid on a landscape utterly foreign to it. He's done a brilliant explication and re-interpretation of explorers' journals, showing how they interpreted certain landforms via their English knowledge and literally didn't see what they saw.

CONNOLLY ¶ That sounds amazing.

HOSPITAL § So we both joked that we would do a book about this, so it's partly the outcome of a joke with Paul Carter that I would write a town that was off maps. But when I actually got out the government surveyor's map of the state of Queensland the markings stop in a certain part in the Outback, and they do print little paragraphs on the map: "Motorists are advised not to proceed past this point." And there's just dotted lines. Rivers are marked but they have no water in them, and so on.

CONNOLLY ¶ Is it just because the conditions are so extreme?

HOSPITAL § Well, it's not unmarked to aborigines, of course. They know every little detail. They can see immense differences. But because we bring a certain concept of landforms, if those markers are missing— rivers that keep flowing and mountains that stay constant— we don't know how to read that landscape. It reads like miles of nothing.

I wanted to play with that idea. We treat maps like some kind of divine absolute. We have a map, we know where we are. But in fact a map is just an imposition of a certain concept on land that may not be so receptive to that kind of thinking.

Coyote Lives

THOMAS KING
by Jeffrey Canton

THOMAS KING has twice been nominated for the Governor General's award— for his children's book, *A Coyote Columbus Story* (1992), and for his second novel, *Green Grass, Running Water* (1993). A film of his first novel, *Medicine River* (1990), was broadcast on CBC-TV. King is also the editor of *All My Relations* (1990), an anthology of short fiction by Canadian Native writers. Of Cherokee, Greek, and German descent, King was, until 1993, chair of American Indian Studies at the University of Minneapolis. Previously, he was professor of Native Studies at the University of Lethbridge, Alberta, for ten years. His most recent book is a short-story collection, *One Good Story, That One* (1993).

JEFFREY CANTON ¶ One of the themes that surfaces over and over again in your fiction is the question of identity: "What does it mean to be Indian? What does it mean to be Canadian?" Why do you think you keep coming back to those questions?

THOMAS KING § It's not a question that concerns me all that much personally, but it is an important question in my fiction. Because it's a question that other people always ask. Readers demand an answer to it, and it's part of that demand for authenticity within the world in which we live. It's the question that Native people have to put up with. And it's a whip that we get beaten with— "Are you a good enough Indian to speak as an Indian?"

For Native people, identity comes from community, and it varies from community to community. I wouldn't define myself as an Indian in the same way that someone living on a reserve would. That whole idea of

"Indian" becomes, in part, a construct. It's fluid. We make it up as we go along.

Some people don't see me as an Indian at all. I live in the city; I don't speak a Native language; I've never spent any large amount of time living on a reserve. But I'm not concerned with how people perceive me from the outside. I'm concerned with what I know and feel about myself. And for many Native people and groups, that's the identifying characteristic. We identify ourselves— and this may sound self-serving and solipsistic— and that's what counts.

And the community in which we exist defines us. Tomson Highway is a Native person because he is a part of that more traditional community he comes from, but also because he's part of the Native arts community here in Toronto, and we recognize and understand him as that.

In the story "Borders," in *One Good Story, That One*, the mother has never identified herself as anything other than Blackfoot— that's all she understands herself as— and it's the outside world that is unwilling and unable to see her as that.

For Eli, in *Green Grass, Running Water*, coming back to the reserve, he realizes that although he's been away for a long time, his place within that community is still there. But it's a changed place. It's not the same place that his sister Norma occupies.

CANTON ¶ In *Green Grass, Running Water*, Lionel learns that he doesn't have to question whether he's living up to what a "good" Indian is because he sells televisions. Nor is Charlie necessarily a better Indian because he's a successful lawyer. I see your fiction breaking down some of those stereotypes from the inside as well as the outside.

KING § I wanted to make sure that people understood that Eli and Charlie and Lionel and Portland are all Native people doing various things with their lives. I wanted to emphasize that the range of "Indian" is not as narrow as many people try to make it.

In *Green Grass, Running Water*, you have Portland going down to Hollywood because he wants to be an actor and work in "B"-westerns. And he winds up succeeding. He went after what he wanted to be and he's done it. We do people who don't conform a disservice. Portland didn't have to go to Hollywood to be defined as an Indian.

Eli is an Indian and Charlie is an Indian and Lionel and Portland are Indians. The variety is infinite, and we'll continue to reconstruct that definition of what an Indian is. As times change, those constructions change.

Now, what remains the same is that firm base that we have in places— even if sometimes the places aren't our own to begin with. I'm Cherokee from Oklahoma, but I don't think of Oklahoma as home. If I think of any place as home it's the Alberta prairies, where I spent ten years with the Blackfoot people. I'm not Blackfoot, but that feels like the place I want to go back to.

CANTON ¶ And you've explored those prairies in both your novels and in several of your short stories.

KING § Don't ask me why. I hate the wind. It's so dry that your skin cracks open like a lizard in the sun. It's conservative. A lot of redneck activity goes on out there. I have no idea why I find it as intriguing as I do. Partly it's the people— the Blackfoot people in particular— but also the landscape. It's magnificent, and it draws my imagination. Whether it draws me back there, I don't know. But whenever I start to see a landscape in my imagination, that's the landscape I see.

CANTON ¶ You're a Canadian citizen and define yourself as a Canadian writer, but your most recent fiction seems to be more pan-Indian in its scope.

KING § Consciously so, too. I can't really write about the reservation experience, but I can write about the experience that contemporary Indians have in trying to manage living in the more contemporary world while maintaining a relationship with that more traditional world— without even trying to define what those worlds are.

There are issues— not universal— that are important to take a look at. Authenticity is one, for me. Identity, in a very general sense, is one. And the issue of borders. I hold Canadian citizenship and think of myself as a Canadian writer because that's all I write about. At the same time, I hold

US citizenship, too. I can flop back and forth across the border like a big fish.

The novel that I'm working on now is set on the border. Two towns: one on either side of the border; one Indian, one white. It should be interesting to see how I play that out and how I make it work. There's a bridge in this novel that got half-finished and then they stopped. You can't get across unless you walk. And it's pretty dangerous to walk, but it's one of the few ways you can get across, back and forth, to these towns. They're separated by a river called the Shield.

The other issue that I can play with is that border between men and women.

CANTON ¶ In many ways, the women in your fiction are so much more intelligent than the men. In *Green Grass, Running Water*, I think of Norma and Latisha and Alberta. And the four old Indians who wander through the contemporary landscape were originally women who have taken on male identities...

KING § ...but may still be women. They're just dressed up as men.

It's not so much that the women are smarter than the men. Eli is quite intelligent, and so is Charlie, though he might be a bit of a sleaze. Lionel is just a little lost. My sense is that within society as a whole, men are simply more privileged and with that privilege comes a certain laziness.

The women in my books don't take things for granted. They work pretty hard to get what they want and have to make specific decisions to make their lives come together. For Alberta, the question isn't, is she going to have a child— she damn well knows she's going to have one. Norma is like so many Indian women on the reserve who knew how a life should be lived and weren't afraid to tell you.

Lionel has had a pretty easy go of it and he hasn't made anything out of it. It's more a question of privilege and the effect that privilege has on you.

CANTON ¶ Do you feel you have a responsibility to accurately portray the Native community in your fiction?

KING § That sense of responsibility is very important. As a Native writer—if you imagine yourself as that— there are certain responsibilities that you come away with. Within my fiction, there are things that I feel I can do and things I feel I can't do. Not because I'm forbidden to do them, but responsibility tells me I should not.

For instance, I don't think that I need stay away from some of the problems that Native communities face— alcoholism, drug abuse, child abuse— but I do have a responsibility *not* to make those such a part of my fiction that I give the impression to the reader that this is what drives Native communities. I'm very much concerned about that. It's my responsibility to make my readers understand what makes Native communities strong.

It doesn't serve the community to constantly have it held up for ridicule because of those problems. Those problems exist within non-Native society, too.

In *Green Grass, Running Water*, there is a scene at the Sun Dance. I know that the Blackfoot don't allow cameras at the Sun Dance, and that includes the kind of camera that fiction turns on the event. You won't see any description of the Sun Dance itself, although you are there at the Sun Dance grounds. What you see is the communal milling around. I don't talk about how the men are dressed, or how they move, or the drum. All that's left to the imagination. And that's very purposely done. As a writer and as a non-Blackfoot, I don't feel that I have any business describing that.

CANTON ¶ One of the most rewarding aspects of your fiction is the way you explore the Native traditions of storytelling. How much of what is in *Green Grass, Running Water* is the result of research?

KING § That's hard to say. I hate doing research. I do damned little. But when I was a graduate student working on my PhD, I did a section of my dissertation on oral stories. I did a lot of reading.

The other part is just in talking— not about oral stories or oral literature— but just talking to people. Every so often, somebody will say something, or they'll tell a story.

Harry Robinson was an influence. The oral work that he put into written English became very important to me as I went through *Green Grass, Running Water.*

What I learned from storytelling— from oral stories— was that those stories help to create a fantastic universe in which anything can happen. You're free to create that as you will. Which is freeing in the same way that I imagine magic realism and surrealism are freeing.

Oral stories taught me a little bit about repetition and the kind of cadences that you can create in a written piece of work that you normally only think of as associated with poetry. They taught me technical aspects of writing— not so much giving me the stories themselves.

Although sometimes the relationships that appear within the stories— those were key. How are those relationships established? How are they pushed forward through the story? Is there an adversarial relationship between the major elements and the major characters? Are there regular climaxes in those oral stories that you see in contemporary European-North American literature? And the answer to some of those questions is "no."

Green Grass, Running Water in many ways becomes a very flat book. It comes up to a particular level and tries to maintain itself at that level all the way through. It's not the climaxes of the novel that are important, it's what the characters do. They don't have to do big things— it's the little movements that tickle me. And I love puns. Talking to storytellers and to Native people in general has taught me the value of a good pun. Like the Nissan, the Pinto and the Karmann-Ghia.

CANTON ¶ Or Dr. Joe Hovaugh. Or the host of celebrities who pass through the Dead Dog Café. You have a lot of fun with those characters.

KING § I picked those characters quite carefully— Jeanette MacDonald and Nelson Eddy, E. Pauline Johnson. And in addition to their power as entities within history, within film and literature, they also blur the line between reality and fiction and between what we think of as history and just gossip— between Indian and non-Indian. I love doing that— putting the reader on the skids. Especially if I can get them to go along with it.

CANTON ¶ Coyote plays a significant part in *Green Grass, Running Water.* Was it difficult to bring this traditional Native character into your novel?

KING § The Coyote in *Green Grass, Running Water* is not a full-blown Coyote. My friend and fellow-writer Gerald Vizenor was disappointed by the Coyote I created in my novel, because it seemed a shadow of the real Coyote. Vizenor works with Coyote, and Vizenor's Coyote is much more complex than my Coyote.

What I needed in this particular novel was a sacred clown. Someone who could point out the fallacies in situations and arguments and who made sure that nothing stayed done. Whatever you tried to do, that particular figure would take apart. My Coyote wants to see the world in a slight state of turmoil.

CANTON ¶ In what way doesn't your Coyote go far enough?

KING § There is a real range to Coyote— everything from benevolence to malevolence. Coyote is always in a state of flux. He has these huge appetites— sexual appetites, appetites for doing good and for doing bad— an entire range that I don't cover.

I use Coyote as a sacred clown, as a part of the chorus, if you will, and, in some ways, as a creator. But I use him within narrow lines, as a reaction to what's happening in the fiction. That was all I wanted to use Coyote for.

I don't think I'll write about Coyote again. One of the things I like about fiction is that you're not obligated to go back to the same topic time after time. *Green Grass, Running Water* is different from *Medicine River,* and the next novel will be different from *Green Grass, Running Water.* I don't think I'll ever do a novel like *Green Grass, Running Water* again.

CANTON ¶ The humour in *Green Grass, Running Water* certainly has a double edge.

KING § There's a great danger to humour. In general, people think of comedy as being not serious. I don't think this was true two hundred years ago. I'm thinking of Restoration comedy, Shakespeare, the European models, without even getting into the Native models.

If you write humorous material, or if you write comedy, the great danger is that they will not take you seriously. I think of myself as a dead serious writer. Comedy is simply my strategy. I don't want to whack somebody over the head, because I don't think that accomplishes much at all.

There's a fine line to comedy. You have to be funny enough to get them laughing so they really don't feel how hard you hit them. And the best kind of comedy is where you start off laughing and end up crying, because you realize just what is happening halfway through the emotion. If I can accomplish that, then I succeed as a storyteller.

But I think this is tied up with the way we read. There are so many distractions. Unless you make the effort to sit down with everything else off and nothing going on in the house, you don't come away being as good a reader as you might be.

I think the number of good readers is probably limited. Whenever I get on a plane, for example, I never see somebody reading Cormac McCarthy or even Margaret Atwood. Normally, I see people reading Tom Clancy, or something that you can buzz through because you know nothing is going to happen in the narrative. Nothing's going to happen in the construction and the syntax of the sentence. You're not going to find yourself saying, "What a turn of phrase!"

For me, that's what fine fiction is about. It's in the sentence. It lies at the heart of syntax. I think most serious writers are very much concerned about what each one of those sentences do. How they work within an almost stanza-like construction. That's what I go for.

Poetry may be an economical way of creating these wonderful effects, but good fiction is not far behind it. It's a quality that you try to strive for in fiction. Poe said that poetry should aspire to the quality of music. The same holds true for the fiction that I do.

Did That Character Choose Me?

JOY KOGAWA

by Sally Ito

JOY KOGAWA, poet and novelist, was born in Vancouver in 1935. Like many other Japanese Canadians, she and her family were forcibly removed from the west coast and interned in the BC interior during the Second World War. *Obasan*, her first novel, is a fictional recounting of that experience. Published in 1981, the book was an enormous success, garnering the 1981 *Books in Canada* First Novel Award and the Canadian Author's Association 1982 Book of the Year Award. Kogawa's second novel, *Itsuka*, published in 1993, chronicles the Japanese-Canadian community's battle for Redress from the Canadian government. *The Rain Ascends* was Kogawa's third and most recent novel.

SALLY ITO ¶ *The Rain Ascends* is your third novel, the first to deal with an issue not directly related to Japanese Canadians. In an interview with Janice Williamson, you talked about being burdened by an identity, particularly the identity of a Japanese Canadian. Your political involvement with Redress and your two novels *Obasan* and *Itsuka* obviously marked you as a Japanese-Canadian writer. However, *The Rain Ascends* is a novel about white Anglo-Saxon characters. How did the experience of being so thoroughly "other" differ from your experience of being Japanese Canadian in your other novels?

JOY KOGAWA § I'm not aware of any imaginative difference. Either way, I was entering the lives of human beings who are and who are not me. Perhaps the more "other" a person is, the more challenge there is to "know" the reality of that other. I am reminded of the story of the lost sheep— that there were a hundred in the fold and one that was lost and the shepherd was most intent on seeking out the lost one. In our society today, there is, I find, no-one more demonized, more "other" than the pedophile. And why did I, as an author, choose to make that character an Anglo-Saxon? Why, rather, did that character choose me to relate his story? A friend of mine told me of a science-fiction novel he was writing in which all the characters of a certain planet were psychically connected so that any pain felt by one was felt by all. My guess is that we are a planet in the process of recovering our memory that we are One. Even Hitler, you ask? Well, was Hitler a human being? We demonize others so easily, especially when we are afraid. And we elevate ordinary people into monstrosities of power by idolizing them. *The Rain Ascends* attempts to see the "other" as familiar, as family, as human; the character, Charles Shelby, gradually came into focus one day when I was walking up Charles Street and thought, "why not Charles?"

ITO ¶ How did personalizing that "other," personalizing evil in this case, change the way you looked at it? Your other novels dealt more with bureaucratic evil or systemic evil.

KOGAWA § I am still today primarily interested in targeting systems rather than persons, but this does not negate personal, individual responsibility. In 1964, when I was struggling with the problem of evil, I was brought to a point of peace when I was able to affirm my trust in— what shall I call this— the Presence? Love? A benevolent universe? I put the problem of evil somewhere on some back burner in my mind. I was able to do so because the fear of evil, which had made it such an urgent issue, was diminished by my prior trust in a good God. I could trust that since God was good, evil could remain a mystery, but not have to be a consuming mystery. In *The Rain Ascends*, the problem was back on the front burner. And the only prism through which it could be seen was through Mercy's energy and prayers. Not my own. Hers. In confronting the problem of evil directly as embodied in a character, I struggled internally to take the character into myself. That process brought Millicent to the edge of her known moral universe. I walked there with Millicent, and, like her, leaned out into outer space, "where there is wailing and gnashing of teeth." Hell. To be able to go down to hell and discover the Presence of Mercy is to be rescued, and I have found strength.

ITO ¶ Millicent seems to have found a middle path through writing out her story, as if articulating it will make her come to terms with it. This experience of wanting to *write* out her story shows to me the uniquely artistic solution Millicent has sought to deal with her dilemma. Millicent talks about fiction being the "sacrificial ram," where "the will to truth meets the will not to harm." Is Millicent's experience a metaphor for your own experience as a writer?

KOGAWA § The part of your question that interests me is the one that deals with the sacrificial ram. Millicent, as a Christian, would believe that somehow the truth would make her free. In coming to terms with *her* truth, she found that what could be slain on the altar were her fictions. She could kill some of the lies, the creations, the fictions, the imaginings, the stories, by which she had made her life bearable. All these "rams" would be the lesser truths that are slain so that the deeper truth is freed.

Do I, as a writer, seek the release of my deeper truths? Maybe so. The pen, for me, is a tool for the journey, and the journey is one of trust, towards greater freedom.

ITO ¶ Sin is a word strangely absent in this novel, and yet there is great sin in it. But the characters seem so weak and unaccountable. Reverend Shelby, in particular, seems to feel no remorse or penitence about what he has done, as if all his sexual acts took place in an innocent inner garden. At one point, you even talk about "uncomprehending criminals." How accountable do you think humans are for their sins? Or are we all just victims of our weaknesses?

KOGAWA § How accountable are we when we are weak, blind, unfeeling cogs? I have recently read Nelson Mandela's autobiography, *Long Walk to Freedom*. At one point, when he is in prison, he says that however much he is unjustly treated by people, he does not hate them, but that he has an intense hatred for the systems of injustice. I think that we do live in great cauldrons of sinfulness and are born into systems of injustice so complex we can hardly see them. I think we are to "grow where we are planted," right in the dung heap and the snake pits. I think we can turn towards the light even from deep down underground, even when we are buried alive in our own slime. I think the power to do so exists in the human condition.

But your question is about those who do not turn to the light. All of us know what it is to turn away from doing the right thing. How accountable are we, you ask. I don't know. I'm grateful that I don't have to judge myself or anyone else. It's enough just to be on the journey, and to know that the name of my road is Trust.

ITO ¶ Yes, you're saying what Christ says— "Judge not that ye not be judged." However, Millicent does indeed judge her own father, even as she examines her own "sins." Is it ultimately up to Millicent to be the conscience of her father?

KOGAWA § I do not think any of us can be the conscience of anyone else. However, in our individualistic society, I believe we divorce ourselves too readily and easily from one another. We do it by demonizing and scapegoating the "sinners" among us, and when we do this, we act to destroy the fabric of community, which is to acknowledge our commonality, to embrace the outsider among us and the outsider that dwells within us.

ITO ¶ But when Millicent acted by confronting her father and then going to the Bishop, did she act for herself, to expiate her own culpability in being silent? I saw Millicent grappling with the choice to deny and the choice to act. Was she practising the "judgement of mercy" when she went to the Bishop?

KOGAWA § When Millicent goes to the Bishop, she is running blind into the wind, out of her horror and dread and confusion. She is conscious of neither judgement nor mercy. She is betraying him. She is, at the same time, crying out for help. She is in the whirlwind. It is not a time of reflection, but of desperation. She hardly knows what she is doing. Her action has within it some hope, some wild hope that a way will be shown out of that hell.

ITO ¶ Was that "wild hope," that "desperation" that Millicent was feeling when she went to the Bishop, a way of practising divine abandonment— that is, the abandonment of herself so that she wouldn't abandon her father?

KOGAWA § Hmm. An interesting take on "divine abandonment." The phrase refers to Rosemary Reuther's words at the beginning of the book. And here, I see "divine abandonment" as referring to people having felt abandoned by God in the Holocaust. In *The Rain Ascends*, one could ask, "Why did God abandon Shelby to his sins? Why did God abandon the children?" Reuther is saying that God abandoned divine power "into the human condition." Where I see God today is in that "other" which is most vulnerable among us. The power that flows towards us and through us is the love that springs forth when we are moved to act to save that which is vulnerable. God draws forth our pity and compassion. At Auschwitz, God was a child hanging from a scaffolding. In the Gulf War, I saw God in the heron or whatever that poor bird was as it was struggling through the oil slick. These days I am envisioning that bird trapped within the so-called powerful people who are so powerless to help the poor.

You ask if Millicent abandoned herself in her struggle for mercy for her father. Maybe she did. At any rate, the power of Mercy was presented to Millicent as she walked the mad-making way of truth, and she was able to lean into Mercy. Mercy kept her sane. Millicent had the faith that Mercy would remain present to her as she kept her eyes steadfastly towards Mercy and that presence was enough. It was more than enough. It was to be with the One who stretched himself between heaven and earth without letting either go.

ITO ¶ Mercy, a constant presence in your book, comes as a goddess. In an interview with M. Redekop, you talked about how Christianity was the spiritual window through which you saw the world. In light of that, your invocation of the goddess in the novel seems to point to what is missing in Protestant Christianity— that is, a viable female spiritual presence that embodies the virtues of mercy and compassion. How do you see the goddess figure working in the spiritual window you have grown up with?

KOGAWA § Mary Jo Leddy, in her review of *The Rain Ascends* in *The Catholic New Times*, says, "throughout the book, denial buzzes like a gnat, even as mercy hovers like a goddess." I was glad she put it that way. The goddess came out of a dream. I don't know anything more about her than that.

ITO ¶ In terms of style, this novel seemed to flow like water, moving from one thing to the next: the spiritual, the moral, the events, history eddying momentarily into reflective pools and then flowing out again. How did the writing of this novel come to you?

KOGAWA § I thought a long time, struggled with it a long time, had a number of different scenarios in mind, wondered about the characters, the ethnicity question, the names, made notes, questioned the universe, and then the pen took off. Once it was finally going, it was written— for me— very fast.

ITO ¶ This book is narrated from the first-person point of view, as were *Obasan* and *Itsuka*. In this book, did you ever feel compelled to get into the heads of your other characters by shifting points of view? Reverend Shelby's point of view, I thought, would have been an interesting one to explore.

KOGAWA § I know that each novel so far has limited itself to the narrator's point of view. I think, particularly in the case of *Itsuka*, that the book would have been better served had other points of view been more fully explored. Maybe next time. In *Itsuka*, Aunt Emily's realities were being lived without her inner landscape being revealed. This is one of that book's many flaws, I suspect. And as for Shelby, one can meet him by joining NAMBLA, the North American Man-Boy Love Association.

ITO ¶ Your comment about NAMBLA makes me wonder how much research a writer must undertake in order to get into a character's head. Did you do much research for this novel?

KOGAWA § I looked all over the place for books and found some in Seattle at the university bookstore and in other bookstores there. I also was given the e-mail address for NAMBLA but never made an attempt to communicate. I looked high and low for people to talk to, but it was as if the whole area was covered in a deep fog. Ultimately, the garden I most needed to cultivate was my own soul, and that's where most of the research took place.

ITO ¶ You were at the recent controversial "Writing thru 'Race'" conference in Vancouver. What did you think of the conference? What do you feel is the position of the minority writer today?

KOGAWA § I loved the energy of the conference. When people finally get their chance to come into the sunlight, it's springtime. New growth. Greenness. Joy. Some people from the outside viewed the conference as separatist, militant, and responded confrontationally. I think we need to be aware that there is a time for anger, and there is a time to seek reconciliation. For each of us as individuals and as members of collectives, we need to understand what particular time we are in and to realize that rage or modesty or kindness are not appropriate for every situation.

As to the question of minority writers, I don't think there is a person alive who is not in some way a member of a minority. I feel that one of the important tasks of the minority writer is to practise imagining what it is like to be part of the powerful and the majority. It is much harder, I find, to practise the imagination of privilege than the imagination of marginalization. I find it so much easier to feel the pain within me than the pain within the other, especially if I perceive the other as having more power. As minority writers I think we have a political obligation to support one another as a category of ethnically marginalized people. At the same time, we have the writer's obligation to enter and explore the reality of the "other." This presents us with the peculiar opportunity to become agents of transformation for a society in which even the most powerful are locked inside the mental state of their own marginalization.

Unpunctuated Nature

STEVE McCAFFERY
by Clint Burnham

STEVE McCAFFERY is the author of *Theory of Sediment* (1991), *The Black Debt* (1989), *North of Intention* (criticism, 1987), and co-editor (with bpNichol) of *Rational Geomancy: The Kids of the Book Machine: The Collected Research Reports of the Toronto Research Group, 1973-82* (1992). His most recent book is *The Cheat of Words* (poetry, 1994). One of Canada's foremost practitioners of writing that challenges mainstream literary structures, Steve McCaffery teaches at York University.

BURNHAM ¶ To start off, what do you think of the interview as a text? I'm thinking particularly of the frequent pretence that a live conversation is going on, and that it is all spontaneous and natural, not to mention the dubious value to be gained in going to the author for all the answers to her texts.

McCAFFERY § The pragmatic benefit of the interview is that of catalyzing thought into areas that the safety of the monologic essay might not take. In this sense, the interview differs from the footnote. Where the latter draws off digressionary matter from a main text, the interview is a constant digression, meandering though questions and responses and sustaining a dynamic which contains, yet similarly unsettles, the monologic momentum. I value the risk of the interview's unpredictability, but I ought to draw a distinction between its written and oral modalities. The interview as the exact transcription of a taped exchange is often lauded for its "truth" to the "spontaneous occasion" but a certain speciousness is involved. There's an aura that obtains to transcriptions such as "well, eh, it's like, kind a Modernism puts it best" precisely because the written here establishes a focus on a permanence never intended, nor experienced, in the primary oral transmission. I prefer the edited, written interview whose contractual agreement accords with the temporal dynamics of writing.

BURNHAM ¶ Your work frequently transgresses boundaries: particularly those between poetry and prose, or poetry and criticism and philosophy. And Marjorie Perloff recently wrote about "Lag" that it is really poetry: "To call this text 'prose' rather than 'verse' is thus not, strictly speaking, accurate, the text being made up of equal line lengths." Do genres and their specificities possess any positive value for you?

McCAFFERY § The problem is we tend to think *in genres* rather than *think* genre *through*. Today in Canada, genres have a significantly institutional determination, which is itself symptomatic of bureaucratic rigidity and inertia. Cultural awards are based on generic distinctions, as too are the channels for federal and provincial funding. Anthologies tend to follow this same partition. The larger issue, of course, is the extent to which such institutional caveats actually determine the types of contemporary writing.

Genres function to impress a unity upon a multiplicity of different works and this should be taken as cautionary knowledge. A genre links to power via its taxonomic methodology to establish rules and vectors of compliance. In their favour I'd argue that genres provide a rhetorical and historical ground against which specific writings can be figured, as class to member or, more dialectically, as rules to interruptions. Most useful to me is to situate genre in relation to strategies and tactics. My own work is always produced with the profound awareness of genres and of their potential disruption. To read "Lag" as prose is certainly permissible but will lead inevitably to a reader's awareness of its deviation from several prose rubrics. That awareness, however, can be invested into considering the work's "uncertain" position within existing literary taxonomy and in that way can call back scrutiny to the possible insufficiencies in generic thinking itself.

BURNHAM ¶ In an essay in *North of Intention* ("The Line of Prose"), you write that prose features a "non-appearance of the value of the line"— not so much a *negation* of the line (as "prose poetry" might constitute) but a negation of that negation. Given your interest in the aleatory aspects of text, do you read prose as texts with line breaks?

McCAFFERY § We need to remember that the reader *is not* a subject but a *functional role demanded by any text*. The empirical subject will assume this role with contingent competence and indeterminate motives. (There can be deliberately heretical as well as conventional readings.) Certain texts impose a passive role upon the reader, but this required model can be ignored or subverted.

I don't have a single formula for reading but rather bring to the task different intentions and desires. I recently read Scott's *The Fortunes of Nigel* for its sheer transparency as plot. Obviously, I wouldn't read Levinas that way. On a more general note, there is a way in which certain grammatically under-defined prose works do yield non-prose qualities. I'm thinking of works such as Karen MacCormack's *Quirks and Quillets*, Fred Wah's *Music at the Heart of Thinking* or my own "An Effect of Cellophane," in which the unpunctuated nature of the prose suspends genre and creates a temporal continuum that elicits, of necessity, a biologically determined phrasing within the durational expenditure the reading involves. Such phrasing is indeterminate, will vary from reading to reading, and yet will be unavoidably present. In all these works it's the withheld assertion of the line-break (which I call phrasing) that's returned to the reader-function as an unpredictable effect modified by the empirical accidence of breath, attention and the intersection of reading (as a psychic activity) with duration as its temporal condition.

BURNHAM ¶ Do you think that avant-garde or experimental poetry, with a dialogic focus on issues of language, foregrounding the signifier, and rendering the text one less "authored" by a subject than constructed by a reading, that this would also constitute a genre in terms of a contract with the reader?

McCAFFERY § As argued earlier, genre is a coercive concept that suppresses multiplicity in favour of a taxonomic oneness, and so to answer your question affirmatively would be to endorse that coercion. What characterizes formally investigative writing is its tremendous variety and ability to both enter and destroy generic constraint. Ron Silliman's writing that utilizes the "new sentence," for example, is simultaneously prose and not prose. I would also caution against erecting a similar contractual agreement with the reader-function as a genre. Certainly, Silliman's, like Charles Bernstein's or Lyn Hejinian's texts, return the reader to a more productive, less consumerist relation with the sites of meaning, yet this is insufficient to warrant the category of genre, as that same reader-function striates texts to those that exist within stable genres like "prose," "poetry" and "play." The contract with the reader you refer to is pertinent to the sociological and political spheres (in the sense that the material form the writing takes is in itself political) but not the field of genre.

BURNHAM ¶ Your work, in common with current post-structuralist theory, distrusts the idea of the subject as an origin or centre. Thus, at the conclusion to "Deliberate Follicles" (in *Theory of Sediment*), you write, "The Characters we are compare the foliage to a frozen cipher that speaks. From the system of latent quanta everything postulates its own advance. The water is grey at the moment the Subject discovers the water to be blue." (178) Instead of seeing literary characters as some version of "people" (the humanist/Forster paradigm), we "people" are ourselves only characters— frozen ciphers that speak. And then, what the subject "discovers" is a mistake. Do you agree with this interpretation— or is it a further mistake to allegorize your work's thematization of language and philosophy?

McCAFFERY § The passage you quote is constructed upon several semantic ambivalences that must be encountered before a cogent "allegorization" can take place. A key aspect in the quoted passage is the function and value of the pronoun "we." In linguistics this is termed a "shifter" and Heidegger calls it a "dasein designator." It's worth reminding ourselves of Roman Jakobson's discovery that pronouns do not enjoy a primordial status but should be treated as pragmatic indices whose meaning is strictly determined by the linguistic context. Pronouns are also the last linguistic acquisitions of the child and one of the first language losses in aphasia. Bearing this in mind *should* complicate an innocent allegorizing of the passage. A second point is the double meaning of the word *character*. The word refers not only to a human figure (real or simulacral) but also to written marks and by implication to writing itself.

It should be clear then, that the phrase, "The Characters we are compare the foliage to a frozen cipher that speaks" is irreducible to a monosemic, semantically unproblematic level. The reader might treat "we are" as a substantive modifier of the plural noun "characters" and invest this reading on a literal level in which case the "we" might refer to either humans identified as characters or to the written marks of writing itself (the "we" being the letters). Whilst wishing to decentre the subject, I'm also insisting on the subject's partly linguistic constitution, alluding to a belief I share with Heidegger that language speaks through us and not us through language.

BURNHAM ¶ One of the most successful theoretical implications of LANGUAGE writing in the past fifteen years has been (roughly speaking) the aligning of realism and referentiality with a Marxist critique of the commodity-fetish. This realignment has been in no small part because of the efforts begun by you in the "Politics of the Referent" issue of *Open Letter* (3.7, 1977). Is realism discredited? It seems also apparent that realism will still have importance for various subaltern groups— women, gays and lesbians, workers, post-colonial peoples— both to document their oppression and to create a subjectivity for the reader.

McCAFFERY § Narrative, as de Certeau pointed out, is a device of continuity that legitimates established forms and norms. In its *modus operandum*, narrative realism produces "stories" which serve to order and severely limit the field of experience. This innate conservatism incriminates every use of narrative. But you articulate quite rightly the practice of narrative onto the non-theoretical domain of concrete social groupings, and this naturally requires a qualification of what I've just said. Narrative is not the cultural property of any one group: neither subaltern nor imperial. Yet its conservative production is invariant and that "surplus value" needs to be assessed in any specified case.

I'm in agreement with Laclau that "the struggles of the working class, of women, gays, marginal populations, third-world masses, must result in the construction of their own reappropriations of tradition through specific

genealogical efforts." Yet such struggles are less consolidated than compet-
ing struggles whose multiple sovereignties reflect the very groundlessness
of our society. My own inclination is to disclaim a happy pluralist equation
("I'm okay, because you're okay, too") and petition something like
Lyotard's judicial concept of the *differend*. The dispute (over realism) is
presented as a dispute between two groups and can't be settled by appeal
to a higher, transcendent arbitrator. Additionally, I would present as
evidence the fact that some gay and lesbian writers have turned to
LANGUAGE writing through their own serious misgivings with narrative
realism. They realize that to adopt a narrative method is to deprive their
writing of the possibility of presenting cultural difference by way of
concrete, embodied form.

Is realism discredited? I think not. But its range of valid application is
definitely questioned and its absolutist nature is extremely weakened.

BURNHAM ¶ You often couple a mischievous interest in chance-driven
composition/scholarship with a tremendous resource of erudition. I'm thinking of the essay on Fred Wah where, in a footnote, you see as an Ur-text of
bpNichol's *The Martyrology* a passage in Victor Hugo's novel *Les travailleurs de
la mer* (in which the hero swings on a giant H). Are you saying, then, that the
momentary lapse of a romantic novel into concrete poetry really casts doubt
on the entire realist-narrative project? (Is the critique of realism also a fetish of
the letter— language as some absolute ground of discourse?)

McCAFFERY § It's interesting the way your question engineers a footnote
into some major statement. The information you decant should not be granted
the weighty value you ascribe, and probably is best read as a slightly humorous
digression from the main argument. However, the question does provoke a
response to the precise status offered to the single letter. The strategic use of
the letter as a method for narrative generation deserves separate and detailed
consideration and I would suggest the interested reader turn to the novels of
Raymond Roussel (1877-1933), the theoretical writings of the Lettriste
Movement and Michel Pierssens' excellent study of logophilia, *The Power of
Babel*.

I accept the Freudian notion of a "split" subject, one divided into conscious and unconscious orders. The basic lesson Freud teaches in his theories of dream-production is that the letter frequently enjoys an autonomous operation in the unconscious, where it detaches from binding signifieds and transforms according to the two rules of metaphor (i.e., substitution) and metonymy (i.e., contiguity). This operation of the single letter beneath the signified is vital to any articulation of the unconscious motility of language onto its conscious operations. The unconscious, though, must not be taken as some primordial, hypo-conscious organism, but considered solely and precisely as a linguistic disposition. This unconscious insistence of the single letter lies at the core of this footnote you quote. I should only add that all of this is to *theorize*, not *fetishize*, the letter. As a critique of realism it would function to question the ideological grounding of narrative on a unitary, rather than a split subject, and would offer itself to a project of writing grounded in the unconscious disposition.

BURNHAM ¶ One of the great limits of Saussure's work on hypograms is the inability to find some origin for the presence of formal rules of combination in Vedic and Latin texts— if the origin is religious, then it certainly is assignable to a socially constructed intent; if the origin is poetic, then intent is not negated, but rather assigned an aesthetic function (as in rhyme or assonance: Starobinski, *Words Upon Words*). In commenting upon Saussure's problem, you remark that he "evades the issues of a general economy"— do you see the abundance of "paragrammatic moments" in texts as an indication that the structure— Bataille's general economy— is the ultimate agent of discourse?

McCAFFERY § No. Not an agent but rather a disposition in discourse and one that's unavoidable in any extended alphabetic combinant arrangement. And there's no hierarchy involved which would facilitate appeal to ultimates and penultimates. The paragramme, as a non-intentional disposition within the written, helps constitute the paralogical and contradictory nature of the intentional. Moreover, it is usually transphenomenal and not experienced as such in conventional reading habits. Yet a perspectival readjustment allows the reader to write these multitudes of slippages and losses, to recover them to non-paragrammatic writings that inevitably contain new ones. The paragramme of course links to entropy and the general drift towards randomness, and, like entropy, is a non-perceptible disposition, a production-as-a-loss outside of conscious intentionality.

BURNHAM ¶ You've been criticized (by Alan Davies, "Steve/steve" in *Writing* 25) for your appropriation of Bataille's vocabulary of rupture, transgression, excess, and libidinal— all as metaphors for writing. Do you still see Bataille's work as a useful source (among the many you exploit, of course)— I'm thinking of recent criticisms of Bataille as coming dangerously close to a kind of occult fascism in the thirties (Anna Boschetti, in *The Intellectual Enterprise*), or as "transgression" as a bourgeois attempt to come to terms with one's privilege (Bourdieu, *In Other Words*)?

McCAFFERY § I'm struck by the enormous disparity between Bataille's radical ideas and their tame embodiments in his fiction. Bataille "writes theory" but also enacts the theories as aspects of plot in orthodox and unchallenging novels. Bataille never risks his texts by staging the general economy as an intrinsic poetic governing the writing's production. Rather than appropriating Bataille's language and ideas, I've tried to take on the blind-spot frontally and apply the theory of loss and waste to the actual formulation of my writing. I should add that I do not believe a writing can be based *exclusively* on the general economic operation. As I've argued elsewhere, inevitable waste and the loss of meaning occur as interruptions within its closure and are felt as slippages outside of the semantic. My own interest in Bataille's theory of general economy came directly out of my rethinking the nature of "open" and "closed" poetry. The former, promoted by Charles Olson, dismissed devices of closure but never tackled the implication that without constraint loss is inevitable.

I'll not comment on Bataille's proximity to fascism but I will remark that I find a distasteful sexism pervades his narrative writings. But my interest has never been in supporting Bataille the person, nor with the entire corpus of his writing. Rather with working through and testing selected theories as a base for an operative poetics.

BURNHAM ¶ For the longest time, you were the most prominent Canadian in the LANGUAGE school— but in the past five or six years, magazines like

Writing, Raddle Moon, Motel, and *hole,* as well as the concrete activities of the Kootenay School of Writing, have created a poetic/critical climate quite open to your work— do you find this changing the conditions (audience, colleagues, the idea of "being an influence" on younger writers) of your own work?

McCAFFERY § I've long felt that there is something fundamental to writing that withholds reciprocity and thwarts the social gratification of tangible response. This is the fundamental solitude that underlies my most "social" texts. A work is written, completed, then published, and apart from the few reviews or essays that appear, that's that. So to speak of "influence" strikes a novel note to me. Certainly the younger writers in Vancouver (Jeff Derksen, Nancy Shaw, Lary Timewell among others) impress me by their successful fusion of formal innovation with a strident commitment to place as social space. I see this more a working through of the socio-topical issues in Charles Olson and *TISH* than as a direct influence from me. What we share is a belief in the inherent politicality of linguistic form. Not emerging (so far) in their writing is a collateral corpus of theory, without which their writings could be criticized as "derivative" from older writers like myself. I personally do not hold this objection and feel that the marked absence of theory is index to a deliberate disinterest in it and perhaps a feeling of its ultimate irrelevance.

The conditions of my own work have certainly changed since the early seventies. Especially the amount of critical attention it's been given by recognized academic critics. This, of course, is always a mixed blessing, but it certainly hasn't affected my writing. My own tendency has been to treat each new book as a totally new project.

BURNHAM ¶ Finally, what links do you see with your theoretical enterprises and progressive politics— do you agree with the Jamesonian view that the "prison-house of language," while offering useful critiques of bourgeois ideology, cannot, in the end, offer a sufficient theory for socialist practice?

McCAFFERY § The relationship of theory to praxis is extremely complex and is certainly not a structural issue. The effectiveness of theory's application is totally dependent on the hierarchical placement of the theoreticians in the dominant ideological apparatus. Where theory radiates from a position of power, then its application is simple and efficient. The two best examples of this would be the biological racism of Hitler's National Socialists and the elimination of the intellectual class in Pol Pot's Cambodia.

In less totalitarian contexts, the official promulgates its power through its own phenomenological reticence. Power moves invisibly in capillary fashion; it intersects with bodies at its weakest points (traffic wardens, tax collectors) and power never settles on a symbolic focus (the Führer or the Sun King). Accordingly, abuse of power is detected, but not confessed. It manifests as leaks in systems and is remedied by replacing the human conduits by less faulty ones. We "plug the holes in democracy" but never replace the entire system. A political poetry should be committed to this detection, to making overt the covert workings of power and its abuse. One way is to defamilarize the orthodox and to confront all habitual modes of thinking, reading, working. Another is to engage innovatively the sociological implications of address and readership. All of this involves a radical address of the political as immanent in poetic form and style. These answers to your questions in their phraseology and vocabulary make a class statement (without the writer necessarily belonging to that class). Certainly, I'm in agreement with Jameson that poetry alone can never offer a "sufficient theory" for socialist practice. Yet such a practice manifests not only in *grande histoire* but also through *petites histoires*. These latter need not be narratives but can be transient social acts within the contracts of literature, in reader–writer relations. It should be stressed, too, that a critical discourse need not be confined to the textual or linguistic, but can manifest as one of several performative implications in the written.

Where the Personal and the Historical Meet

MICHAEL ONDAATJE
by Cary Fagan

MICHAEL ONDAATJE is a poet and novelist. His novels include *Coming through Slaughter* (1976), *In the Skin of a Lion* (1987), and, most recently, *The English Patient* (1992). He teaches at Glendon College, York University.

> "... it is from my mother's side that we got a sense of the dramatic, the tall stories, the determination to now and then hold the floor. The ham in us. While from my father, in spite of his temporary manic public behaviour, we got our sense of secrecy, the desire to be reclusive."
>
> — *Running in the Family*

Over the telephone from Rhode Island (he has been teaching at Brown University) Michael Ondaatje hems and haws. He doesn't like talking about his work, he says; its meaning is self-evident. Rather guiltily I push a little harder. He agrees to the interview, but asks politely that I not run it as a straight question-and-answer, as he's bored of those. I promise to intersperse the talk with some commentary.

Michael Ondaatje was born in 1943, the son of "two of the best known and wealthiest families in Ceylon," as he writes in his memoir, *Running in the Family* (1982). He went first to England in 1954, and then, with his mother, to Canada in 1962. Ondaatje became involved with Coach House Press in Toronto, which published his first books of poetry. But I wish to talk to him about his novels: *The Collected Works of Billy the Kid* (1970), *Coming through Slaughter* (1976), and especially *In the Skin of a Lion* (1987).

It's possible to include *Running in the Family* as a novel, for it emerges out of the same sources—photographs, journals, historical documents. And it is so fantastic at times that it reads like fiction. Ondaatje seems to need that grounding in history from which to take off, to fly.

Ondaatje comes into Toronto for a few days to attend rehearsals of the revival of the stage adaptation of *The Collected Works of Billy the Kid*. He emerges from rehearsal into the lobby of the Tarragon Theatre, smiling, in jeans and a sweater. There's a lot of grey in the hair and beard now, and his blue eyes actually twinkle. We troop upstairs into an empty room.

ロ

CARY FAGAN ¶ Looking back at the novels, it's possible to see a progression in the use of historical material. *Billy the Kid* is a collage, but that same kind of material gets more and more assimilated into the books by the time of *In the Skin of a Lion*.

MICHAEL ONDAATJE § Yeah, with each book I've felt more confident with how I've put everything into the next. In the first book I had no concept of form. I wrote poetry. I wrote prose. I had photographs. I was very involved with the shaping of the thing, but that came later. What happened with *In the Skin of a Lion* was that I had enough of a voice to incorporate all the bits and pieces. It's not a feeling of assurance because I don't really have that. I felt very nervous and tentative when I was shaping the book. In *In the Skin of a Lion* I wanted a kind of seamlessness, because there are so many shifts and characters, a voice to reach over the gaps. And partly because it's more historically set around us, as opposed to a fantasy or something like that. It had to be more believable.

FAGAN ¶ One of the things I find exciting about all the books, but especially *In the Skin of a Lion*, is that you've managed to write novels without succumbing to more conventional kinds of narrative. You still maintain the strengths that you have as a poet, where you began. But at the same time the books do tell a very compelling story. Were you always uninterested in trying to write a conventional narrative?

ONDAATJE § I think it would be impossible for me to write a conventional narrative. My mind is so fucked up! [laughs] The only letters I write are fictional letters. I can write an ordered letter in a book, but if I'm writing a real letter every sentence goes off in a different direction. I know I can write scenes, but I'm not quite sure where they can go. I don't really plan beforehand.

FAGAN ¶ Do you surprise yourself a lot?

ONDAATJE § Uh-huh. I don't really know what's going to happen. I didn't know what Patrick was going to do at the end [of *In the Skin of a Lion*]. I didn't know that the nuns were going to appear. Those things kind of grow organically. I don't have a scheme for the novel when I sit down.

FAGAN ¶ I can't help wondering what the origins of *In the Skin of a Lion* were. It's clear from all the books that photographs are important to you as inspiration. There's a line in the book about the American photographer Lewis Hine, about his photographs being rooms that one can walk into. I'm thinking of the photographs that you describe of the building of the Bloor Street viaduct. Did you see those?

ONDAATJE § Yeah, I saw them. I went looking for them when I was researching that period. I think when you write you create a photograph in some way. So there was not one photograph that I looked at more than any other. There were so many, first of all. So you kind of look at them and put them away and remember the steam condenser or that image of a guy on the edge of a parapet. It's like remembering pieces of your own past or present. I think I was looking for an ideal photographer who was in Toronto in the twenties and I didn't find that. The ones that were most interesting were the official government photographs.

FAGAN ¶ By Arthur Goss?

ONDAATJE § Goss. Very straight. You know, seven garbage trucks in a row. They weren't statements the way the Hines ones were, so I had to impose that on those pictures.

FAGAN ¶ That's part of the rewriting of history for fictional purposes.

ONDAATJE § Yeah. But even though it's a straight photograph, you know it's not a straight photograph. It's a commission: this guy was sent to photograph a tunnel. You have to see what's the social context behind that. I used to imagine these guys walking the tunnels and then Goss is sent down there and everyone has to stop and pretend to be shouting something for ten seconds and then get back to work and Goss goes home. That kind of context behind the photograph, or what happens after the photograph is finished.

FAGAN ¶ Most people here don't have a strong historical sense of Toronto. That's one reason why the novel is so marvellous. Is a sense of the history of the city something you cultivated, or just felt?

ONDAATJE § I don't think I cultivated it. After I'd begun the book I realized it was a book about the city. It wasn't going to be about just one individual and that meant it was about five or six people instead. And the building of the bridge got me into the whole thing about the Macedonian community, the Italian people— who were the people who actually worked on the bridge and the tunnels and the waterworks. I was just very interested in it; it wasn't a plan to write a book about Toronto. It just became more interesting than the Ambrose Small character, which is how I began the book. There was a lot of formal and technical stuff that was fascinating to me because it was kind of unspoken. If you look at the archives of Toronto— it's all so neutral, factual. So much sand was used, so much concrete, as if that was all.

FAGAN ¶ Some people think that Toronto is too prosaic a city to have a literary identity. Maybe with your background you bring a more exotic sensibility to the city.

ONDAATJE § I'm sure that was a big influence. When I first came to the city I didn't like it at all. But when I moved here in 1970 I was excited not by the formality of the city, but by the Cinema Lumière or Coach House or this falafal house. They were secret places. It was a sense of a community that was unofficial that really excited me about Toronto.

◻

In the Skin of a Lion is one of the few works of fiction that makes Toronto something more than itself, a city of story and image. I am amazed how many people I know have read it. And *loved* it. When I tell Ondaatje this he becomes shy and uncomfortable, but says that it is the book he himself feels closest to and that the favourable response "cheers me up when I'm really depressed about what I'm doing right now."

In *Running in the Family*, Ondaatje describes being caught along with other boys urinating on the tires of Father Barnabus, a teacher at St. Thomas College Boy school in Ceylon. "A communal protest," he calls the act, "the first of my socialist tendencies." The identity that Ondaatje gives to Toronto in *In the Skin of a Lion* is inseparable from the novel's affection for the working people whose labour built the city. One of the book's central images, the water filtration plant being built by Public Works Commissioner Harris, is depicted as being grotesquely and immorally lavish in comparison with the workers' salaries. But at the same time it is admittedly beautiful, a conflict the novel provides no clear answer for.

¤

FAGAN ¶ In the novel you show the building of the Bloor Street Viaduct and the water filtration plant. Did you realize that you were recovering their history, exposing parts of the city that had been invisible?

ONDAATJE § Not consciously. Towards the end of the book I was very worried that somebody else was writing a novel about the viaduct! [laughs] Because it was like a main character by then. The sculptor Robert Fones had once mentioned the viaduct and how beautiful it was and I had driven under it about eight hundred times. And so I looked at it and thought, it is a beautiful place. And then I discovered that Harris had also been involved in the waterworks. So I started to find out about him. But none of the books mentions this guy or talks about the waterworks or the bridges. They became, in a way, love objects as I went on.

FAGAN ¶ Harris is an interesting character. Thinking of him and Ambrose Small, I was reminded a little of E.L. Doctorow's *Ragtime*.

ONDAATJE § I don't know. I loved *Ragtime* when I read it years ago. Along with thousands of other books I've been influenced by. I was using historical characters before I read *Ragtime*, so it wasn't so much that. I think I liked the voice, kind of light and witty. The characters weren't real and that was the problem for me. I wanted Harris to become more complex than that. The fact that a character is a symbol of A or B happens by the end of the book. Harris seemed to be going in the direction of total villain and then he got muted in that role.

FAGAN ¶ There's a point where he realizes that he's really small change.

ONDAATJE § And that's pretty accurate. Historically he was quite a sweet guy. He was a photography fan. And he was very moral, very honourable. There was another political figure in Toronto who hated him and who kept trying to get him into trouble. Harris would go to Chicago and they'd send up a hooker to his room and try to catch him. But he was a very straight arrow.

FAGAN ¶ One of the epigraphs that begins the book is by John Berger. "Never again will— "

ONDAATJE § "— a single story be told as though it were the only one."

FAGAN ¶ It's a beautiful line, from the novel *G.* It seems that *In the Skin of a Lion* and *G.* are relations in a way, loving cousins.

ONDAATJE § Oh, yeah, very definitely. I loved *G.* when I read it. It was the first book of Berger's that I read and it knocked me out. I like a lot of his writing. The recent essays on art, which are very personal. His take on history, too, which is not so much straight Marxist any more but where the personal and the historical meet. That edge. I'm sure that book influenced me a lot, unconsciously probably. I almost didn't want to use a Berger quote because it was so central to me. You know, I'd quote Berger drunkenly at parties. And the last thing I put into the book was the epigraph because it helped how you read the book. And justified its scattered approach. [laughs]

FAGAN ¶ Both Doctorow and Berger are left-wing writers. Without trying to classify, *In the Skin of a Lion* has strong political sympathies. But it's not in any way polemical. Is that a writing problem, determining which province is politics and which is art?

ONDAATJE § That's such a central question today, and it's not one that I know how to answer. Everyone is going through a stage now where there is so much debate about all these issues. Like the whole Vision 21 thing, which is really interesting. And everyone's making grand statements that it should be A or B. When I don't know what the answer is. So it's a kind of listening time. Novels that give you the right way to do things I just don't trust any more. The problem of what does someone like Patrick do, what does someone like Temelcoff do. That's so closely bound with character— human character, as opposed to politically correct behaviour.

If there was a kind of direction in this book, it was making sure that something got said, to write about that unofficial thing that was happening. There were a lot of strikes, just as violent and extreme as anywhere else, but you hardly ever read about that in Toronto history. I think Dorothy Livesay's book, *Right Hand Left Hand*, is one of the few literary books I've read that talks about political involvement. In the CanLit canon there's very little of that. It's just background.

FAGAN ¶ Scholars are already writing academic papers on this novel. Does that seem strange?

ONDAATJE § Yeah. I think that's the most dangerous thing for Canadian literature right now. The best writing comes when you're not self-conscious, and to think that there's somebody out there listening for something becomes pretty ominous. I just don't want to think about it in those terms. It's nice in a sense, but I don't think it's helpful to the writer at all. I'd much rather the book be enjoyed as opposed to studied.

Holding onto the Core

ALTHEA PRINCE
by Robyn Gillam

Antiguan-born writer, sociologist, and university professor ALTHEA PRINCE has lived in Toronto since 1965 and published essays, poems, and stories in periodicals and magazines for many years. She is also the author of two children's books, including *How the East Pond Got Its Flowers* (1991) which was chosen for the Children's Book Centre. Prince's collection of short stories, *Ladies of the Night* (1993) established her as an important voice in Canadian fiction; her two novels will be published in the near future.

ROBYN GILLAM ¶ Would you describe yourself as a storyteller? And is it fair to say that the idea of "story" has a special meaning for you?

ALTHEA PRINCE § Yes, I would describe myself as a storyteller as well as a writer of fiction, because all of what I do is storytelling. I think of storytelling as a particular genre within the style, tradition, and heritage of my mother and my grandmother. They were storytellers, and the stories they told were specific to a particular region in Antigua— Bolans, the village that my mother and grandmother come from— and specifically in the Anansi tradition, but they did not only tell Anansi stories; they also told stories that had a trickster at the centre. I do tell those stories and I do write fiction.

GILLAM ¶ In a *Border/lines* article, you talked about the idea that "story" is the story of a people and their whole cultural tradition.

PRINCE § Exactly. I used "story" in the sociological sense to speak of a people's way of perceiving the world, of epistemology. When I talk about "storytelling," I'm talking about a particular collection, a particular body of stories. When I talk about Our Story, I use a capital "O" and a capital "S," and I do that very essentially from a political place because I'm very concerned that we begin to own our own stories, own them very vocally, so that we don't run into the issue of First Nations peoples and Métis, of people actually stealing their stories. People are beginning to talk very, very stridently about our stories, and we are going about bringing our story to the academy and we, as a people, are doing something very proactive about how they are treated in the academy; and I see a sense of urgency about this because people are beginning to look at our stories. People should deal with their own stories. We haven't even begun to deal with these stories in an intellectual, scholarly way, so we don't even know how to begin to deal with other people dealing with our stories. It's a connection that we need to make and we need to make it fast.

GILLAM ¶ You have referred to the Trinidadian writer and theorist C.L.R. James, and his prescriptions for the formation of an authentic Caribbean culture with reference to content, language, and the undertaking itself. How does this process play out in your own work?

PRINCE § We were speaking in very different language, James and I, but we were talking about the same thing. He hit on the core of the issue and began to identify that there were writers speaking in an authentic voice, who could speak with the language of the people. I'm using very clichéd terms, because I'm speaking of a very existential thing. He recognized that out of the colonial process had come a colonial voice, but there was also another voice which had managed to hold onto the root and the core. People are beginning to try to write the real voice as opposed to the colonial voice. People are writing from who they really are. And so this doesn't mean that people have to write in Caribbean language; it's not about other languages... one can write in standard English and still be real. What James had suddenly realized after reading Heidegger for the first time, was that "the authentic" was an incredible political tool, that "the authentic" could actually empower. If you speak with an authentic voice, if you write with an authentic voice, you really don't have to worry about being overtaken by a dominant hegemony. There's no grabbing at authenticity; you already have it. People want to hold onto their core, and if somebody's saying *I've found your core* and if that someone comes from that part of the world that carried out the colonial oppression, it feels odious. So it's wrapped up with taking a step forward in life. You have declared your step. You take a step in which your foot comes firmly onto the ground; it's stamping your foot, which is a very Antiguan way of describing somebody exerting their power, of planting themselves in the world. It's also saying, *I am, I am here.*

The issue of language is really interesting for me because I'm fluent in both standard English and in Antiguan language, and I'm very comfortable writing in both. Both define me; I'm a product of both. I went to an English girls' high school in Antigua. My father was Dominican, brought up in the Dominican patois, and he emigrated to Antigua. My mother was a rural girl who did not go to the matriculation stage of high school. It's a kind of schizophrenia; to speak and perform in Antiguan language is a very different process from performing in standard English. Any story I do in Antiguan language is going to be very different, the presentation of my body, even, because the body is involved in the language, the voice, the way you look at people as you are speaking to them— all are very different in Antiguan than in standard English. It's the narrator who will speak in standard English in such a story.

GILLAM ¶ I noticed, particularly in the children's stories, *How the East Pond Got Its Flowers* and *How the Starfish Got to the Sea*, that although you're telling the story in standard English, if you're talking about a character and you're using indirect speech for what they're thinking or doing, then you use Antiguan English.

PRINCE § It's not a very contrived method as much as it's natural, reaching for what is authentic. And that, I think, is authentic in terms of a society that was born and raised and nurtured in colonialism and is now trying to reconstruct itself out of this amalgam.

GILLAM ¶ Many of the narratives in *Ladies of the Night* depict women pitted against each other. How can this be explained from a feminist and post-colonial perspective?

PRINCE § The stories come out of lived experience, mine and that of other women in the society around me. I wanted to give those women a voice.

They don't have access to feminist-style theory, they're not in a feminist-style relationship, and they have a story. I felt very comfortable telling their story— the story of women betraying each other— that's real and it's interesting to me. Young African-Canadian women responded with outrage to women who had actually been so unprotective of each other. They were shocked; they didn't know; it's a generational thing. They want to feel good; they want strong women to triumph in the end. But in my stories the woman doesn't necessarily triumph in her life situation, although in some instances she triumphs in spirit. And the life that she lives or lived was maybe marked by, experienced through, Antiguan spiritual values. This would be the majority, because the working class is the majority and these are working-class women.

I needed to talk about class, I needed to talk about race, although I didn't want to do it directly. I wanted to present a situation, and present it in such a way that it was clear these women had these experiences because they were African, they were definitely not women of the lighter-skinned, moneyed class. It is a time capsule because things have changed. It is a time capsule that is not presented anywhere, and there was outrage— that's the right word for it— from many men.

GILLAM ¶ When I saw you reading from *Ladies of the Night*, you said, well, I'm afraid people won't like this for Black History Month because it's not positive enough.

PRINCE § I expected that people would be upset because, in Black History Month, men make poetry about their Nubian princesses and women talk about their Nubian princes, and we are one and we are African and African people must talk about their heritage and so on. And that is as far removed from these women I am writing about as can be. They never experienced the lifestyle of a Nubian queen, pan-Africanism was not a practical reality. However, they are African and in a particular life situation because they are African. And that's my own diplomatic intervention, to remind people that this is what we should be talking about because this is a part of history that is not talked about.

GILLAM ¶ I think these concerns are important to everyone, especially those raised in the story "Ladies of the Night."

PRINCE § Yes, and some of my white friends in Canada have told me they have recognized it in their own life. A woman who came from Nicaragua said she cried. She said the story had a lot to do with women in Nicaragua, not her own life. It's a silencing, and I hesitate to use this word because it's so clichéd, which is unfortunate, you know. I guess I prefer to say giving back, speaking about what is and what isn't found in the silence. The people who react are either the people who are doing the silencing, or people who have been hiding their own silence.

GILLAM ¶ Another story which I thought was very powerful was "Sister Friends Is Sister Friends." A devastating ending, but a very true story. These stories have a wide currency.

PRINCE § They're wider than Antigua. And it makes me very happy to hear women who are not from the Caribbean, women who are not from Antigua, say, "I really can relate to these stories," when they haven't had this experience, but there's enough of this experience around to make me glad that it's been talked about. The other thing about *Ladies of the Night* is— and one that I should return to in print— a thing that has been critiqued a lot, is the fact that the stories are about men and women. They're not just about women, and one of the things I wanted to show in at least one of the stories was that men do feel and men do experience pain in relationships. In "On the Gallery," the father tells his daughter what he has experienced in his relationship with his wife. I thought it was a rescue mission for men. They have emotions, yes, they do, and they're real. I really know men because I had seven brothers and my father was as much my caregiver as my mother was— maybe even more so— because my father retired when I was small, so the headspace of the men in my family was something to which I was very close. My father was very nurturing; in fact, more nurturing to me than my mother was.

GILLAM ¶ That's the figure of Papa Biggis, the storyteller in *How the Starfish Got to the Sea*.

PRINCE § Yes. He comes also from my mother, who told me that when she was growing up she had two storytellers in her life— along with her mother— and they were both men. One of them was the postman who used to come to the village on his donkey; he would tell her stories. But there's this other image of the storyteller as being a woman, and this image of the Caribbean family being mostly female-centred, where the single parent is the mother, and I didn't have that experience. So it has happened that people who did not have my experience are asking where that came from. I really came of age in Canada and I learned not to apologize for my particular when it fell outside of the general, and my particular included the father who bathed me, who cooked, who went to market, who bought fish and cleaned them and was a very liberated man, which is unusual for his generation. But it was my experience, you know? So it is not easy to bash the man and say that he didn't do any of those things, and that's why I present that other man as well. And that's where I think that storyteller character comes from.

I actually welcome criticism of *Ladies of the Night* because it gives me an opportunity to talk about so many things, to tell people to think about the fact that we, African-Caribbean people and African people in general, can now put ourselves in a position where we do not only present the best of who we are because of where we are located in this society. Black people really do want to present the best face. And this is crazy-making. Who can write this way, who can paint this way, and who can dance this way? It's very restricting. Don't think I'm suggesting that an artist can afford to do art for art's sake and not be aware of where we are living and who we are, because that's another danger, where one can say, well, I'm just a writer who happens to be black, or I'm just a writer who comes from Antigua. What I'm saying is, I can't afford to write a story that doesn't have a criminal because the *Toronto Sun* has criminalized all black male youth, because there may be a story that requires one, because that's the way my imagination will take me, and I guess I have grown out of being reactive to the dominant society. Nothing I do can really come from a place where I am reacting to the dominant society.

GILLAM ¶ A lot of people are working on erotica now, a lot of women writers. Did you make any particular decision to work on this? How did you get into this area?

PRINCE § I've always written erotica, but I've never tried to publish it before.

In fact, the first work I wrote was erotica— in Antigua in 1984 or so— and nothing came of it. I had many discussions with other Caribbean women about it. There was around it a sense of secrecy, because our society doesn't really allow for us to talk about it. And Caribbean writers do not write about making love. It may be referred to, or spoken of in a distancing kind of way, but there is no description of people actually being intimate. I didn't set out to do this because of that, actually.

GILLAM ¶ There is a passage in one of your stories, "Junice and Stanley," where the male character can hardly bring himself to say the word "sex," and yet he's having affairs with all these women.

PRINCE § Yes, yes. Hypocritical, but very English. It's amazing that a society bred in the way that Caribbean society was bred could actually end up with these kinds of taboos about talking about sex, talking about the sexual relations between African women and the planter class— a planter class that would have had marriages and wives from England, then they would have children with African women, and it would be the norm and it wouldn't be hidden at all. Yet they managed to lay on society all these Victorian rules of the game— very interesting. And what we're left with is that people will not discuss their sexuality and sensuous things.

Male writers talk about sex, about getting a woman, having a woman, having sex with a woman. Women writers just didn't deal with it. They talked about loving a man, and being with a man, and liking a man, but they never talked about the lovemaking. And one of the things that I think may have prevented that is being eroticized as black women. Black women were being thought of as having all this sexual power. It was the black woman who seduced the planter, who was a good man until some sultry black woman came along and tempted him. I think black women were afraid to perpetuate that eroticization by writing it. I see a kind of liberation in not reacting to the fact that you eroticize me. I have an erotic self— this is my erotic self.

People are not used to having that voice. *Waiting to Exhale* hasn't helped. It made it into commercial entertainment, written by a black woman, the first black woman's voice on sex. And it is sex as opposed to sensuality and love, and we haven't really progressed. It's all a part of the imaging; they make us the mother, they make us sexual partners, and so on and so on and so on. We have left a part of our voice out of the picture. Dionne Brand's new novel, *In Another Place, Not Here*, contains erotic writing.

My stories seem to have a life of their own. The ones set in the Caribbean seem to be driven by water, sea, sand, earth, trees, rain and sun. They're very connected to nature. The ones that are set in Toronto are more substantive, I guess, in terms of the relationships.

GILLAM ¶ I noticed that in *Ladies of the Night*. The stories set in Toronto are more down-to-earth, very hard-edged.

PRINCE § Concrete surrounds them, and people just start to eat each other up. With more of the earth around them, people can treat each other pretty much as the things on the earth relate to each other, and those are the stories about people's intimate sexual experiences. I feel as if I am trying to define, in those particular stories, how we can regenerate the society.

GILLAM ¶ Is this also connected with sex and procreation?

PRINCE § Yes. How are babies created? That's interesting to talk about, the circumstances that went into that particular child really impact on what that child goes on to do in life. It's just so simple, it's phenomenal. There's a story where a child comes from a union that comes like a harvest after the work, in the coolness, in the shade, in the shelter of the trees, and it's a very protected kind of procreation; not protected as much as nurturing because there are all kinds of natural things around the couple when they are making love and conceive this baby. So it's almost as if God willed it and that baby is a very important baby in the next story. That baby goes on to be a woman who refuses to let her child be sold into slavery. The child was sold into slavery three times and she walked from one estate to the other to get it back. This is real, by the way, this is in the colonial records, where she's named as a slave woman, and I've named her Ashah. But she sets a precedent, her case, because after this had happened three times, the man who had actually bought the baby, the plantation owner, said that he was losing the use of his property that he'd paid for, and the judge said to the two men, what's the matter with you? Don't you realize that a mother's love is clearly stronger than your transaction? Give the woman back her baby. It had never happened before. And she walked, and if you see the distance today in Antigua, you think, wow! But if you think of the distance at that time, it's even worse, because there weren't any real roads. The island was huge; she kept going back for her baby. Then my political sociological head came in and said, there's my responsibility as an African person writing the story, saying, where's the father of that baby? I could easily, I think, have belittled her, and made the father the planter, but I made the father an African man. Because he was a driver (they had gangs and each one had a driver), he could not have gone with her because he would have been missed; the driver is the most important worker. He had to take charge, he had to direct the work, so I made him the driver. And I also talk about how they fell in love.

GILLAM ¶ So this isn't just erotica; it's a holistic thing.

PRINCE § It's not Anaïs Nin. The erotic part of that story is when Ashah, and Jeremiah, the man who fathers her baby, meet and fall in love and make love, but not when they have their baby. The birth of their baby needed a nurturing environment of its own, but Ashah needed to become a Great One because when she was born it rained.

GILLAM ¶ At a time when reality and representation are inextricably blended in mass culture, does the dichotomy of autobiography and imagination present a particular challenge for the writer?

PRINCE § I'd have to say no, all writing is biographical, but I really talk about ethnographic material, because it really is ethnographic fiction. And the academy is beginning to recognize that ethnographic fiction is on the same level as anthropologists' ethnographies. Because ethnographic fiction presents the rhythm of life, it presents relationships in the family, in wider communities, it does all the things the ethnographer does. I'm not a pioneer. Zora Neale Hurston did that. She was an anthropologist, and after a while she realized that there was much more that she could say in fiction than she could in anthropology. So it's all very natural for me; in fact, I started to write fiction instead of my dissertation.

GILLAM ¶ This seems connected to a phenomenon of writers who come to writing from the academy rather than from journalism or wherever.

PRINCE § Yeah, especially in a discipline like sociology. One is writing all the sociological formalities that could be fiction. But that's not how I feel about my writing... I guess I'm aware of the fact that I'm dealing with issues, but because the stories come from another spiritual place, I feel them as writing the spirit of a particular people.

Normally, empirical research would not be done necessarily by people inside the culture, but ethnographic fiction is written by people inside the culture. You are not then going to say that the fiction is not valid because it is fiction: that is crazy. So I had actually to make a case for my use of the fiction in my graduate work as a manifestation of a state of mind, as opposed to conducting an enquiry: how do you feel about the world?

I don't feel like a sociologist who is writing fiction. I'm a fiction writer who has trained in sociology, and I think that's because I was always a writer and I trained in sociology. In "Henrietta," my lens widens to include politics. Not in very direct ways, but to speak about the condition of the streets and maybe about the plight of an old woman and include the fact that there are no social services to help her be old in her neighbourhood, to be old in comfort, and that is something that happens at the societal level: the fact that the streets have holes, that when she hobbles down the street to the shop, she walks on a sidewalk with holes. With the narrow lens you look at her emotional issues, the heart, the mind. But the issue is really emigration and lack of social services. I didn't feel that I blamed the daughter, but maybe I did. She's sort of redeemed by her tears at the end.

Recreating Paradise

NINO RICCI
by Jeffrey Canton

NINO RICCI is the author of three novels that form a trilogy: *Lives of the Saints* (1990), *In a Glass House* (1993), and *Where She Has Gone* (1997).

"I came to writing from a desire to tell stories rather than from a concern with style and technique," Nino Ricci says thoughtfully, "but I spent most of my undergraduate years studying poetry rather than fiction, and came to a kind of epiphany through that about the ways in which language and imagery affect people. That concern, I think, does show up in my work now.

"*Lives of the Saints* is not especially innovative in form or technique; it is written in a high realist style and relies on a detailed representation of the world of the story for its effect. In the second book of the trilogy, I am trying to move into more complex psychological territory; more material in that novel will be internalized. In the third book, I hope to begin experimenting more with structure and form. However, the kind of aesthetic that comes through in *Lives of the Saints* will remain a kind of base line through my writing."

Nino Ricci's first novel, *Lives of the Saints* (Cormorant), was the first volume of a projected trilogy. Critical acclaim greeted *Lives of the Saints*, which won the Governor General's award as well as the 1990 W.H.Smith/*Books in Canada* First Novel Award.

Ricci has remained surprisingly modest despite all the attention that *Lives* has brought his way. "I was finding my own voice and style as I was writing *Lives of the Saints*," he explains. "It was my apprenticeship, in terms of developing simple skills such as getting a character from Point A to Point B with a minimum amount of unnecessary work. Also in terms of trying to find the material in the book that was actually necessary to the unfolding of the story.

"Just before beginning *Lives of the Saints*, I finished reading Thomas Pynchon's *Gravity's Rainbow*, which I would describe as an encyclopedia of the world. I was very impressed, and quite influenced by it; I started out with grand plans for the amount of material I would be able to integrate and the issues I would be able to deal with in my novel.

"It took me several drafts to whittle it down to what was really the story I wanted to tell," he chuckles. "I was imposing a great deal of material on the novel that I would never have able been to integrate into a unified whole. As my thesis at Concordia, I submitted an early version of *Lives* which was approximately one hundred and fifty pages longer than the final version. Afterwards, I went through and cut off the first eighty pages, much of which was simply exposition or was not crucial to the story line. I found that much of the writing I did on *Lives of the Saints* was more for myself than for the reader and I was able to omit a lot of it when I came to do the final version of the book."

Lives of the Saints is the story of Vittorio Innocente, a small boy growing up in the rural Italian village of Valle del Sole. The novel begins from the perspective of Vittorio as an adult, but the narrative the reader follows is developed from his perspective as a child— a mixture of the ruthless objectivity of a child's innocent observations with a child's sense of wonder and magic.

Writing from that perspective wasn't easy for Ricci. "I found it difficult to write from the perspective of a child. It wasn't something that I wanted to do. When I started the trilogy, what I had in mind was a single novel that would be written from the adult point of view. It would have dealt mainly with the relationship between the narrator, Vittorio, and his half-sister in adulthood.

"What has become *Lives of the Saints* was a prologue to that. When I began working on that prologue, however, the world of Valle del Sole and of Vittorio's childhood took over. Initially, I wasn't able to resolve the distance between the child's perspective and that of the adult narrator. In earlier drafts there was a greater sense of intrusion from the adult narrator and hence a lot of material that didn't work.

"One thing that helped me was focusing on other characters in the novel: for example, on the character of his mother, Cristina. In this way I was able to bring out Vittorio's psychology through his perceptions of the world around him. I do think that children think more in terms of images and how they link together, rather than analytically or logically. So I tried to bring across Vittorio's character by focusing on what images were impinging on his consciousness, how he combined those images, what kinds of stories he created from them. That is how I resolved that narrative problem.

"Vittorio's sense of wonder about the world," adds Ricci, "is something that would be much harder to capture from an adult point of view; that sense of wonder was hard to leave intact, without judging it. From that adult perspective, you immediately get into judgements— about superstition or backwardness, and you would miss the magic that it is possible to convey through the eyes of a child. I think that wonder keeps these ideologies strong in these communities in the first place. It gives sense to their world, populates it spiritually, and is therefore a very hard worldview to give up."

Ricci is quick to differentiate between the voice he has created in *Lives of the Saints* and his own. He doesn't want readers to necessarily hear the same voice in the second volume of the trilogy.

"I don't believe in the necessity of having a single and recognizable voice that runs through all the writing that you do, although that has been drilled into many of us— that need for a writer to find his/her *own* voice. I don't think that a writer needs to always write in the same voice. There are voices that might be appropriate for some material and not for others.

"As this trilogy unfolds, the voice will change. In the first book there is a sense of distance and irony that comes precisely from the distance between the narrator and the child. As the cycle moves towards the third book, the narrator will have much less distance from his own experience, and whatever irony occurs will be more the product of what the reader sees, but that the narrator isn't necessarily controlling.

"One of the reasons," he explains, "I wanted to start the trilogy in Italy, was to give readers a sense of people within a community where they are not marginalized as ethnic. Ethnicity will be a major issue in the second book, and I wanted my readers to be able to enter into that community and see the strangeness of that label— ethnic— for someone who is living it from the inside.

"In the second book, the anger and humiliation that the narrator experiences in his life will impinge on him in the present and will be more difficult to deny. I envision other books beyond this series where I will deal with different sorts of characters and different voices."

One of the novel's most striking achievements is Ricci's village of Valle del Sole. Where did that evocative portrait of this pocket of rural Italy come from? *Lives of the Saints* is not an autobiographical novel; Ricci did not grow up in the Italian Appenines.

"It would be hard to separate fact from fiction in the portrait of Valle del Sole. Valle del Sole is loosely based on my mother's village, which I've visited several times. The first time, I was twelve, and I didn't like it much— to me, it seemed backward and barbaric. There were flies in the kitchen. None of the houses had modern bathrooms. That is what affected me most superficially.

"But at the same time, there was something extremely alluring about the country, and when I left, I had a much stronger sense of what it meant to be Italian and a greater appreciation for it. At some level that world registered in my mind and imagination and became elaborated as time went on and as I returned to Italy over a period of years.

"I drew from my reading of Freud and Jung in imagining how that kind of community would operate. I also joined my reactions to my mother's village with my own experience growing up in a very close-knit Italian community in Canada. Many of those people came from the same area in Italy, so they recreated, in a sense, the kind of politics that you would have found in a small Italian town or village. So I was able to integrate my sense of the dynamics and politics of it into Valle del Sole."

Sociological studies, fiction, and film all added to the type of world that Ricci wanted to conjure up in *Lives of the Saints*. Research that he conducted also helped him to get a sense of a rural Italian community. "When I was at university, I interviewed approximately one hundred and fifty Italian immigrants as part of a project, although it's very hard to get Italians, or anyone from that background, to be perfectly frank with you when you have a tape recorder in front of you and it's an 'official' function. Usually the most interesting material would come once I had turned off the tape recorder.

"What came across most strongly was the sense of people having lost a sense of their wholeness, especially people who had come over when they were older. They wouldn't call it that, but that is what it amounted to. They had lost a sense of a world where they were completely at home, where they didn't question things. A world where they knew they could speak to their neighbours; where they knew that people knew who they were, and shared a common history; they didn't have that in Canada. And they would never have that again— not even if they returned to Italy, because they would be outsiders there as well. That fragmentation impressed itself very strongly on me."

Ricci is careful to emphasize that *Lives of the Saints* was generated by a desire to bring the immigrant experience into a larger context. "The fact that there is a mythology attached to the experience of immigration," says Ricci, "connects it to the whole history of Western mythology. To Ulysses and Aeneas, for example, and the Fisher King legends. That, I think, is very much operative in the immigrant mind— that sense of an unacceptable present and a golden future, of a grail that one is going to find. The reality, though, doesn't match the myth. But the myth remains operative, even when there is sufficient reality to begin to test it.

"It was probably hard in a village like Valle del Sole to get a real impression of what it was like 'over there.' I noticed, for example, when my family travelled back to this village, in the seventies, that North Americans have a very strange status. You are the person who has done it— who has gone over, who is wealthy in terms that can't precisely be understood. At the same time, you are treated with a measure of condescension— you no longer understand the world you once came from—

and perhaps even resentment, because you are the one who left while the rest stayed behind.

"I wanted to tie into that larger mythology. To look at a world that was on the point of transition between a kind of medieval worldview and modernity. While immigration is providing this escape, it is also destroying a certain way of life."

That myth of the "other place" will still be very much on Ricci's mind as he works through the two remaining books of this trilogy.

"What I intend to do in the third book is to have Vittorio return to the village of Valle del Sole, and I hope to deal with the inherent flaw of the myth of return. That other world that appears to a lot of immigrants before they leave as 'paradise' often becomes, upon arriving in that other place, 'hell.' Most of the people I interviewed said that if they had had the money to return to Italy in the first month, they would have left Canada in a minute. And over time the paradise they imagined they were coming to is replaced by the paradise they imagine they left behind.

"It hasn't altogether surprised me, but one of the most common responses to *Lives of the Saints* from Italians in Canada has been a sense of pleasure in having that world recreated for them. Ten or fifteen years ago, perhaps, they might not have had that same sense of pleasure, because the novel would have seemed too critical a portrait of where they had come from and they would probably have taken it as a criticism of that world. But now, at this distance, from the perspective of the success they have achieved in this country, a kind of nostalgia for that lost world has taken form and that world has become romanticized. While they reached a point of realistic happiness here in Canada, after their various struggles, there is still this sense of a world that has been lost."

Lives of the Saints is not just Vittorio's story. It is also the story of his mother's rebellion against the traditions, values and superstitions of Valle del Sole. Cristina defiantly transgresses the established order, flaunting her contempt for the backwardness she sees everywhere in Valle del Sole.

"In Italy," Ricci points out, "there has always been a resistance to any form of authority, and this is certainly true of people's attitudes to the Church. The strong adherence to the beliefs of Christianity was mixed with a lot of anti-clericalism, resistance to priests, to the wealth and corruption that the Church came to represent.

"That, perhaps, explains the attachment to saints. They represent an undercurrent of pagan beliefs which was never completely eradicated. The everyday world verged on the miraculous and on this underworld of spirituality which the religion itself didn't give people directly. It imposed laws and codes of behaviour but tended not to incorporate this more magical, imaginative level which had been a way of organizing the world before Christianity was imposed. I think you find this often in cultures that are more isolated."

The parallels between Cristina and her patron saint were very consciously drawn by Ricci. "To the point," he says, "where it's almost over-obvious. I didn't mind doing that because these myths are so alive to the people who are living in Valle del Sole that it seemed fitting.

"What Cristina does is what Santa Cristina had done before her. Santa Cristina lived in a Roman world. She rejected the Roman gods and created her own way in rebellion against the society that surrounded her. In the novel, Cristina similarly rejects the Christian values and the superstitions of Valle del Sole and tries to create her own personal morality. In that larger sense, she is a saint. But there is also the more superficial sense in which she has committed adultery, has broken the laws, and is therefore a sinner. I wanted to play with the construction of morality— of acceptable behaviour. And the values that go beyond those moral systems that society has constructed."

Who does Nino Ricci read? "I have favourite books rather than favourite authors. Alice Munro's *The Lives of Girls and Women*. Elizabeth Harvor's *If Only We Could Drive like this Forever*. Robertson Davies' *Fifth Business*. That novel was very influential and is still one of my favourites. The opening paragraph of *Lives of the Saints* takes a lot from the beginning of *Fifth Business*— the image of the stone that Davies introduces there and carries through the trilogy."

"My reading tastes vary. I've never, for example, attached myself to a single writer and said to myself this is what I want. That's partly the influence of Northrop Frye, who advocated that you simply expose yourself to as much possible and make as much sense out of it as you can.

"The real strength of literature is its complexity, its ability to integrate vast amounts of material in a way that doesn't necessarily arrive at any particular solution to a given problem but makes you aware of the many facets of whatever problem is under discussion. I like to move between contemporary fiction and older works of fiction— not necessarily classics— I think it's dangerous only to focus on what's coming out in the current year. You lose a sense of the overall progression and continuity of literature."

Northrop Frye also provided a key for Ricci's exploration of myth, ritual and superstition in *Lives of the Saints*. While Ricci now finds Frye "somewhat totalitarian in his worldview," he is nonetheless indebted to Frye for his investigation of patterns of mythology in literature. "Frye gave me a broader way of understanding storytelling which I tried to explore in *Lives*. I wanted Cristina's life, on one level, to tie into these mythological patterns. That was one of the reasons why I wanted this death and re-birth at the end of the book— a motif that runs through the novel. And I also wanted the immigrant experience to tie into the larger 'quest' motif that writers like Frye and Joseph Campbell talk about in relation to myth.

"I hope, in the third book, to come back to some of these patterns that I've explored in *Lives of the Saints* and begin to problematize them as well, to look at them a little more closely, and allow the reader to see how the adult narrator has himself, in some sense, been buying into these mythologies and using them to structure his own life, and his memory of it, because that is the way that he has learned to give meaning to his experiences."

Ricci is currently in the midst of the second part of his trilogy. "I'm nearly done the second book— I've put about three years into it." *Lives* ended with Vittorio and his half-sister arriving in Halifax, on the verge of entering both a new world and a new life.

"*In A Glass House*, the second book, concentrates on Vittorio's relationship with his father. The half-sister is in the book but she becomes marginalized. She will return in the third book, which focuses on her relationship with the narrator. That third book will come back eventually to Valle del Sole. I hope to tie everything together without too much artificial closure."

As Ricci points out, where to publish in Canada envelops writers in a catch-22 situation. "Larger houses in Canada have the budgets. Publishers such as Random House of Canada, for example, have shown a commitment to Canadian literature and literary excellence. But budgets for literary fiction are the first things to be cut when you enter a period of economic hardship such as we now face; the small presses are doing all the groundwork."

I ask how he feels about winning the Governor General's award.

"I feel honoured to have had this recognition from my peers. Despite the various controversies that have surrounded the Governor General's award, I feel that it is an important prize, that it has value and meaning.

"Pragmatically, of course, winning the award is very helpful. And I think that is part of the intention of these awards— to give authors more prominence.

"There is," he smiles, "however, an odd edge to the legitimacy that being a Governor General's award winner gives you— I'm not sure that you can be as avant-garde or out-of-the-mainstream when you bear the label 'Winner of the Governor General's award.'"

Versions of the Truth

MORDECAI RICHLER
by Robyn Gillam

MORDECAI RICHLER lives in Montreal, where he was born in 1931. Richler is the author of ten novels, including *Cocksure* (Governor General's award, 1968), *St. Urbain's Horseman* (Governor General's award, 1971) and *Barney's Version* (Giller Prize, 1997). Three of his novels have been made into feature films.

ROBYN GILLAM ¶ *Barney's Version* plunges right in, *in medias res*, and there's this character who starts off with a diatribe against an enemy of his, and this is why he's writing the book, and then there's this incredible stream of reminiscences and all these tiresome little footnotes, and then the narrative starts, and he complains how everyone hates him and is trying to get even, and he doesn't seem like a very sympathetic character, but as we go through all the flashbacks and digressions and practical jokes, I felt that Barney was a very sympathetic character, and you begin to feel outrage that people think that Barney is a terrible person, and then I thought of the title and I thought, wait a minute, it's Barney's version, maybe he's making this up and he's really the awful person people say he is. Is this book about textual truth? Are you talking about a text as a truthful thing or a text as just somebody's version? Are you trying to make people think about truth?

MORDECAI RICHLER § That's a very reasonable and intelligent question. It's really for the reader to decide whether he's telling the truth or not. But everyone has their own version of the truth, obviously, and this is his version. Depends whether you credit him with veracity, if he's a man who tells the truth or not. It's certainly not self-serving, but I wouldn't follow it around with an explanation. There is it is. The reader has to make up his or her mind.

GILLAM ¶ When someone tells you something, you should think about it, and when you read a text, for example, like the Bible...

RICHLER § That's full of lies as well.

GILLAM ¶ Well, that's what makes it interesting.

RICHLER § Of course.

GILLAM ¶ The idea of memory is important in the novel, and the question is whether people remember things because they can remember them, or more importantly, because they choose to. And this goes back to the difference between Barney's version of what happened in Paris, or McIvor's, or Clara's, and so on. Is his memory just what someone happens to remember, or is it a deliberate editing...?

RICHLER § We all edit our memories to a certain extent, and, I'm sure you know that Barney and McIvor had different versions of what happened, if he was being followed or avoided... and then readers have to make up their minds... and the footnotes are there to serve a purpose.

GILLAM ¶ In the beginning you wonder what the footnotes are doing, but later it becomes clear. Even though there is this objective fact of him losing his memory, you start to question— well, I forget all kinds of things, we all do.

RICHLER § Yes, of course.

GILLAM ¶ You referred to the recovered memory racket... I don't believe in it myself; I think if something important happens to you, you remember it...

RICHLER § That wasn't meant to send any message.

GILLAM ¶ The whole idea of memory has become really important to people in the last few years and it's being used in this way.

RICHLER § Well, you know, if five different people have been to a dinner party, they all have different memories of happened.

GILLAM ¶ The Rashamon phenomenon.

RICHLER § Yes. And this is the first time I've written a novel in the first person. Kind of liberating...

GILLAM ¶ Why did you decide to do that?

RICHLER § Well, why not? I'd never done it before. A new game to play, and it has its own rules, and its own discipline. Once you find the voice, it's a lot easier, but until you get the voice, it's... difficult. But, I think I got the voice and then it just seemed to flow.

GILLAM ¶ I was completely drawn in. It was just like meeting a person; at first you didn't know what to think of him, you're a little wary of him and then... Why didn't you write a novel in the first person before?

RICHLER § It just hadn't occurred to me. It just didn't fit. It certainly didn't fit *Gursky* which had all kinds of voices and versions; I would never have been able to do it... I guess *Duddy Kravitz could* have been written in the first person...

GILLAM ¶ A lot of writers don't think except in the first person... very solipsistic...

RICHLER § Well, this is the first time... I think I'll do something different next time.

GILLAM ¶ Second person?

RICHLER § Ha ha.

GILLAM ¶ I'm not sure second person really works... it's really just the first person, you're just distancing yourself.

RICHLER § Yeah.

GILLAM ¶ In this book and elsewhere, you often put your characters on trial, literally or metaphorically... Why?

RICHLER § I don't know... but I must confess I've done it more than once...

I just don't know; I couldn't answer that now. But it's something I've done before. I guess I'm not going to get away with it again.

GILLAM ¶ Throughout the Ancient Near East and in Early Christian times, the next world is a law court and you have to plead your case and I maybe just wondered if you had some ideas like that in the back of your mind.

RICHLER § Well, possibly. I had a very rich religious upbringing when I was a youngster and I guess it stayed with me... but I've used it in a literal sense... but sure, we're on trial...

GILLAM ¶ That's true.

RICHLER § I don't know about a final judgement...

GILLAM ¶ But, in a sense, this is what happens to Barney...

RICHLER § One request. Please don't give away the ending.

GILLAM ¶ You know, it was funny, but just a few days before I started reading this, I went to the Air Show and they had these water bombers there— the planes that figure in the book. You know, I'd never seen them before.

RICHLER § Oh, yes, oh, yes... Well, I tell you, what happened was that I was sitting out at our place on the lake one day and I saw those water bombers. That's when it occurred to me.

GILLAM ¶ Oh, yes. It'd flatten you, wouldn't it?

RICHLER § That's right...

GILLAM ¶ One of the things I like about the book is your humour, and humour is very two-edged; it's awful, and it's comic. This is, of course, what makes humour work, and what bothers people about it... This is what gives you a controversial standing with some people. Barney's not exactly a politically correct character, is he?

RICHLER § No.

GILLAM ¶ I think he's a good person.

RICHLER § I think so, on balance, yeah.

GILLAM ¶ Barney says, I'm not really talented, I'm not really creative, what I do isn't worthwhile, I'm not really a success, I've had a rotten life and I've done a lot of rotten things to people. But he's no worse, certainly, than most of the people he knows. And that reflects on the kind of society we live in— you believe people who toot their own horn, who say, I'm good, I'm wonderful, and it works...

RICHLER § It's very sad.

GILLAM ¶ What do you think will get people exercised about this book?

RICHLER § The truth is, I never know. I really just don't know how it's going to land. You never know. It's a very tricky time; you don't know how it's going to strike. I couldn't answer that. I think some people will strongly object to it being politically incorrect... I don't know; these are such odd times.

GILLAM ¶ I do think that special interest politics has a valuable role in our society, but I also think there's a tremendous opportunity for real hypocrites to get out there...

RICHLER § I think there might be problems with some feminists. I don't know. It's a story about a man who's truly in love with a wonderful woman, so I don't know; it's pretty difficult.

GILLAM ¶ And who regrets being negative about letting her go back to work.

RICHLER § Right.

GILLAM ¶ I guess you can't predict, but what do you think it is that bothers people about your work?

RICHLER § Well, in the nature of things, I'm a satirical writer, so I make fun of just about everything or anybody. I'm fair game myself. No one's obliged to applaud or approve; I'm not owed an audience or anything. I do my work as best I can, I send it out, and I wait and see what happens, but I'm not owed anything by anybody. This book ridicules so many things that some people will respond very strongly.

GILLAM ¶ I can imagine people taking those letters that Barney writes to the Clara Charnofsky Foundation for Wimyn in a not very good way...

RICHLER § Yes...

GILLAM ¶ I thought they were quite funny...

RICHLER § And some pillars of the Jewish community may object to that man who keeps welcoming anti-Semitic incidents, I don't know. I thought it was quite funny myself. I just don't know.

GILLAM ¶ Do you think this is getting worse, or do you think that people have always reacted negatively to satire and humour?

RICHLER § They've always reacted negatively to some extent, but other people have obviously enjoyed it, responded with pleasure, or nobody would read my books.

GILLAM ¶ I think you're practising satire out of a moral position...

RICHLER § Well, every satirist is essentially a moralist.

GILLAM ¶ Yes, and I think you see some things in Canadian society that really bother you, in fact, maybe, outrage you.

RICHLER § It's not so much Canadian society; I use Canadian society because that's what I've written about, but most of it's true of American or British society... it's not that different from other western societies really.

GILLAM ¶ Except maybe Quebec and that kind of thing.

RICHLER § Yes. But that's really in the background, Quebec.

GILLAM ¶ In the book, they go and watch the Referendum, but since then, there's noise, but there's not much happening. What do you think will happen in Quebec?

RICHLER § I think people are getting rather bored with it all in Quebec and I really think they peaked in the last referendum...

GILLAM ¶ They did really badly in the last federal election, the Bloc.

RICHLER § Well, it wasn't a big issue, it's deceptive. You know, Bouchard is a very intelligent man and I don't think he'll have a referendum unless he's sure of winning big, and that's very unlikely because he knows as well as anyone else that if it's 50-50 either way, it's a just a mess, and he doesn't want that. So I rather suspect that Bouchard will lead the Parti Québécois into the next election and then leave rather than be the man who lost another referendum... And without Bouchard it will sink, but still you have 30 to 35% of the francophones in Quebec who are hardcore separatists and whether or not one agrees with them, they've worked for thirty, thirty-five years for this dream of theirs, and there're going to be a lot of depressed people in their sixties who spent their whole adult lives working for this, so it's a very delicate situation all the same. That's a very substantial part of the population. I think we need some kind of healer in this country, and it's certainly not an office that could be filled by the dreadful Preston Manning.

GILLAM ¶ I wish he'd just go away.

RICHLER § With the meeting of premiers, the ghost in the room was that dreadful Manning, and they had to appease Manning, who, I think, is an appalling man. Everything right-wing and ignorant in this country and all the buffoons are attracted to his manner, and they are anti-Quebec and I get sick and tired... Dreadful people.

GILLAM ¶ You're lucky you don't live here in Ontario.

RICHLER § Well, happily, they didn't do that well in the federal election here. But I'm sure in small-town Ontario, they had a considerable following.

GILLAM ¶ Basically, Mike Harris has copied the Reform Party. It's like having the Reform Party.

RICHLER § Yes, it's true.

GILLAM ¶ Now, he's getting ready to disembowel Toronto.

RICHLER § Oh, Toronto is a hell of a lot better than it was thirty or forty years ago, when it was a real Orangeman's town. It's really a decent place now; a lot of Italians came here and Greeks and all kinds of people have come here— they've done a lot for the city. It's a far more enjoyable city than it ever was.

GILLAM ¶ Even when I came here in 1981, it was pretty bleak. They didn't even have outdoor patios.

RICHLER § Or outdoor displays of food... now it's a lot more sensual and a lot more pleasing.

GILLAM ¶ Still, I like Montreal better. I'd like to be able to live in Montreal, but I don't speak enough French. There's no economy there any more.

RICHLER § There's really been a rapid decline, which is too bad.

GILLAM ¶ You mention all the empty shops in the book. That adds to the air of melancholy, because you situate the action in a time and a place.

RICHLER § No. It's certainly taking place in a city that's shrinking day by day.

GILLAM ¶ The whole tone is very much more downbeat than the earlier novels, isn't it?

RICHLER § Yeah.

GILLAM ¶ People these days seem interested in fiction as thinly disguised autobiography or journalism. Do you think this trend is becoming more pronounced?... I think there's tendency to see fiction in this way.

RICHLER § There'll be that tendency with *Barney's Version* because it's written in the first person.

GILLAM ¶ I think, perhaps, there's a cultural failure of imagination here, and people have difficulty telling the difference... because in journalism, especially in TV journalism, you have this bleeding of categories, like fiction and documentary.

RICHLER § Well, there was an excerpt from this novel published in *Saturday Night*. I don't know how many people have said, "I read your article in *Saturday Night*."

GILLAM ¶ They can't tell the difference. I'll give students some sort of non-fiction piece to read, and they'll say, if it's a *book*, it's a novel. As if they can't figure out what the difference between them is.

RICHLER § As you probably know, we lived in London for twenty years and when I came back in '72, I taught at Carlton one day a week. I taught one of those suspect creative writing courses. And I interviewed students who wanted to be in the course. I was only taking fifteen kids. And I asked each one of them— what's the last novel you read?— and one of them— these were all English majors— absolutely endearing— said to me: fiction or non-fiction? I thought that was a gem.

GILLAM ¶ Students don't want to do any real academic work; they just want to be entertained.

RICHLER § I do believe the novel should be entertaining. And I do write for the serious reader. There's a lot of literary references in this novel that I guess a lot of people won't get, but I don't care. Thirty or forty years ago you could count on your readers being educated and understanding a lot of things; you can no longer take that for granted, that people are familiar with the Bible or they've read their mythology. It's a different generation. It's not that they're not bright, it's just that it's all brought down to the lowest common denominator and when they get to university they're not educated. They have to play catch-up... university's a bit too democratic. Everyone goes to university and so the standards are lowered.

GILLAM ¶ And back in high school, you're not allowed to fail anybody.

RICHLER § I was over here in 1961 and I was at Sir George Williams College for one term, and they were all into this, there shouldn't be marks, and I said, I'll tell you what I'll do, I'll put all your names into a hat and there'll be passes and failures and As and Bs... you take what you get. And, oh, no, no, I couldn't do that. They were quite shocked, because this was a creative writing course, which was a Mickey Mouse course, and I failed a lot of them. And they were really startled. And I said, look, I don't want you to waste your time writing, because you can't write. I'm doing you a favour.

GILLAM ¶ With something like *Solomon Gursky*, do you get irritated with people's determination to see it not as fiction but as something else?

RICHLER § Well, you know, I've been around the block a few times. I no longer get as agitated about these things as I used to. So depending on my mood, I can be angry, but for the most part I just let them wash over me.

GILLAM ¶ I think when people are younger they care too much.

RICHLER § But it's good to care...

GILLAM ¶ *Barney's Version* is another one of those Imaginary Montreal novels. What's the next one?

RICHLER § I never talk about that.

GILLAM ¶ Is there going to be another one, or is it going to be completely different?

RICHLER § I hope it'll be something completely different...

GILLAM ¶ Maybe we can look forward to more of them?

RICHLER § My theory is that we all write one novel too many, but I don't know if I've done that yet.

GILLAM ¶ I think you have a way to go.

RICHLER § But it's a wasting business... I'll just go on, I guess.

GILLAM ¶ Do you think writing is a debilitating profession?

RICHLER § No, I think there's far too much self-pity about writing. We're not drafted, we all volunteer. And if I found it so horrendous, I should do something else.

GILLAM ¶ You've had people criticize you for not creating sympathetic or convincing female characters... and you've said somewhere that it's difficult to do it.

RICHLER § I think, in fairness, there have been some. The character of Hannah in *St. Urbain's Horseman*, and a few others, but I've always found it difficult.

GILLAM ¶ I don't think this is a big suprise. Why should you be able to do it?

RICHLER § Someone who does it very well is Brian Moore. He's done it very well from the very first novel, which was *Judith*...

GILLAM ¶ I've never read any Brian Moore, actually.

RICHLER § Well, he's really done it remarkably well, I must say. I found it difficult.

GILLAM ¶ I don't think it should be something to reproach you with. In this book, especially, with it being in the first person, I don't think it's such a problem. Everything is Barney's version; it's his version of every person.

RICHLER § You can also say that's a cop-out.

GILLAM ¶ Yes, but artistically consistent. Perhaps Miriam came across as a little bit too idealized, but he was horrible to the Second Mrs. Panofsky.

RICHLER § I think she's a triumph, myself.

GILLAM ¶ One of the things I love about the way you write is how you transfer spoken into written text and it actually looks funnier on the page.

RICHLER § Those telephone conversations went on about eight more pages each because they were so much fun to write. I looked at them and thought, look, this is really going on. I cut them back. The whole novel would come to a stop, so I really cut back.

GILLAM ¶ It's funny, putting a cigar on the cover... I don't know if you have any control over what they put on the cover.

RICHLER § Yes, yes. They certainly sent it to me and asked what I thought and I said, that's great. The British jacket is different because initially I called the novel *Barney, like the player piano*. And this was very difficult because a lot of people didn't understand what it meant. And someone says to him, you're like a player piano, you pick up everyone else's ideas. And, of course, in England it's called a pianola, not a player piano. Then my wife came up with this title, and I thought, fair enough.

GILLAM ¶ I think it's good because it makes you think. At one point I was completely taken aback and thought, wait a minute, he could be some lying bastard. How do we know?

RICHLER § Well, that's good. I believe in ambiguity and all.

The Idea of Story

VERONICA ROSS
by Melissa Hardy

Born in 1946, VERONICA ROSS emigrated from West Germany to Montreal when she was six years old. She spent a number of years in Nova Scotia, where many of her earlier stories are set; now she lives in Kitchener with writer-photographer husband Richard O'Brien. She has published widely in both commercial and literary magazines and is the author of four story collections— *Goodbye Summer, Dark Secrets, Homecoming,* and *Order in the Universe*— as well as the novels *Fisherwoman* and *Hannah B.* Ross is associate editor for the *Antigonish Review*, and has served terms as writer-in-residence in Thunder Bay, London, and Kitchener. She is the author of the Carolyn Archer mystery series, which includes *Millicent* and *The Burden of Grace.*

MELISSA HARDY ¶ What did you want to be when you grew up?

VERONICA ROSS § I didn't think in terms of wanting to be a writer. When I was seventeen or eighteen I very much wanted to be a painter. I'm glad I didn't pursue it— it was a romantic notion. But writing was something I just did. There was nothing I enjoyed more.

HARDY ¶ When you read, what do you look for?

ROSS § Life. Original voice. Something that means something to me; that moves me. It's quite an event to find a writer whose work you fall in love with. But I'm less happy than I could be with contemporary writing. There's so much sameness. I don't read so-called "serious" writing so much when I'm working. Then I read a lot of escapist stuff— mysteries and biographies. I've been reading a lot of history lately— perhaps because I'm thinking of writing something vaguely historical. The idea's still misty. Biography and history present a very clean, clear read, whereas a book that is— I hate that word— "serious"— is like a door on a new room. Opening it requires an effort.

HARDY ¶ Whose books do you reread?

ROSS § Oh, Tolstoy and Dostoevsky— just like everyone else. Margaret Laurence. Alice Munro. Early Doris Lessing. Some German writers.

HARDY ¶ What do you conceive of as your role? Are you a storyteller? A societal mirror?

ROSS § Storyteller. I don't want to be a societal mirror. I really like the idea of story. I think it's been lost.

HARDY ¶ Is this because of postmodernism?

ROSS § Oh, yes. You know— this sounds terrible— but a writer I really enjoy is Stephen King. He tells such wonderful stories. Real yarns. People want stories. We don't tell enough of them.

HARDY ¶ So you think that the literary consciousness with which many contemporary writers infuse a piece of work can weigh it down?

ROSS § Don't get me wrong. Reading a pot-boiler and a novel with some depth are entirely different experiences, but there's no reason why a good novel can't also be a good read. Take Thomas Mann's *Magic Mountain*. Or *Buddenbrooks*. Large, well-written novels, with different levels and layers, and a great story... We need more of those today. That's missing.

HARDY ¶ Do you perceive yourself as having a number of voices that you regularly employ in your writing— a set of stock characters?

ROSS § I think Margaret in *Fisherwoman*— the strong, older woman who's been a steamroller (I love that word: "steamroller")— has appeared a lot. And I have this male character who's very puzzled. You mentioned earlier that I had two types of men, the more rough-and-tumble, straightforward kind of man, and the softer type. But both of them are really puzzled.

HARDY ¶ Like Jacob in "God's Blessing"?

ROSS § Poor Jacob! Yes. He's so confused. He has a lot of innocence. But I just write about these people. I don't set out to write about The Confusion of Men in Our Society.

HARDY ¶ Could you describe your work habits?

ROSS § I write my first draft on paper, then I revise on a computer. I revise and revise. I love to write at night. I like darkness. Darkness and warm weather. I think writing in a hotel would be tremendous— I've always liked hotels. The feeling of anonymity, like you have no other life except writing. And I have this vision of a house by a lake somewhere. Not back to the land. A very comfortable, little house. I like the idea of water. Being in the country but near a city. It's a clichéd, I know.

HARDY ¶ Do you write a set number of pages, a set number of hours?

ROSS § Usually the momentum of what I'm writing carries me along, but sometimes, if I'm really passionate about a piece I'm writing, I'll just write it flat out, up to sixteen hours at a time.

HARDY ¶ When you write, do you feel you enter a different space?

ROSS § Don't you?

HARDY ¶ *Fisherwoman* is your longest published narrative. How did you pace yourself in order to write that?

ROSS § I started that book several times. It was so stupid. Then, when I finally found out how to do it— that I should use first person— it just followed.

HARDY ¶ How do stories come to you?

ROSS § I start with people, I suppose. For example, last night at the restaurant we were at, there were two people, a mother and daughter. Well, maybe not. Anyway, an older woman who was quite proper but rather dowdy, and this slovenly looking younger woman sitting slumped in her chair, unhappy to be there. And I was looking at them over your shoulder, thinking, "Who are they? Are they a mother and a daughter? Are they lovers?" Well, maybe in a couple of years those two people, as I remember them, or the people that they've created for me, will come together with an idea, and then I'll have a story.

HARDY ¶ You are very respectful towards your characters. And they are very ordinary people, most of them.

ROSS § Don't you ever see people on the street and have this feeling of suddenly seeing a person as a very unique individual? For example, you see a woman struggling with shopping bags, tired, bedraggled, over the hill, and there's something noble and sad and maybe a bit funny about her, too? And not feeling sorry for that person, but admiring her strength and determination? Recognizing her life force?

HARDY ¶ But you're not a sentimental writer.

ROSS § I don't like sentiment. A few of my earlier stories were sentimental, some of the stories in *Dark Secrets*. I would write them differently today.

HARDY ¶ Not infrequently you have a male protagonist, and, because you go in and out of your characters' heads so much, that's tantamount to adopting a male viewpoint. A lot of women writers aren't willing to do that.

ROSS § It seems quite natural to me. Last night I couldn't sleep, and I lay in bed wondering if I could write a first-person narrative from a male viewpoint. I haven't done that as far as I can remember. But I'd like to try it.

HARDY ¶ You don't see viewpoint as sacrosanct, so that only a Native or a black woman can legitimately write about Native or black women's experience?

ROSS § I think that there are certainly cases when that's more legitimate—because of historical abuses and tragedies. But I don't think it's necessarily wrong or even inappropriate. It just depends. That's different from male and female. It's nuts that a woman shouldn't be able to write about a man.

HARDY ¶ Unless you were to say that women have been abused and damaged throughout the centuries...

ROSS § And they have. They have. I think sometimes men have been abused, too.

HARDY ¶ What effect has postmodernism had on your work?

ROSS § None that I'm aware of. I'm not even sure I understand what postmodernism is... I'm not sure I want to.

HARDY ¶ Well, do you consciously try to subvert language or conventional forms...

ROSS § Maybe in my German novel.

HARDY ¶ This is the novel you wrote after your trip to Germany...

ROSS § Part of it's written in the second person, which is difficult.

HARDY ¶ What is it about?

ROSS § Now that I'm removed from it to a certain extent, I would say that *Hannah B.* is about the illusion of history and the history of illusion. Don't I sound like a prim little moralist?

HARDY ¶ Do you think that the subject matter— post-war Germany— might have dictated that it be handled in a more postmodern way than you typically would?

ROSS § Could be. Really, I don't like making those sorts of judgements about *my* work *now*. I'd rather leave them to somebody else twenty years from now. It just felt like the novel I should write. And I loved writing it.

HARDY ¶ Are some things hard to write? Like pulling teeth?

ROSS § I don't write things that are hard any more. I used to when I was just starting out and desperate to publish. But it's stupid to do that. If I don't feel passionate about a story, if I don't care about the people, I just don't do it. It's a very emotional process, not intellectual at all.

HARDY ¶ You say that you were desperate to publish?

ROSS § You reach a point when you feel the need. And it's hard. I hate to think there's an unpublished Hemingway or Malcolm Lowry out there. Isn't that scary? I still have faith that people with a real gift will publish. I'd like to think that. Maybe I'm wrong.

HARDY ¶ How interested are you in language or style?

ROSS § Not very, though that's not the case with *Hannah B.* I think I was more conscious of using language there, and in my later stories as well.

HARDY ¶ Some of the stories which will appear in your collection, *Order in the Universe*, have a German element in them, and they are very different from your earlier work.

ROSS § Things shifted for me because of changes in my personal life... I went to Germany and lived there for a little while, and after about three months I found it almost impossible to speak English. I couldn't get my tongue around it. And English is my main language— I think in it. Then when I came back, the writing had changed. I think I did come to terms with something there.

HARDY ¶ It's a commonplace that immigrants, particularly if they're children, go overboard to absorb the culture of their new country. In your Maritime stories you sound more down-east than a Maritimer. Yet you have this European background, and you spent your girlhood in a big, cosmopolitan city...

ROSS § I felt very comfortable writing about the Maritimes. I liked the Maritimes.

HARDY ¶ In the German stories your sense of reality becomes more European. More flexible. I don't like to use the term magic realism.

ROSS § I hate that term. I know what it means, but I've yet to find a good definition of it.

HARDY ¶ When you write the German stories, do you find your mindset is different?

ROSS § Yes. Schizy, isn't it?

HARDY ¶ If I hadn't known you had written *Fisherwoman* and *Order in the Universe*, I would say they were written by different people.

ROSS § You see! I could have a double life!

HARDY ¶ When you write, is it like transcribing a scene that you see in your head? Or is it like remembering?

ROSS § I like that. Remembering. Yes.

HARDY ¶ Because you're a writer, do you look on experience, on life, differently?

ROSS § Hey! Come on! We shouldn't take ourselves so seriously. I just love writing stories. I also enjoy doing other things. Putzing around in the garden. I like to cook. The need to write... It's a terrible need. Sometimes life would be easier without writing. I could work at McDonald's.

Oral Tapestry

GAIL SCOTT
by Beverley Daurio

Born in Ottawa, GAIL SCOTT grew up in a bilingual community in eastern Ontario. She worked as a journalist for several years, contributing regularly to the *Gazette*, the *Globe and Mail*, and *Maclean's*. A founding editor of *Spirale*, Scott is on the editorial board of *Tessera*. She is the author of *Spaces like Stairs* (essays,), *Spare Parts* (stories,), and two novels, *Heroine* and *Main Brides*. Scott's new novel, *My Paris*, will be released in the near future.

BEVERLEY DAURIO ¶ Your three works of fiction, *Spare Parts*, *Heroine*, and *Main Brides*, could be read as the charting of *a* woman's progress from girl to mature woman, from heterosexual to lesbian experiences, through the sixties, seventies, and eighties... Images from *Heroine* return in *Main Brides*—the soldier Xed out in the picture of the Portuguese bride in the photo-shop window, for example. Do you think that this is a useful way to look at your work in fiction?

GAIL SCOTT § It's true that I often write about clearly delineated time periods. But the word "progress" implies a movement forward, which is not exactly how I perceive experience or writing. I try to see things, rather, as a field of meaning— I get an image of flowers and grass waving in a summer breeze— where there is a complex set of relationships between various elements, including time and space. Example: time progresses chronologically (alas), but also circles in *un retour éternel*. I mean, the way we go back to the old knots, old wounds, but also to the old sites of pleasure, desire. This *retour* is profoundly human.

The reappearance in *Main Brides* of the bride in the photo-shop window from *Heroine* is, in fact, an instance of how that works in my narrative processes. This way of thinking forces me to cross genres in novel writing. It has to do partly with the displacement of the writing subject from a position of certitude towards one of doubt, ambivalence. Ambivalence opens the space for constant slippage, questioning, which is the real work of poetic language. It confounds the art-as-therapy approach and belies the notion that writing directly mirrors experience. In fact, I sometimes suspect the reverse: that life choices are made quite unconsciously, by artists, in terms of their art— whence a tendency I discern in some of us to be greedy for experience, to never say "never." Well, "never" up to a point: my next book shall be written largely in male voices— and I'm not planning a sex change!

DAURIO ¶ *Main Brides* is, among other things, a series of portraits of women. Would you discuss your intentions with regard to "character" in this book?

SCOTT § Lydia is both a female character naming, creating other characters, and a person of somewhat undefined boundaries, merged with her other characters in a kind of Cubist portrait of a figure of a woman at a certain point in geography, culture, time. Her sexual ambivalence permits me to play with all sorts of codes. For instance, dress codes that one might think of as principally heterosexual, and which represent broader notions of "pleasing," coupled with explicit, sometimes obsessional desire for women. Would Lydia desire men, as well, had she not seen the body of a girl in the park earlier?

I saw this kind of reticence, anger, in women after the Montreal massacre. These portraits are "tropes" (Lydia's favourite word) of the social context in other ways, including "statistically" (although Lydia distrusts statistics). Example: almost one third of the portrait subjects are rape/incest survivors (I was being conservative). But in taking on the task of portraiture, Lydia feels a certain guilt, which she attributes to her voyeurism.

Julia Kristeva says somewhere that voyeurism is the other side of abjection. That the voyeurism starts at the point where the writing stops (I take writing here to mean creation, including self-creation). This moment is a parenthesis I open in the novel without closing.

DAURIO ¶ You have spent more than fifteen years living bilingually in

Quebec, involved in both the English-speaking and québécoise literary/theo-retical feminist "worlds." How do you see the differences between these milieux? Janice Williamson once asked you about the difference in *rapport d'adresse* between your work and Nicole Brossard's.

SCOTT § I first heard the notion of *le rapport d'adresse* applied to writer/reader reception in discussions with Nicole at the time of making the film *Fire Words*. At issue was a sense that, in certain contexts, the "male" editor, critic, loomed in the woman writer's mind, snuffing out style, voice. This remains, of course, an issue for many women writers (I see it in creative writing departments sometimes).

But it's much more complex than that— the inhibiting superego can mask any kind of dominant voice, be it elders (Mother!), people of other races, classes. Which is why young writers need peer groups, sympathetic readers who share their deep concerns and are prepared to give them the space to try their new wings, voices.

Unfortunately, peers in radical political movements, hungry for mes-sages, often fail to fulfill this function— although, paradoxically, at the same time, the very existence of the movement opens the space for radical questioning. This contradictory dynamic is the subject of my essay "A Feminist at the Carnival" in *Spaces Like Stairs*.

Also at issue for me on the subject of whom I address when I write is the bicultural nature of my imagined audience. The big challenge in *Heroine* was to try to synthesize experience issuing from two diametrically opposed cultural situations (Quebec/Canada). For this book, I found it easier, as if the contradiction had been integrated into style— but the French-English dichotomy definitely makes it harder to write, and is one reason my writing takes so long.

DAURIO ¶ Few Canadian feminist writers have written, as you have done in your book of essays, *Spaces Like Stairs,* about theory, politics, and writing. There has even been something of a backlash against the idea that politics and aesthetics are linked.

SCOTT § The backlash isn't surprising given the extreme conservatism of the late eighties, early nineties. It's hard to understand how politics might relate in a profound, urgent way to aesthetics when operating from a reformist or, worse, depoliticized context. Like any other application of experience to writing, the urgency of the issue has to be felt. It's only when rebellion becomes a profession that it seems necessary to worry about whether your work has any relationship to what's moving out there. It's *because* you're thinking in structures— that is, in terms of changing social structures— that you start thinking form might be an aesthetic issue as well.

For me, in the particular Quebec context in which my writing started (which context, in time, has altered considerably), the interest in theory was concomitant with the desire for profound change.

DAURIO ¶ The narratives in *Heroine* and *Main Brides* are not strictly chronological, conventional structures; yet they are impelling, active, moving. Could you discuss the narrative strategy in your novels?

SCOTT § Narrative is my obsession, but I come at it with something of the mindset of a poet. It is a constantly elusive thing I am trying to grasp, as one tries to find, under a dream's manifest content, its censored latent content. This requires giving up the control of the sentence at the outset, finding some new way of writing it that permits discovery. As the sentence changes, the paragraph changes, and ultimately, the narrative structure. This is a lifetime's work.

In *Main Brides*, I needed sentences that would make the voices palpable in the text, voices of lust, hope, desire, but also pain, menace— *plus* a "story" to hold it all together. The *Sky* sections, which provide the narrative link between the seven portraits of the book, although simple on the surface, are the hardest things I have ever written. I think this is because they operate on a point where novel and short story meet.

I've often wondered why I need to write narrative as much as I do when language poetry is one of the forms I most enjoy reading. I think finding a narrative or story is my particular way of pinning down hope. Anna Karenina (because of the train image) shattered by the revolution and coming together in some new kind of montage, minus the moralizing, the sentimentalism.

DAURIO ¶ *Main Brides* revels in depictions of the streets and cafés of Montreal— the "real"— but at the same time alludes often to surrealist theories.

SCOTT § The business of writing from place is something I experience so intensely that I can hardly discuss it. Montreal is so much part of who/what I am as a person and writer. I settled here as a young writer because it offered two things I needed: to have French in my ear (which is how I grew up); and a context of rebellion.

But it is not an easy place to live, often shattered as well as dynamized by difference (which is maybe why Lydia resists revealing her ethnicity, although she participates in the rhetoric of difference constantly). As *une anglaise*, I am both of, and not of, the place. Anything surrealist that surfaces in my writing probably relates to this: the ambiguity, irony, of my position. The understanding that the "line of reason" changes depending on the language spoken (just read the different headlines in the French and English papers). Certain notions of surrealism are still technically useful to me— the insistence on "objective chance," and the importance of dreams. But surrealism is also problematic in the way it objectifies the Other.

DAURIO ¶ Though the action in *Main Brides* ranges over North America and Cuba, the narrative voice speaks primarily from a café, a still place from which the consciousness then wanders wherever it pleases...

SCOTT § I suppose it is often unclear in novels where the narrator is positioned, although it often seems to be looking down on its subject. Here and in *Heroine* the narrative voice is personified in a way that suggests, I think, more layers of narration than the classical author, narrator, text structure. In *Heroine* she is somewhat collapsed with the voice of the author. In *Main Brides,* one senses that Lydia, who is narrating the stories of her portraits, may be another voice, narrating her. And so on— a chain where the boundaries between the different narrative levels are somewhat unclear. Narrative as metonymy rather than as cause-and-effect.

DAURIO ¶ What do you think about the current arguments about political correctness? Can feminist and other theory strangle free expression?

SCOTT § The word "correct" reminds me of all the *dos* and *don'ts* of my Protestant childhood, as if "politically correct" stemmed from some kind of old-fashioned moralism that develops in political movements not willing to go far enough. It's anathema to writing. The exploration of new ethics, ways of being, generally arising as well from movements of change, is, on the contrary, fuel for the writer's fire. Any writer with a political consciousness, however imperfect, is caught between the two. We choose our own shackles.

Writing *Heroine,* a radical feminist was leaning over my shoulder repeating "she (that is, 'Gail,' the narrator) is too wimpy." All the same, I was thankful it was she, the feminist, leaning over my shoulder, rather than some guy with Frye boots and a paunch waving the conventions of the canon at me.

I suspect we prose-fiction writers have more problems with the p.c. censors than poets, because, by using sentences, we move towards fixing things in place (making statements). Also, because we create characters who tend not to be p.c., thank god, because p.c. is generally a superficial take on being, hence boring.

But feminism and theory are not necessarily synonymous with each other, nor does being publicly linked with either of those words (apparently both considered bad company in polite circles) amount to being politically correct. My hair stands on end when people say "theory" ruins writing. What theory? On what level are they speaking? Does this mean they never read? Everything we absorb in our environment has some theory linked to it. To pretend this isn't so is to hide one's head in the sand. "Theory" is just another word for understanding systems. If a writer is so poorly constituted intellectually as to be overwhelmed, invaded, by any book of ideas that she reads, she probably isn't a very good writer.

But what I hate most about this position is its profound hypocrisy— for reading is part of writing; most writers read widely. I guess some writers think it makes them look better if they pretend they did it all by themselves.

DAURIO ¶ Could you please discuss how history is addressed in *Main Brides,* and why?

SCOTT § At the end of this terrible century, which has at its heart the

Holocaust and Hiroshima, many people are speaking of the end of history. If it's the end of anything, I prefer to think it's the end of history as we know it; to pretend Lydia is practising, in her mind (and possibly in the making of her portraits), a new way to write history. I believe this is part of a project, almost unconscious, of many women writing today. Lydia's propositions on this score are whimsical, inspired by too many *carafons*.

But in my mind, while writing phrases on history, was a passage from Walter Benjamin's great *Le livre des passages*: "La première étape... consistera à reprendre dans l'histoire le principe du montage. C'est à dire à édifier les grandes constructions à partir de très petits éléments confectionnés avec précision et netteté." The opposite of the battering-ram approach to history— with its laws and principles of dominance that exclude, always, the other, either metaphorically, on the level of discourse, or simply by murder. My intention here was only to posit some method for hope in place of despair, represented in the novel by the sign of the murdered girl's body in the park.

DAURIO ¶ There is some play with palimpsests in *Main Brides*— a French-only sign that does not quite cover an English-Hebrew-Arabic sign, for example— and the related matter of recurring references to New Orleans, Louisiana, which I understood to be a fear-image for the Québécois because of the destruction of French culture in the States...

SCOTT § The word "palimpsest" covers very well how I like to think of narrative— as a space of shifting uncertain meaning, its strength coming precisely from its flexibility. There are little examples of this everywhere in *Main Brides:* in Nanette's fascination for the movement of clouds; in the ungraspable movement of love in "Canadian Girls," in the contradictory movement of fear and brashness in "DisMay." The character Z.'s shifting back and forth between cultures, the shifting of the signs on the sign shop, represent, also, a painful, restless search for the resolution of a problem that many of us wear written on our bodies.

I'm not sure New Orleans is a fear image for Québécois, today— people here wouldn't tolerate that kind of deterioration of their language, culture, when they have independence as an option. I invoked New

Orleans for other reasons: a similar approach to pleasure; also, the fact that it's not easy to be marginal. I read in the newspaper that, of the large continental cities, the two French-speaking ones have among the highest employment rates. Also, not surprisingly, New Orleans and Montreal have things in common, architecturally.

DAURIO ¶ Voices sound, out of the air almost, from time to time throughout *Main Brides*, like a chorus from a Greek drama, with questions, comments, arguments. What do they represent for you in the book?

SCOTT § I do see the voices in the bar as a kind of Greek chorus. The bar's regulars, whose thoughts are tendentiously interpreted by Lydia, but the voices of others, too, passing on the street, or speaking in her head, all add up to a kind of oral tapestry of the particular point in time from which she speaks.

In a sense, the whole book participates in this "tapestry," for every part is influenced by every other part; there are hundreds of tiny reverberations. But the regulars, particularly, represent voices of inhibition, negative predilection, *in Lydia's mind.*

Occasionally, when writing this book, I wanted to turn those figures around, to see them from "their own" viewpoint, more sympathetically. But something about the internal logic of the novel did not permit it. This may be one reason why I intend to try and write "in a male voice" for a change. Of course, it would be my take on that voice, so there is nothing to say I will succeed.

All Those Selves and Experiences

MAKEDA SILVERA
by Jeffrey Canton

MAKEDA SILVERA has written for the Black community newspapers *Share* and *Contrast*, and is author of the resource guide, *Growing Up Black* (1989); an acclaimed collection of oral histories of West Indian domestic workers, *Silenced* (revised 1989); a collection of short stories, *Remembering G.* (1991); she is also editor of an anthology of writings by lesbians of colour, *Piece of My Heart* (1991). Silvera's first novel is *The Revenge of Maria*. She is co-founder of Sister Vision, Black Women and Women of Colour Press, in Toronto, where she is managing editor.

JEFFREY CANTON ¶ Your latest book is the collection of stories, *Remembering G.* Would it be fair to describe *Remembering G.* as "autobiographical fiction"? It's neither strictly memoir nor fiction.

MAKEDA SILVER § The more that I write and enter into the world of fiction, I come to understand that I can't write from pure fantasy or make-believe. Part of my impetus has to be grounded in some experience of my own or in experiences of people close to me. Then you mould that experience and craft it and that is what becomes fiction.

CANTON ¶ Your previous books— and I'm thinking particularly of *Silenced* and the anthology, *Piece of My Heart: a lesbian of colour anthology*— have not been fiction. What made you take the leap into the "world of fiction"?

SILVERA § I write to understand self, society and my place in society and the place of the people I am very close to within society. I felt I could best write about and come to better understand my own growing-up years through fiction.

CANTON ¶ The stories in *Remembering G.* draw on the memories of your mother and your grandmother. How do they feel about the way you have written about their lives?

SILVERA § There are varying opinions and reactions from my family. My grandmother was quite fine with it. As far as she's concerned, this is my work, something I have done and that I've worked really hard at. I have exposed some family stuff that she might not be happy with, but as far as she's concerned, I am the writer and what I've done is fine. She's very supportive.

My mother and some other members of my family, though proud of the book, don't really understand, or are afraid of that honesty that sometimes comes with writing. In terms of my mother, there is a tremendous amount of censorship. She would say to me: "You could have written this differently," or "I know this story and this is not the way that it's supposed to be told."

CANTON ¶ How do you feel about the world of *Remembering G.*, that you left behind and are no longer concretely part of?

SILVERA § When I wrote the stories in *Remembering G.*, I looked at it purely from the point of view as a child. That's how I saw the world as it was, twenty-odd years ago. All the characters and everything just came back and this was Jamaica and that was this world.

In the book that I am working on now, that changes dramatically. I'm looking at Jamaica and the Caribbean very much as an outsider, as somebody who goes back and forth and is trying to find a place and doesn't really belong. Most of the experiences are from here, but always going back there, and not being as grounded as the young girl here.

CANTON ¶ Within the stories you played with the distance of a story, a memory— especially in the title story, "Remembering G."— from that childhood world. Did you find it difficult to write from the perspective of a child?

SILVERA § I didn't find it difficult. I really enjoyed it. For me, the most difficult story in terms of myself as that child was "Remembering G."

CANTON ¶ Why was that more difficult? I would have thought that a story like "Gem"— which is a precursor to your coming-out story— and which is immediately followed by the terrifying "Jack-the-Painter," where you deal with sexual abuse, would have been more difficult emotionally. For me, "Jack-the-Painter" spoiled the mood left by "Gem": it felt like an invasion of sexual privacy.

SILVERA § I'm not good at analyzing my own stories, even though I write to find some kind of truth or illumination or whatever. In some sense, "Gem" and "Jack-the-Painter" were easier for me to write because I've worked through a lot of that stuff. "Jack-the-Painter" is something that happened and it was an abuse but I feel that I've worked through all of that. I understand it as an issue and know that it still happens, but it is not something that has handicapped me and kept me in a state of fear. I've understood it and I have gone beyond it.

CANTON ¶ Did the oral histories which you collected in *Silenced* help you in writing *Remembering G.*? It strikes me that through your work runs a common thread— the need that we have to share our stories.

SILVERA § Working on *Silenced*, I never thought of the book *Remembering G.* It wasn't there. I never thought that *Remembering G.* was an extension of *Silenced*. But a writer tries to seek truth and to share that experience. To bare oneself. After re-reading *Silenced*, to some extent I thought, if these women could do this, so can I, because I also have a lot that I can share with other people.

CANTON ¶ In the introduction to *Silenced* you write, "Language is a powerful aspect of culture. When it is taken away from an individual, it is an act of disempowering that person." I felt that *Remembering G.* was your way of re-empowering—

SILVERA § ...with that language...

CANTON ¶ — your own childhood and culture. Would you agree?

SILVERA § More so because of the age I was when I came here. At twelve, at thirteen years of age, being immersed in the school system with that language— that so-called disability language. And having to try to integrate and to prove oneself. It was really important for me to deal with that language.

Also knowing that there are a lot of youths in the school system who have had that experience, who are afraid to speak up, who see no reflection of self anywhere at all. I have two children, young women, who go to Oakwood Collegiate in Toronto, and I went there to the Afro-Canadian class to read. It was wonderful and one of the best rewards for writing *Remembering G*. The students were saying "Wow! This is what *I* have experienced. This is what happened," and it created a forum for them to publicly speak about language, dialect and experience."

CANTON ¶ In your resource guide, *Growing Up Black*, you open the first chapter, "Getting to know ourselves," with a quote that sums up one teenager's experience of immigration— "I came here from Trinidad when I was four years old. I really have no memory of Trinidad but I'm familiar with Trinidadian food and culture because my parents talk and eat Trinidadian." This must be a common experience for children of immigrants and this is one of the things that makes *Remembering G*. such a resonant book. Would you agree?

SILVERA § Most definitely.

CANTON ¶ One of the interesting aspects of *Remembering G*. is your use of the Jamaican language.

SILVERA § That was very important in terms of the transition and moving across different cultures and different worlds. To make oneself visible— to be able to say "I am here. This is how I speak. This is what I have to say. This is really valuable and important." Yes, I'm telling a story and I do have a community and I am grounded, but I want other people outside that community to learn and understand and move. I don't always have to speak in someone else's corner.

CANTON ¶ Would it also be a question of taking pride in that language and the culture? In terms of writing these experiences and re-capturing that world, your voice celebrates the diversity of that world, too.

SILVERA § A lot of that is grounded in my experience as a young adult living here, where all of that was taken away from me. All of my self-confidence and worth. Moving here at twelve or thirteen took a lot of that away. It's a different culture. You are no longer in the majority. It's no longer a community that you live in where so-and-so knows your mother or grandmother.

You are taken out and dumped somewhere here and there's complete and total alienation from even your parents. Because they don't understand the system. They are caught up in a web of prejudice and racism and are also trying to find themselves in that system. It creates a real block for children.

It was important for me to take that journey back in understanding that happens when you come here or when you move something that is living and breathing. It was important to take that journey and to go back there— what was it like? who was this child? who are these children— these happy, normal kids? And what happens when you take them somewhere that they are not familiar with and where they are alienated with growing up Black?

CANTON ¶ Growing up in *Remembering G.* entails an exploration of sexuality. "Out de Candle" celebrates the development of a sexual persona— it is full of fascination with sexuality. It is also full of warnings— about sexual abuses, sexual prejudices.

SILVERA § It was important to me that all those selves and experiences be in there. The sexual abuse, the awakening sexuality, exploring different sexual aspects with friends of your own sex, and, as in the first story, "No Beating Like Dis One," exploring sex with a boy.

It's that point in growing up where you don't really know. You have not formed anything, you have no opinions about anything. To bring all of those experiences together and all of the stuff that young girls go through at that age and also, as you get older, what, somehow you begin to censor and what you don't. To explore this freshness and blossoming. What we take and what we don't take and why.

CANTON ¶ In your essay in *Pieces of My Heart*, "Man Royals and Sodomites: Some Thoughts on the Invisibility of Afro-Caribbean Lesbians," you talk about the need to "imagine and discover our existence, past and present" and "to create wholeness through our art... to share our histories and record these histories..." so that we can "create a rhythm that is uniquely ours— proud, powerful and gay, naming ourselves, and taking our space within the larger history of Afro-Caribbean peoples."

SILVERA § In the society that we find ourselves in sometimes, as minorities, you can't usually do that in a public space. To me, this is why writing is so powerful. You claim space, you take space, you take what you want. You are alone, isolated— you're writing. It's not like being in a public space where you are standing up and giving a speech, or where you have to make allowances for all the different groups that are around or the power structure.

CANTON ¶ Did you find it difficult to write in the Jamaican language from this distance?

SILVERA § It was more difficult to write in it than to speak in it. To find some kind of grounding and commonality in the spelling of words so that others could understand it, because sometimes what you hear and what's on paper are two different things. Doing this in dialect— with the glossary— was a continuing journey and education for myself. It's also an area that I want to continue to explore, to have that freedom to go back and forth between standard English and dialect. I took it quite seriously as another language.

CANTON ¶ Do you see the act of giving voice as a political act?

SILVERA § Yes. Whether it is English or a dialect or whatever, we do speak in different languages; that is something that's not recognized. When you don't speak in the language of the other or of the establishment, you are silenced and you feel silenced. You have to take that and turn it around and make sense out of it and be powerful.

CANTON ¶ How do you feel about the Caribbean from your perspective now? For example, how do react as a feminist to the more patriarchal attitudes prevalent in the Caribbean?

SILVERA § It's interesting. I am a feminist but I don't have a different feeling because I am a Black feminist. I live in Canada but I feel that I live in a Third World section of Canada; Canada is divided. I have a community which is Black, which is Caribbean. I have extended family, I have friends and this is the life. I have friends who are not feminist who are involved in this kind of lifestyle who have been transformed from the Caribbean to here. It's still, for me, based in a lot of reality. When I write in that way or when, in *Silenced,* I chose to present that in print in a formal manner, it is because it is a reality to the women that I'm writing on behalf of. It is their lives and these are things they talked about that were important to them.

If these people are going to read the book and to reclaim their power and their community, then it's important to say that in print so that they can relate that and it can become some kind of dialogue or discussion. This is different from where we live or from this society— how is it different? How are we going to change it? Do we want to change it or are we satisfied with this? Or we're dissatisfied with this and we have this other model out there. It opens up space and room to look at things differently. It's important that it be out there and in print. It's a reality. Even if you are a feminist, you still live in your community.

CANTON ¶ In a special 1983 issue of *Fireweed* that examined the lives and experiences of women of colour, you took part in a dialogue that examined the state of women of colour in Canada. You say at one point in the discussion, "We live in a racist society and I'm reminded of that every day, every hour of my life." Do you feel more optimistic now, nine years later?

SILVERA § It's a complex question. In terms of Sister Vision, it's true that it's been able to give so much voice to a lot of women who would never have had access to being taken seriously as writers, to being published and space to read in public. Through Sister Vision and a lot of hard work. In terms of that literary stuff, it's changed a wee bit— as much as Sister Vision can with its resources and also as much as enough pressure has been put on other publishers to open up space.

On the other hand, for people who are not artists, who work nine-to-five or work in a factory, it hasn't really changed. The issues and the circumstances might be a bit more volatile because there are more people of colour every day. The population is growing so some of those issues are being put on the table. But I wouldn't say that it has changed. It hasn't.

Because there are more people, because the voices will not remain silenced, I would say that more whites, more people from the dominant society, are beginning to listen a bit more than they did ten years ago.

When I look back at my own life, in retrospect, growing up here and going to high school I was totally alienated. I had no sense of self and was ashamed of self. The end result of that was that I dropped out of school and got involved in gangs because that was where I could feel a sense of self and worth.

I look at high schools today— those gangs, made up of kids who are trying to protect each other, to find power in themselves as outcasts, are still there. So what has really changed? What happened on Yonge Street earlier this year— twenty years ago when I was in high school that didn't happen; it was more internalized— and now it's out. But there's been no change in the actual structure, in the society itself.

CANTON ¶ When did you co-found Sister Vision?

SILVERA § In 1985. With Stephanie Martin.

CANTON ¶ How do feel about your work in publishing?

SILVERA § Really great. There are some moments— because it is publishing and publishing is really hard— when you want to walk out of that door and be totally invisible. On the whole, however, I feel good because we have given voices to people who would not necessarily have a voice. For example, we've recently published a revised edition of a children's book by Lenore Keeshig-Tobias, *Bird Talk*, and we wanted to do a translation into Ojibwa. And she's told me since how much this has empowered her. You feel a lot of a reward.

Hell, we're doing something, not just publishing within the establishment; we're breaking ground and doing things that have never been done in Canada before.

CANTON ¶ I'm curious about the plight of the domestic workers whose stories make up your book *Silenced*— have there been changes, for example, in the Employment Visa?

SILVERA § There have been such small changes that *Silenced* could be reprinted tomorrow without many alterations. The lives of the women are just the same. Any changes have been merely cosmetic and do not really impact on their lives because a lot of them live in individual homes, where there's a certain kind of intimacy. It's not a workplace, it's not a factory where you clock in and clock out. Until domestic workers can come to Canada and have the choice of living in or out, nothing will change.

CANTON ¶ What writers have influenced your work? At the end of *Growing Up Black*, you list writers such as Toni Morrison, Alice Walker and Jamaica Kincaid—

SILVERA § They are all people I especially enjoy reading. Toni Morrison is a writer I respect. I love her work. As a writer myself, I know how much time that it has taken her to mould her stories.

I read a lot of Alice Walker as a young woman and it inspired me, though I don't think I actually took any directions from her, because she was writing from a Black-American experience. And I was an Afro-Caribbean woman on my way to becoming an Afro-Canadian woman and there were no Black writers in Canada that you could take anything from.

I think Jamaica Kincaid's first two books are quite fine in the exploration of a young girl growing up, but I feel that my story was a different story that had to be told in a different way.

CANTON ¶ What kinds of books do you most enjoy reading?

SILVERA § I get caught up as a reader with the lives of writers, more so, than what they have written or analyses of their work. The kind of journey that they have made to write and the stumbling blocks they faced. I tend to read many autobiographies of writers.

James Baldwin is a writer I absolutely fell in love with when I was eighteen, when I didn't even know where I was going in terms of my sexuality or writing. I'm reading a lot of old classics by white male Europeans that I totally rejected in my early years, when I read writers like Claude McKay, Richard Wright and Baldwin.

CANTON ¶ Why did you decide to write?

SILVERA § Growing up here in the early seventies, I was really hungry for some sense of self. But most of the Black writers were male, like Austin Clarke, and I had the sense of something missing in terms of women. When Black women writers from America started writing, there were things I could relate to but there was still a part missing. Even when I became aware of Caribbean women writing, there were gaps around issues relating to sexuality and around being a North American Black— a lot of the values are different. I came to realize that there were no books around— you have to create them.

You have to write them yourselves with that passion and that knowledge, that sense that "I want to do this, I want to be a writer and to create."

CANTON ¶ You are working on a new book...

SILVERA § Yes, it deals with experiences in Canada. I am exploring issues like censorship and family, issues that I'm dealing with that happen every day but are also painful. Where in *Remembering G.* there is a bit of pain, it's still really sweet and a celebration of self and growing up; the new book is the reality of just being here, and it's hard.

Ideals and Lost Children

AUDREY THOMAS
by Robyn Gillam

AUDREY THOMAS' novels include *Graven Images* (1993), *Songs My Mother Taught Me* (1973), *Mrs. Blood* (1975), and *Intertidal Life* (1984). Born in New York State, she has lived in British Columbia since 1959. Thomas' extensive travels included a period of residence in western Africa, the setting for her most recent novel, *Coming Down from Wa* (1997). Also the author of many radio plays and a number of short story collections, Thomas has won several literary prizes, including the Marian Engel Award and the Canada-Australia Award for fiction, and has been shortlisted for the Governor General's Award.

ROBYN GILLAM ¶ What made you decide to write a novel from a male perspective?

AUDREY THOMAS § It was a challenge. That's why I did it, partly. It was a challenge because of the way men use language. I'm not a semanticist or a linguist, but I bet if you broke down sentence patterns, the equivalent male and the equivalent female, you'd find the sentence patterns quite different. Notice he's a young man, he's very sensitive. I made it easier for myself. It was really fun to try and see if I could make him at all convincing. I've been going around asking men who have read the book, and they believed in him.

GILLAM ¶ Is there anything else you noticed when you were creating this male character?

THOMAS § I had to try and see how he would look at women. I found that very interesting and I did ask a lot of men some very pointed questions. There's a scene in the book where William is in the blazing sun, when they're at a border. They're crossing into Ghana from the Ivory Coast, and he wants to get out of the sun; he goes round to the back of the long distance bus he's been travelling on to get into the shade and there are all these young and not-so-young women nursing their babies, and he's so embarrassed. When I wrote this scene, I took it to men, and they said, this is completely unbelievable, it wouldn't have bothered us, and I thought, you're lying through your teeth. The women are nursing their babies. Their breasts are being used for a non-erotic function. One man said it wouldn't have bothered him in the least. Meanwhile, his face was getting redder and redder. Such a liar! I was trying to think up themes that would show the difference, where a man would feel quite disconcerted.

GILLAM ¶ Part of William's character is feeling that he wants to be an artist, and he can't be.

THOMAS § People have talent for different things, and William does not have a talent for drawing. He's fixated on it; and maybe you do the thing you can't do. It's always the impossible ideal, because you can't do it. That's why he remembers this girl that is so pretty, who said she'd give up all her good looks to be able to sing like Edith Piaf for one day.

GILLAM ¶ So the protagonist is looking for something he can't have?

THOMAS § I think so. There's a book that influenced me profoundly, which I every so often read over again— Conrad's Lord Jim. Jim is the ultimate romantic; he's always going to be heroic. He always sees himself as a heroic person, which is very different from being romantic, and yet he jumps ship when he thinks the ship is sinking. The ship doesn't sink and he has to carry this shame with him and he keeps going farther and farther into the remote far east, in order to hide his shame, because he can't live up to his romantic conception of himself, and, then, of course, he does become Lord Jim, he does find a place to stay, and sort of dies for his romantic ideal. I've always found that book very, very interesting. And I think William is a dyed-in-the-wool romantic. He's on a kind of archetypal quest: a quest for knowledge, a quest for a father... and he is observant. He does appreciate the landscape through which he passes. In some ways he is an artist, but he doesn't know that. I haven't imagined where he will go from here. He might do something with cloth, because he keeps buying up all this cloth, which has these amazing colours put together. He may use it as a designer.

GILLAM ¶ Are these quests perpetual?

THOMAS § Yes, I think it's that old Descartes thing. One of his arguments for the proofs of the existence of God is that there must be perfection, since we have such a ton of imperfection. Where do we get this idea that we're imperfect? Where do we get all this idealism from? Why are we always yearning? I don't know. I think it's part of human nature. A big part. What's in *Portrait of the Artist*? Remember that Lucifer was God's brightest angel till he fell. Maybe we're all just fallen angels, and, therefore, always yearning for the ideal. I think you can be fulfilled for a period of time, but I think happiness is a word that is, in a way, retrospective. If you're stuck saying, *oh, God, I'm happy,* you're probably in trouble. If you look back at happiness, it's a reflexive word, in a way. I mean, there are moments of pure joy, but that's a different thing.

GILLAM ¶ Like *Graven Images, Coming Down from Wa* revolves around a mysterious incident that poisons relations within a family. If we think of the family as a kind of writing, does that make it a mystery rather than a romance or a history? What relationship does *Coming Down from Wa* have to *Graven Images*?

THOMAS § Well, it doesn't really have any, but I am an avid reader of mystery, particularly psychological mystery. I read a lot of Ruth Rendell even though she tends to give me the creeps, particularly when she's writing as Barbara Vine. I think she's really in love with the psychotic personality. Those are not books to read alone at night, they really aren't; sometimes they're absolutely terrifying, particularly when they're in the first person. A friend of mine said, I do believe that every writer only writes one story. Hemingway writes about personal courage, but what he really writes about is the lack of personal courage. The women are sort of incidental. It's about personal, manly courage, about definitions of courage. We now know that he himself had a real problem with physical courage. It was his obsession. Fitzgerald writes about money. That's his great obsession, money. A friend of mine said that my big obsession is, and I don't know why, the lost child. He said, if you look back at all your books, they deal with the lost child, using that very generally. And that would be the link between *Graven Images* and *Coming Down from Wa*. There's no real direct correlation at all, but they do both deal with lost children. In fact, they deal very specifically with loss... and lost innocence. I also have orphans in my stories; I'm not an orphan, I'm not adopted. I don't know why I've got to work on the lost children.

GILLAM ¶ What fascinates me in this novel is the mystery and how the quester is drawn into it; they come into this thing at the heart of a maze. But it's always more and it's always less than they imagined.

THOMAS § Oh, absolutely, it's always more and it's always less. And when William thinks he's got the answer at one point, he doesn't. The answer is what the mother has to say. And we don't know how much of the story she's really told him.

GILLAM ¶ I thought it was very disturbing when William decided to send his parents a postcard that just said, *I KNOW.* You know that this is his low point, and then he loses his money.

THOMAS § That actually came out of an incident in Greece. I'll take anything and transpose it anywhere. I was with my youngest daughter in Greece one summer. We'd had coffee at a little open air café. The hundred drachma note looks like a hundred dollar bill, and I handed this young waiter what I thought was a hundred drachma note, and we wandered off down the road. He came running after us, and he said, what's this? I'd given him my hundred dollar bill, my emergency hundred dollar bill. Thank God he was honest. I kept that incident, thinking, that would be a really good incident for a story, where you give someone the wrong money. I was trying to think of something that would take William into a kind of crisis. As he says, it's terrible to throw stones at children about money, about anything, but particularly about money. There are a lot of biblical references in the novel; let he who is without sin cast the first stone. Now he, too, is a sinner.

GILLAM ¶ I think people who are reading the novel may be wondering if you're saying something about the developing world. What about the issue of voice? Was that something you were thinking about when you wrote it?

THOMAS § Well, I did think about it. When William's up in the north and he realizes that it isn't Gideon's Bible, it's the Koran in the night table, and he wants to go out and shout, I am Salman Rushdie... because I've always found it really interesting; we wear these buttons here; nobody's going to kill you for wearing a button. But what would have happened to him if he had gone out there, in this extraordinarily Muslim society, and just shouted out something like that? Probably nothing. They'd say, who is Salman Rushdie? They'd just look at him.

GILLAM ¶ *Coming Down from Wa*, in contrast to some of your other works, like *Intertidal Life* or *Graven Images*, seems to foreground dialogue and narrative and dramatic situations, rather than the wordplay and literary allusions that we find in the other novels.

THOMAS § They're not as blatant. It's probably the most linear novel I've ever written.

GILLAM ¶ And I was wondering if this comes out of your work with radio plays and so on.

THOMAS § I think a lot of my fascination with dialogue comes out of that. When you're writing radio plays, and I've written a lot of them, there are two things. One is that you are essentially writing for an audience of one; I don't find it very different to write a radio play than to write a short story. Everything depends on dialogue, everything, and you can't look back and say, and what was that guy saying? as you can with a book; you have to get it right the first time. I am fascinated by dialogue, and I am quite good at it and I've gotten better and better. The more radio work I do, the better I get at dialogue.

GILLAM ¶ Because some of your short stories have become radio plays and vice versa.

THOMAS § Absolutely. And one of my radio plays is becoming a film script, called *Change of Heart*. It's a comedy about heart transplants. It's a lot different from the radio play. The central premise started with someone I know getting a heart transplant years ago, maybe eighteen years ago; she got a boy's heart, as I recall. Everybody was saying, she's going to be different; I was going around being rational and saying the heart is only an organ, it doesn't matter whose heart it is. It's an organ, it's muscle, it's not even an organ. She not going to be any different. And then I began to think, because I like country-and-western music, about all this stuff about the heart, about the fact that your heart speeds up when it sees the loved one or the bear. We do feel like the heart is the centre of our soul, somehow.

GILLAM ¶ *Coming Down from Wa* seems to hark back to *Intertidal Life*, in that it's about exploration. You suggest in the earlier book that this activity might be recast from a female position. Here we've got a male explorer, but he's stripped of his potency, in the shape of things like maps, navigational instruments and self-confidence.

THOMAS § And he's very sick, too. He's stripped in another sense. He gets very, very ill; he gets completely washed out, purged. That's really important. But it's funny you should say that, because I'm working on a book set in Orkney and in Rupert's Land, what is now Manitoba, and it has to do with a woman who disguised herself as a man in order to work for the Hudson's Bay Company.

GILLAM ¶ In the introduction to *Good Bye Harold, Good Luck*, you said that people accusing you of not being feminist did not see that it was implicit in your writing.

THOMAS § You can't add feminism to your work. You're either a feminist or you're not. And in that introduction, I say it's not like vanilla; you don't go, tsk tsk, needs a bit more feminism, and you put some more feminism in. It doesn't work that way. And if you want to write polemic, which is a different thing altogether, you should be writing non-fiction. In the feminist movement, in the sixties, some of the really strong writers were writing non-fiction, because they knew perfectly well they couldn't do it in fiction without writing crummy fiction. So they were writing non-fiction, which is exactly what they should have been writing.

GILLAM ¶ Whereas in the case of fiction, it's structural.

THOMAS § Yeah. And I think the kind of women I'm interested in are women who are struggling with these questions about what it means to be a woman. What does that really mean? I mean, what advantages and what limitations are put on them in the second half of the twentieth century?

GILLAM ¶ What do you think of, for want of a better word, post-structuralist, postmodern criticism, which is looking at women's writing as something that particularly engages language; in particular, things that Linda Hutcheon has written about your work, and how people associate you with Aritha van Herk and Nicole Brossard?

THOMAS § That is such nonsense. I'm not any of those things. If I'm a deconstructionist, it started at the age of three, before the word was invented. I don't think or write any differently than I did at three. I just have a bigger vocabulary. I've always used collage, I always used those kinds of techniques, I've always played around with words. Playing around with words is what I do. There's something so deadly serious about all this real language-oriented stuff. But I understand it from the Quebec women, because we've taken a lot of the gender problems out of our language. Now, if I were a professor in a French university and I had to be called "le professeur," in a classroom with six girls and one boy, I think I would get pretty interested in those questions, too. But, I think, in English, we've dropped a lot of that, and so maybe I don't feel as strongly about some of those problems as I do about other problems. I just really love playing with language, and I can push it, too, you know. Someone was talking to me the other day about my manuscript and I said, excuse me, you have to call those womenuscripts. I just wanted to see what his reaction would be.

GILLAM ¶ This has become political to a lot of critics because, to a lot of men, a lot of male writers, a lot of male academics, playing with words used to be considered rather childish, unless it occurred in Shakespeare or James Joyce, where it was okay.

THOMAS § That's the best play there is... I'm not language-oriented in the philosophical way; definitely in the plasticine way. I love playing with words; I'll never stop.

Distance Will Reveal Its Secrets

LOLA LEMIRE TOSTEVIN
by Barbara Carey

LOLA LEMIRE TOSTEVIN is a Toronto writer who has published many reviews and essays, as well as four books of poetry— *Color of Her Speech* (1982), *Gyno-Text* (1983, which also appears in *The Long Poem Anthology*, edited by Sharon Thesen (1991), *Double Standards* (1985) and *'sophie* (1988). She is the author of a collection of essays, *Subject to Criticism* (1996), and a novel, *Frog Moon* (1992).

BARBARA CAREY ¶ As a child, you spent seven years in a convent. What effect has this experience had on you as a writer?

LOLA LEMIRE TOSTEVIN § I didn't think it had had any effect when I was writing poetry. But when I began writing *Frog Moon* I realized I needed to include part of that experience. And I keep buying CDs, music, that go back to the chants of the mass, although I don't practice religion any more.

CAREY ¶ So there's something about the ritual that still appeals to you?

TOSTEVIN § I think "ritual" is the key word. There's something about the ritual that I've never been able to get through. I still like that sense of communion, of communication, although I don't believe in the dogma. Also the kind of formation the nuns gave us— reading St. Thomas Aquinas and all those texts— you can't help but be influenced by that. Someone once said that I thought like a Jesuit. Not that I took that as a compliment, but I think what the person was referring to was a kind of formation which has never left me. My education, to the end of high school, was with nuns, and it was strict.

CAREY ¶ Do you think that your attitude towards language itself is marked by that experience?

TOSTEVIN § I'm sure it is. Except for two or three brief periods of recreation each day, the only time we were allowed to speak was in a prayer or Scripture context. Other than those brief periods it was either silence or prayer— or singing. But I was told I was tone deaf, so I didn't sing. Language, in part, became connected to liturgy, to prayer. And I have kept that sense of ritual around language, I think.

CAREY ¶ You've written four books of poetry. What made you turn from poetry to the novel form?

TOSTEVIN § I wanted to experience language at another level, the longer line. I wanted to work language at a more narrative level than what I'd been doing. I was apologizing to my parents once for speaking another kind of French in front of them— because I was talking to someone who spoke French differently from them— and I was feeling snobbish. One of my parents said, to know a language is to know it at all its levels. And this is what I would like to do in my writing, explore language at different levels. Although I'm aware of the irony that I'm doing this in English—

CAREY ¶ Why *did* you choose to write in English rather than your native French?

TOSTEVIN § It wasn't a matter of choice. I realized when I started to write that my first language had become English; my maternal tongue had become a second language. I believe there was a conscious moving away from everything French when I came out of the convent. My education beyond high school was mostly in English and my boyfriends were English. I didn't want to have anything to do with Catholicism which, I realized later on, was identified with being French. When I first sat down to write it was so painful writing in French... so I put writing on the back-burner for many years because of that. It was only when I decided to write in English that I finally felt free enough to write.

CAREY ¶ The narrator of *Frog Moon* seems to feel real regret about having lost her French to some extent, as if she's also lost part of herself: "...as if some emotions can only be expressed in the language closest to those emotions."

TOSTEVIN § The narrator of *Frog Moon* has lost part of herself. And she feels guilty because of it and she also feels caught between two languages. Some of her emotions translate spontaneously into French. There are moments, for me as well, in which I'm aware that I'm reacting to something that was learned, conditioned in French.

CAREY ¶ And yet you have to write them in English?

TOSTEVIN § If I write about them then I have to do it in English. Or if I'm in the middle of a conversation with an English person, then yes, the emotion has to be translated.

CAREY ¶ That seems like a very difficult position to be in.

TOSTEVIN § It's schizophrenic. I used to think it was unique to me. But then someone from Jamaica, who speaks a very proper English, told me that whenever she got angry she spontaneously reverted to the Jamaican *patois*. So I suppose there are certain emotions that are so close to our basic formation that we react in the language closest to that formation. That's not to say that when we sit down to write about the emotion we write it in *patois*. Most *patois* languages don't exist in writing.

CAREY ¶ There's an interesting juxtaposition of the young girl's convent experience where, as one nun puts it, "words are useless," with her father's boyhood in a lumber camp where stories played a big part in the camp's sense of community.

TOSTEVIN § Yes. The narrator realizes that she has spent much of her childhood in silence and in isolation, whereas her father has spent a lot of his childhood with the telling of tall tales. So there is that dichotomy, where one gender grew up one way and she grew up another way. And there are the stories her mother told her as well. But at convent, speech was often a sin—

speaking in class, speaking during study periods or in chapel, was a sin. Whereas the father was surrounded by tall tales.

CAREY ¶ The value of speech was reinforced for him, too, because the men in the camp who could tell the best stories were highly regarded.

TOSTEVIN § Yes, they were the official storytellers. I was so excited when my father used those words. When he said they had official storytellers who'd take their place at the table every night and continue spinning the tales as the winter went on.

CAREY ¶ In fact the young girl uses language, her vocation as a writer, to rebel against her community in the convent. She uses what had been, for her father, an instrument of cohesion in his community.

TOSTEVIN § Yes, but I want to emphasize that it wasn't only the father who used language. Her mother did as well, but in a different context. That played an important role in the vocation she eventually chose.

CAREY ¶ This is a very unconventionally structured novel, for instance, in the way that folk tales and expository prose passages are embedded in the central narrative. How did you decide on the form the book would take?

TOSTEVIN § I knew I wanted an intertextual novel of tall tales, folk tales and the character's own narrative. But I didn't want to use these in a linear narrative. Nor did I want to write a history book about the small town the narrator came from. I'm interested in what Françoise Lionnet calls *métissage*, from the word *métis*: the different sources, history, anthropology, literature, shuffled like a pack of cards to arrive at character, human nature. *Collage*— Lévi-Strauss called it. But I didn't want it to be too fragmented, either. I wanted to keep some of the tall tales embedded in the narrator's voice, so I decided to present them as exactly that. Some are tall tales, some are from other sources, always embedded in the narrator's voice. Through various sources she's able to construct a background to her life.

CAREY ¶ When you write the story of someone's life you're borrowing other stories to make sense of theirs, aren't you?

TOSTEVIN § And to make sense of the main character as well. I wanted to emphasize that. I also wanted a definite break from story to story; to make it clear each time that it is another person's story she's re-telling. The stories interweave with her own, as a little girl, a middle-aged woman... I suppose it's like Freud's hysteric; the disrupted narrative trying to disengage itself from a dominant narrative. I don't feel one can tell a story in one long narrative. Well, one can, but it's also a construct, a framework, which doesn't have anything more to do with reality than any other construct. And it's not one that appeals to me. As with language, I like to explore other possibilities.

CAREY ¶ I liked the way the elements of traditional folk tales are echoed in the narrator's own stories.

TOSTEVIN § Those folk tales and tall tales were part of her formation. The book is constructed with a title for each chapter with each title reappearing and connecting. I was pleased when I hit on that. I didn't want to leave each story as an independent story. I wanted something that would say, I've taken these various tales and constructed a novel with characters.

CAREY ¶ The narrator uses these stories to discern patterns in her own experience; she learns from them.

TOSTEVIN § Yes, that was her background. Her father came from an oral tradition and her mother was just discovering books, the literary tradition, which was a vehicle of transition for the daughter. And her parents wanted her to be educated. That was why they sent her to a convent— so she could get the best education they thought was available.

CAREY ¶ At another level, the tradition of tall tales is like the Christmas customs that the family in the book observes. Both bear a history and convey a sense of community.

TOSTEVIN § Yes. I think her family looks forward to Christmas as an excuse to perpetuate the rituals. But no one in the family is very religious, so it has nothing to do with religion. It's a reason to come together. The religious term "communion" means, to me, "communication." The communion of Christmas has been replaced by the family getting together. And of course it was very important to the main character as a child, because it was the first time she went home since having left in September.

CAREY ¶ I'd like to read a few quotes from the book, and ask you to comment on them. First, "you begin a novel imagining your main character different from who you are in the hope distance will reveal its secrets."

TOSTEVIN § Sometimes you need distance to understand situations better. In the first section of the book the narrator says that being nine years old and being eighty is part of the same waiting. She's neither nine nor eighty, but she imagines herself down the road, once her parents are no longer there, once the few opportunities to speak French will no longer be there. What will be left? It was important to me that she be old at the beginning and at the end. Writing is a kind of burial. There's one passage in the book where she's in Paris and walking in a cemetery. To me the book became like one of those tombstones: the concretized inscription of memory. I couldn't go on to other projects until I buried some of this.

CAREY ¶ "The foreign tongue of prayer... pleads for the restoration of a part of us that's been lost."

TOSTEVIN § I studied Latin in the higher grades. But in the earlier grades we repeated prayers in Latin over and over again without knowing what they meant. Of course this could apply to French as well. It reminds me of Julia Kristeva's theory around the levels of language: one level where we use it to communicate and another level that's closer to the rhythms of the body. The chanting and praying in Latin became a rhythm that was a lot of fun. We've lost our awareness of how closely language is tied to the body. We're always looking for narratives in content but we forget that other aspect of language, which to me is pure poetry. Too many poets ignore the substance of language, the rhythm of the line, in their haste to communicate messages.

CAREY ¶ I'm interested in the process of writing this book. Flannery O'Connor wrote that writing a novel is "a plunge into reality and very shocking to the system." What did you learn through the experience of writing *Frog Moon*?

TOSTEVIN § It was painful in some ways, and joyous in others. A lot of what I thought I'd buried resurfaced. One of the most painful experiences was facing the fact that my parents *are* old. I want to keep them with me forever. A lot of the book was fun, too. I did a bit of research— came across names vaguely familiar from my past— the Prophet of the Rand for example, in an old *Maclean's* magazine. The writing was really what Kristeva calls "subject-in-process." It was having to write a few hundred pages so I could get on with writing something else.

CAREY ¶ Do you remember how it actually started? Because you had been writing poetry to this point.

TOSTEVIN § I always had in the back of my mind that I would write short stories or a novel. I also knew that it would have to revolve somewhat around the fact that the narrator had been in a convent, because there were so many things to resolve around that experience. I don't know if they're resolved, but I think they're partially resolved. There's a line at the beginning of *Double Standards*, my third collection of poems: "I wanted to be story." That collection was meant to be a novel or short story, but I was still caught up in experimenting with language, and the book kept forgetting it was supposed to be fiction, kept going into poetry. But when I started *Frog Moon* I knew this was not going to happen. I knew it from the beginning, when I sat with my father until four a.m. on a few occasions and asked him to tell me some of the stories again. At first he was shy, afraid of the written word.

CAREY ¶ Because it has more authority?

TOSTEVIN § It has more authority for him. He barely learned how to write, so writing to him is a foreign language. It has very little to do with speech. As if his words were being translated into a foreign language. Which I did. It's actually a double translation, because I translated his stories into my own and from French into English.

CAREY ¶ The narrator emphasizes that these are not to be understood as his words, but as her rendering of them.

TOSTEVIN § Yes. This is to reinforce the fact that we keep borrowing from others and translate their stories into our own.

CAREY ¶ Throughout this interview, you've been careful to differentiate between you and the narrator, though clearly her experiences are similar to your own. Why be so rigorous in making this distinction?

TOSTEVIN § I didn't write an autobiography, I wrote a novel. The reader shouldn't assume that all the experiences of this book are clearly and autobiographically my own. Of course there are similarities in the process of cultural encoding from which the narrator and I cannot escape. You're never entirely free of your upbringing. But there is a lot of invention in this novel. A lot. If there is anything autobiographical about this novel, it is not how it tells my story, but how it, or any book I would write, invents me as a writer.

Ghosts in the Landscape

JANE URQUHART

by Jeffrey Canton

Poet, short-story writer, and novelist JANE URQUHART is the author of several books, including the novels *The Whirlpool* (reprinted 1986), *Changing Heaven* (1990), *Away* (1993), and *The Underpainter* (1997). She has been the recipient of the Trillium Award, the Marian Engel Award, and the Prix du Meilleur Livre Étranger.

"I had explored the graveyard outside the Brontë parsonage," explains Jane Urquhart, "but on my way out to the moors, I noticed another graveyard, slightly newer. Wandering through it, I saw a tombstone engraved with a balloon, and a woman's name and dates. It's one of the most terrifying graveyards that I've been in. When I went to live in Yorkshire, in the village of Stanbury, which is as close to the site of *Wuthering Heights* as you can get, I asked about this grave, and was told that the woman buried there had been a stunt performer. She took off over the Brontë moors as part of a village gala, and parachuted from the balloon over the moors; but the parachute didn't open and she was killed.

"I thought to myself— of all places to come crashing down, the Brontë moors are probably the best. You might become a ghost, and this would be a terrific place to haunt. You might run into another ghost, and that's basically how the novel began in my mind."

In Toronto to read at Harbourfront and launch her second novel, *Changing Heaven*, Urquhart, in conversation, is as provocative as the fiction she writes. The wild, wuthering atmosphere of *Changing Heaven* seems almost to hover above us. She is constantly shifting about, moving, gesturing, bursting with a restless energy that outraces speech, weaving a web of thoughts and ideas intricately about us.

The tombstone of Lucy Cove that triggered *Changing Heaven*, Urquhart explains, is the kind of image that usually sets her off on her fictional travels. "The idea for a novel," she says, "usually precedes the actual writing. It's something that I carry around with me— I read around it, think about it, visit the landscape. When I was writing *The Whirlpool*, I spent a great deal of time in the forest which is above the Niagara River whirlpool itself. And, I read, among other things, the diary of a woman called Julia Cruickshank, who was married to a military historian who was supposed to be building her a house in this landscape. That was certainly part of the genesis of that novel.

"In addition, my husband Tony comes from the oldest undertaking family in Canada. His family had a little book that belonged to his grandmother, wherein she recorded items found on bodies retrieved from the Niagara River. Like a character in that novel, she also dug up cannonballs and buttons and things when she was gardening; and the funeral home was located on the battleground of Lundy's Lane. I never met Tony's grandmother, and my imaginary concept of this woman was probably very different from the woman she might have been, though I discovered subsequently that I wasn't that far off. Tony's mother also told me stories about what it was like to grow up in that particular environment, so it was real, it was given to me."

Urquhart is bent on exploring fictional worlds, and *Changing Heaven* leads us into the midst of Emily Brontë's fantastic high Gothic masterpiece, *Wuthering Heights*. The spirit of Emily Brontë herself roams the moors in Urquhart's book, landscaping them to fit her moods, and she is joined by the spirit of nineteenth-century balloonist Arianna Ether. Not a spiritualist herself, Urquhart nonetheless adores ghosts. "There is something about the literature of the nineteenth century that suggests a more viable atmosphere for ghosts. It's probably the inheritance of writers like Edgar Allen Poe.

"As far as believing in them— I haven't decided. I'm not the sort of person who belongs to psychic research societies. If I were, no doubt my ghosts might be more ponderous individuals."

She is careful to add, "The ghosts in *Changing Heaven* are ghosts on a metaphorical level as well as on an actual level. In a way, they haunt the book. I like to think of Emily Brontë as haunting her own presence in the story. Emily and Arianna don't manifest themselves as howling, shrieking phantoms dragging their chains behind them. They are not out to drive anyone mad with fear; the ghost of Emily Brontë is very much against haunting. On the whole, they are lighthearted ghosts— but they do talk about serious issues, particularly about women and men and how they regard each other."

Urquhart admits that she is obsessed with *Wuthering Heights*. "I chose Emily Brontë," she says, "partly because of my great admiration for her work, and, accidentally, because of the discovery of Lucy Cove's grave. I wanted to hear, I suppose, what Emily would have had to say about romantic love, for example— a topic that one chooses these days at one's own risk when writing a novel. I didn't have a preconceived plan about what shape her character was going to take, and I was surprised to discover that she became so pragmatic."

Urquhart adamantly maintains, "I wasn't interested in writing a fictional biography of Emily Brontë based on a transcription of nineteenth-century letters and diaries. I wanted her to develop in my own mind. I feel that she was a strong character, a little bossy and with an enormous imaginative scope. Not an ethereal, Emily Dickinson type, but robust— she did spend enormous amounts of time tramping about the moors with her vicious dog, Keeper." *Changing Heaven* also has autobiographical elements. Urquhart makes it clear that Ann Frears, the protagonist of the novel, is not a fictional stand-in for Jane Urquhart; the childhood sections of Ann's story have parallels in Urquhart's life. "If there is any part of *Changing Heaven* that is autobiographical, it's Ann's obsession with *Wuthering Heights*. I read it when I was nine or ten years old. I didn't necessarily understand it— I wasn't that precocious— but I certainly found myself fascinated by the concept of this out-of-control passion that, in the novel, is totally reflected in the landscape. I'm sure that Emily Brontë chose the name Heathcliff because the combination of those two words, heath and cliff, dominate the land there.

"In *The Whirlpool*," she explains, "landscape operates in the same way that the weather does in *Changing Heaven*. The landscape is in a state of turbulence and flux. Granted, that is also to some degree true of the moors, but the moors are earthbound, and the changes and fluctuations that take place on the moors are dependent on atmospheric conditions. Not so with Niagara Falls. That's my husband's part of the world, a part of the world that I visited often. I found that the Niagara region and that river, in particular, were so resonant with meaning. I have a feeling that landscape reflects personality more than we perhaps give it credit. When I looked at the river for the first time, it astounded me.

"I need more than a superficial connection with the landscape I'm going to discuss in a novel," Urquhart adds. "I need to actually live in the place for a while. When I lived near Haworth, for example, I would take long walks on the moors— not because I thought that I was a reincarnation of Emily Brontë and could experience everything she did by being out there— but so as to be able to pick up details of the world surrounding me. You know when you are on the moors that these are Emily Brontë's moors. In *Changing Heaven*, Emily's ghost discusses creating the moors with Arianna, and, in a sense, she really did create them for the rest of us— we will never see them in any other way. They are hers, they belong to her."

Changing Heaven blends the fantastic and the fabulous with the dailiness of contemporary life in Toronto. Part of the novel is three stories that Brontë scholar Ann Frears is told when she stays in Yorkshire. To Urquhart, "Telling stories is an important part of the human psyche. Wanting to shape the events of our lives, to give them order. Transforming our daily lives into the stuff of myth.

"In Stanbury, I lived with my husband and daughter in a little cottage much like the one in the novel, and we met the most wonderful people. Very strong and spiritually rich. They have had incredibly difficult lives, the Yorkshire people, yet they have held onto their sense of self in the most remarkable way. And they are born storytellers, once they get over their reticence about your being a stranger. The stories in *Changing Heaven* are based on fragments that I heard in 'The Friendly Pub,' although they developed into something entirely different from the stories that I heard.

"The Yorkshire people are very practical and down-to-earth, yet they have a strong streak of magic in them, similar to the Irish. They know what their landscape is, they know their community, and they like to add myths to their lives. When I finished *Changing Heaven,* it struck me that the Brontës were probably the wonderful writers they were because they came out of that tradition of Yorkshire storytelling.

"These people in Stanbury," she tells me, "are the grandchildren of the Reverend Patrick Brontë's parishioners. They talk about the Brontës as part of the community that their grandparents knew— 'Oh, that Bramwell, he was a bad lot.' There was one woman who told me, 'The trouble with those girls was they never got married. Because shoes wouldn't and clogs dasn't.' And that meant that people who wore shoes were of a higher class than that of a simple parson and his daughters, while clogs were working class and that class dared not communicate with the parson's daughters on a romantic level. So the Brontës were in a kind of limbo between classes."

Obsession is the stuff of Jane Urquhart's fiction. It is a theme that she explores not only in *Changing Heaven* but in her earlier novel, *The Whirlpool,* as well. "I don't think many authors can write without being obsessed," she explains. "Unless you care deeply about your material, you are not going to have the emotional impulse to pull yourself all the way through the book. An enormous amount of time goes into writing a novel, and usually I'm obsessed from the day I first sit down to write the first sentence until I finish the tenth draft. I'm obsessed with obsessions. I have to be obsessed with the subject and I'll hold it in my mind for long periods of time. And think about it, play with it, talk about it. My friends know exactly where I am in the writing of my next book— I'm boring them all to death talking about the Irish potato famines of the nineteenth century. Interest in the subject isn't enough for me— I really have to know it. Reading and research are only tools— I couldn't have written *Changing Heaven* if I hadn't lived in Stanbury, experienced the landscape, walked it for miles and miles."

Urquhart's next project "centres in part around the whole kind of extended family that I grew up in— this extended Irish family that immigrated to Canada around the time of the potato famine. It will be a new experience for me because it involves many kinds of characters which I haven't dealt with in my fiction to date.

"I want to explore the myth of that Ireland which the immigrants brought with them, that culminated in the romanticization of that land, and that became stronger as the generations moved forward and further away from it. I heard stories when I was growing up that had been literally handed down from my great-great-great-grandfathers! Stories that focused on all kinds of real and imagined injustices, and the difficulty of keeping your sense of self when there's a great imperialist power looming over you. Which I think we can relate to looking south of the border.

"The other side of the book— there are always two sides to my books— has to do with magic. I'm very curious about the concept that the Irish have of a person who is *away*— someone who has been touched by the supernatural world. When such a person returns to the cottage kitchen, that person is not really *back*. The Irish sometimes believe that if a certain person has been touched by the supernatural, that what you have in that cottage kitchen is a supernatural being who has been disguised as that individual.

"I'm hoping to work that concept of being *away* in a supernatural sense with the concept of immigration to a new land. When you are there, *away* from the homeland, the homeland then takes on the aspect of a myth."

Taboos

M.G. VASSANJI

by John Clement Ball

M.G. VASSANJI was born in Nairobi, Kenya, and grew up in Dar es Salaam, Tanzania. He began a successful career as a nuclear physicist in the United States, but a few years after coming to Canada in 1978, he took up writing. *The Gunny Sack*, published in London by Heinemann International in 1989, was the African regional winner of the Commonwealth Writers Prize for best first book. Since then, he has published the novels *No New Land* (1991) and *The Book of Secrets* (1994), as well as a collection of stories, *Uhuru Street* (1992), all with McClelland and Stewart.

BALL ¶ A few years ago you wrote in an essay (in *A Meeting of Streams*, 1985) that the post-colonial migrant writer's first serious act of writing is a reclamation of the past, after which he or she has a basis from which to write about the present. *The Gunny Sack*, your first novel, has been called the first Tanzan-Asian novel. If it is the first, then this would suggest that your particular racial and communal history of Asians in East Africa has been under-represented in literature, and that writing that history had a particular urgency.

VASSANJI § We lived through a period of tremendous transitions and big changes— movements across continents, from India to Africa, and within Africa, and so on— plus the personal changes within our lives— the political changes, colonialism, wars, independence, revolutions— and you just had to find out why you were what you were, what had happened to you. It's like coming out of a state of shock, trying to remember what happened during the last hundred years.

BALL ¶ And this had not been really dealt with by literary authors from your area?

VASSANJI § There were one or two earlier attempts, but since they were the first, they didn't deal in great detail— didn't create depth— with our lives. I think what was needed was a kind of brutal honesty.

BALL ¶ And of course your book has such a comprehensive approach to the history. It takes a very long period of history as its subject.

VASSANJI § Plus it deals with subjects that have never been dealt with before: communal histories, histories which were considered sacred to some people. I remember even back in 1975, when I was a graduate student, wondering, how would one deal with this aspect of life? How would it enter the world of fiction? Because it's so personal; it's so communal; it's so private that you have to break new ground, and you have to worry about the repercussions.

BALL ¶ Were there taboos on making some of that material public?

VASSANJI § Yes, there were taboos, definitely. You don't deal with religious figures, or talk about certain beliefs. And since some of these beliefs keep changing, for a writer they're very interesting. Why do they change? Why do the stories that I was told as a child suddenly become unimportant? And that's important to me, because there are stories— things that people don't want to deal with, and I think a writer has to.

BALL ¶ At one point, Salim, your narrator, says that five years after his father's death, the memory of his father "was receding behind the overgrowth of fresh memories that were appearing with the density and vigor of a jungle." Now, this is understandably the case for a young boy— as we grow older our earliest memories get increasingly vague— but is that also true for a people? Does the recent past, in a sense, need to be pruned in order to get at the distant, ancestral past?

VASSANJI § Definitely, there's so much that people forget; especially when you move to a completely new, western country, where you have to deal with insecurities that in fact come from your own background. So you have to hide some of the history in order to cope with the present. When I wrote *The Gunny Sack*, I didn't write it for the East African-Asian communities, because I didn't think they were interested in the past. What amazed me was the rapidity, the warmth, the enthusiasm with which they picked up that book. Part of it, I think, is nostalgia; but even that nostalgia is an acknowledgement of something that happened, an acknowledgement also with affection. So I think my book did make people more willing to look at the past, to acknowledge it.

BALL ¶ How do you get at a past that has been forgotten, lost? What process did that involve for you?

VASSANJI § I used to listen to people, and for a long time I found myself more interested in talking to older people than younger people, because when younger people talk there's a lot of hot air and they're trying to prove things. Whereas older people have stories to tell, and all you have to do is listen and then probe them a little bit— because the more you get interested, the more pointed your questions become. And then they just open up. I had a few sources and I used to listen to them and they really inspired me.

BALL ¶ As that material becomes more remote, as even the older people may be reporting on stories that they have overheard, maybe second- or third-hand, does it gain a quality that maybe isn't quite history at a certain point?

VASSANJI § It's myth. So, in fact, that's what the author does: you're not a historian— although in some sense you are a historian— but basically you are creating a myth. But you need a source of stories, always, to create a myth.

BALL ¶ So myth, history, memory all become one thing.

VASSANJI § They become one, yes. And in my new novel, *The Book of Secrets*, which I just finished, I have done the opposite of what *The Gunny Sack* does, because what *The Gunny Sack* does is try to give shape to personal and collective memory in the form of the novel. While I was researching that novel, one of my sources was old people, but also you have to look up the past in documents and see what really happened. So, while I was reading up on the history, I became very fascinated with the process of digging up the past as a historian. So I started with a diary, which is in fact one of the documents one uses when studying colonial history— diaries and colonial documents. I started with a diary and a historian who says he's going to be objective, and one step removed from the people he's describing. And in the process of making an objective history, he finds that it's impossible and becomes part of the description.

BALL ¶ The gunny sack itself provides the structuring principle for the first novel. It's a bag that contains objects that act as windows to history and triggers to memory. I think the gunny sack also suggests a narrative logic, which isn't necessarily compatible with the narrative logic of chronologically told history. Is that a liberation of sorts for you as a writer?

VASSANJI § It is. When I began the novel, I had a very romantic image, which was partly personal, of a single person, a young man, who carries a real gunny sack with him, and that bag is full of memories, and he sits down in one place and tries to look at the memories one at a time. And it's that kind of a weight that I felt upon me when I began the novel. But, as the novel progressed, then the novel itself became the gunny sack, and there was a transformation.

BALL ¶ Salim has two ancestries: African and Asian— although he's primarily Asian, seven-eighths as opposed to one-eighth African. Were you looking to make him like Rushdie's Saleem in *Midnight's Children* or like Walcott's Shabine in "The Schooner *Flight*"— a figure of syncretism who could combine multiple cultural and racial ancestries into one figure?

VASSANJI § Yes, but it was not a very deliberate attempt, because a lot of people from India in fact come from communities that are very syncretistic. I come from a community that was converted from Hinduism into Islam, but the memories of Hinduism were very much part of our lives. I was brought up, told stories from what we call Hinduism. But I don't really call them Hindu stories— they were just Indian stories. When they appeared in our community, those stories became ours, they were transformed in the necessary way.

BALL ¶ So it seemed natural...

VASSANJI § It was natural because people are syncretistic, and there are various kinds of Islam, various kinds of Hinduism. On the east coast of Africa, you have the Bantu culture and the Arab culture, and the Swahili culture that was a mixture of these two. You have stories from the Middle East, from

China, which were spawned within the local context. Plus we had English-style education, and our influence from American films, Hindi films, and so on. For me, that is really a wealth of experience that I treasure. Unfortunately, the modern world tries to sort of ethnically cleanse itself, and that's really ugly.

BALL ¶ Your second novel, *No New Land*, is set primarily in Canada, focusing on the African-Asian community in Toronto. One reviewer, in the *Far Eastern Economic Review*, said the theme of the novel was "the awful experience of immigrating to Canada" and that the novel was "essential reading for anyone taking that step." That implies that the novel is some kind of warning. I was wondering if you would agree with that reading of it.

VASSANJI § Not really. The novel was just a treatment of a certain experience. No, the novel is funny in many parts, and it ends on an optimistic note. It looks back because you have to look back at what you are, but not with a view to going back— for these people, at least, it's impossible.

I thought many reviewers in fact saw the novel as a negative portrayal of Canada. What they failed to see were the human beings behind the portrayals. In fact, in the mainstream reviews, it was very disappointing; it seemed people were not interested in the people I was talking about, but in how they lived— a sort of anthropological interest.

BALL ¶ So the characters were representatives of something.

VASSANJI § Yes. Who are these people that you see in subways? One interviewer said that she'd often seen these people in subways and wondered who they were and now my novel gave her an idea of that.

BALL ¶ The audience for your work encompasses so many nationalities, races, and cultural backgrounds, from Canada to the African communities, and the Indian diaspora in the broader sense. Are you conscious of the way people from those different communities read your work, and the different things they'll be looking for?

VASSANJI § Sometimes one is made conscious of that. Some people from East Africa were not happy with the crudeness of some of the characters in *No New Land*, because they see themselves as quite sophisticated. Therefore, if the character is either crude or presents racist attitudes— communal attitudes— then it's a negative reflection on them.

BALL ¶ And of course you're not the first writer to be challenged on that front.

VASSANJI § Just last weekend someone came up and said, "Do Indian writers consciously meet and decide what community image they are going to portray?" And I said, "What community? There are dozens of communities."

BALL ¶ The tension that is a major theme of *No New Land*— between assimilation and acculturation to mainstream Canadian culture, versus maintaining some kind of racial or cultural integrity brought over from the old land— I think that's going to be interpreted differently by different readers.

VASSANJI § Well, if you see how the novel ends, it is quite clear: you acknowledge the past and you move forward.

BALL ¶ Although, while Nurdin's immediate problems may have sorted themselves out with the help of his friend Jamal, he's still not really succeeding or happy in Canada, on his own terms or his family's terms.

VASSANJI § You're always left with certain things undone. I don't think anybody dies having completed his life's project. And for some people— a certain age group who came to Canada in their late thirties— they lived so much of their lives in East Africa— plus the fact that within the East African context they were not very highly educated— so it was hard for them to cope with the new transition intellectually, or even be comfortable with western culture. They would always be incomplete.

But what most people have done, at least as far as I have observed, is formed their own communities, and in those communities they are quite complete within themselves. They are happy— they have their own lives, their own positions— and the novel hints at that. But Nurdin is an exception, because he also likes to look out. He sees a way out but he is incapable of making that step. You could just call him a victim of history or circumstance. His age, where he comes from, his belief system, how he was brought up— he's not going to change completely. He sees the attraction of changing— and he does change to some degree— but he doesn't have it in him to make that big leap. I don't think many people have that. The younger they are, the more easily they can do it. But, of course, they have less to lose.

BALL ¶ The themes of community dissolution— and the consequent isolation of individuals in the wake of political change, modernization, decolonization, migration— these themes link your work very closely with that of other writers from the Indian diaspora: Sam Selvon, Neil Bissoondath, even V.S. Naipaul in some ways. Do you see yourself as part of an emerging tradition of writing by Indians who have moved to the West via another place?

VASSANJI § Well, I see myself that way in a kind of de facto way. First, I have no choice in the subject I write on or the experiences I deal with: you are what you are. I realize that others deal with similar experiences in their own different ways, because every community is specific. Second, it's a strength. I really find it quite exhilarating that there are so many parts of me to explore, so many experiences that are not really integrated within me. And I like that rawness; it's very exciting to have so many different experiences in one life.

BALL ¶ I think that's one of the compelling things about your wuik, and the new popularity of writing by people from Africa, the West Indies— this syncretistic combination of influences that has emerged out of the history.

VASSANJI § Yes. Unfortunately for the younger generation, they have only one or maybe one-and-a-half experiences.

BALL ¶ Yes, your generation is uniquely placed.

VASSANJI § Uniquely placed because we're just between independence and colonialism, and between cultures, and between religions, and between countries. And even in the West, many of us move from one country to another.

BALL ¶ Your most recently published book, *Uhuru Street*, takes you back to Africa after being mostly in Canada in the second novel— back to Dar es

Salaam in particular, and to part of the historical period that's covered in *The Gunny Sack*. Arun Mukherjee once wrote that with the publication of *Uhuru Street* your fictional project is beginning to resemble that of Faulkner, in that the way you are rendering a particular local community repeatedly in your work means that community becomes enriched— we get to know it a little better as each book comes out.

VASSANJI § I was quite surprised by her comparison, because I am a great admirer of Faulkner, and I myself saw that comparison as kind of distinctive. Consciously, but not very seriously, it occurred to me. Also because Faulkner dealt with a very small community, very unsophisticated in some ways— not a mainstream community. But he dealt with it and he made us aware of that community, so even you and I can talk about the Snopeses or whatever. I think Ngugi has done the same thing for his Gikuyu tribe. I am also a great admirer of Ngugi for what he has achieved.

BALL ¶ And as the most prominent and established author from East Africa, he must have been quite an influence on you.

VASSANJI § The only influence, I think, was in the fact that he unashamedly picked up on a tribe and said, "I'm going to be with their experience." And you find that you learn more about that tribe— the tribe becomes part of you. And after all, as a human being, you come from a tribe also. He dealt with their experiences, which had never been dealt with before. He gave you a side of the Mau Mau wars, for example, which you would never have got otherwise. So in that sense I was influenced by his work.

BALL ¶ Both *No New Land* and *Uhuru Street* contain a single instance of horrific inter-racial violence against Indians at a central point in the book. Do you see those episodes— I'm thinking of the subway attack in *No New Land* and the rape and murder of the Indian woman in *Uhuru Street*— as emblematic of a more subtle and generalized violence against Indian minorities in both continents?

VASSANJI § Not really. The two incidents are very different. I wrote about the Dar es Salaam incident because I heard about it, and it really bothered me because it was the kind of thing I'd never heard about before. Dar es Salaam was not a violent place. If that had happened in Nairobi, I'd have said, "Yeah, I remember as a child being afraid of what could happen at night in Nairobi," because it was a violent city. But Dar es Salaam is a coastal place; the people are friendly. I was amazed and horrified that this could happen. That's why I wrote about it— trying to understand what kind of racial attitude the woman would have at the point of being attacked. Once the story came out, many people thought that what I was trying to say was that this is what Indians are going through in East Africa, and that was not my point. My reason for doing that was because this one incident was very unusual.

BALL ¶ It seems unusual in the context of all the other stories, which have nothing like that.

VASSANJI § Yes, but people from the Caribbean, for example, are used to much more systematic racism. I've had people from the Caribbean come and say, "Oh, yeah, I know what you're talking about." So I wrote to one person point-blank: "You don't know what I'm talking about," because it's a very different society, a very different experience. In Canada, I thought also that it was a unique incident because Toronto is a very clean city; even if people were racist, they wouldn't want to be portrayed as people who beat up people in subways. There is a kind of clean front in Toronto. But only last month I found out there was another incident like that. On the Bloor subway line, a Tamil man was beaten up. So, I'm beginning to wonder.

BALL ¶ You've recently travelled to India for the first time. That must have been quite momentous. Can you talk about your feelings and responses?

VASSANJI § Going to India was like going to a place with all your nerves exposed, because I knew everything I would see would bring out a response from me. I would want to understand it in terms of my upbringing, my ancestral memories, and so on. So I was quite numb for a few days. I was pleasantly surprised by the fact that it wasn't an alien place, as I thought it might be; in places it looked very much like the Indian sections of Dar es Salaam. And I felt very comfortable there. I travelled about eight thousand kilometres. I just felt in some ways that part of me was going home— not all of me, but a part of me. I had romanticized India as a student— because that was where my roots were— but after a while, as I matured, I put India behind me, because so much else was happening. When I went to India this time, I realized that I have to go back there again, both physically and metaphorically, and basically reclaim that part of me that I had sort of decided I didn't want any more.

I went during the time of the riots, and the violence that happened there during the riots was so bad, so savage, that although in some ways it was like going home— there was also this outrage, this anger, at all this violence— people were taking it so easily. And when the *Indian Express* asked me to write about my experience, I wrote about these incidents that I had heard about, and I spoke to people who had experienced them first hand. It's something I still haven't got over. The savagery was just too much.

BALL ¶ So is writing about India the next project?

VASSANJI § I'm writing another novel that's set in North America, but that's taking its own time because it's not an easy novel. I'm also writing a travelogue about my experiences of India, and I plan to go back next year. It's a place that keeps drawing me; I don't think I can let it go now.

BALL ¶ Is there an ancestral village for you to visit there now?

VASSANJI § There are ancestral towns, which I couldn't go to because of the riots. I went to Gujarat, and I spoke with people, and some of them in fact witnessed violence. And I wondered, what would it have taken— what historical quirk or coincidence or whatever— for me to be in his shoes, and for him to be in mine? Would I have experienced violence, or would I have been one of these thugs who go around looting and raping? It's something that I try to understand.

BALL ¶ Would you be *you*, in other words?

VASSANJI § Yes. But you are *you*, and that's what I realized: that if you claim yourself to be of Indian ancestry, then you are in some ways responsible for what goes on there.

Afterword:
The Power to Bend Spoons

FRANK DAVEY

in conversation with Beverley Daurio

FRANK DAVEY is a poet, scholar, theorist, and critic. His studies of Canadian society in transition, including *Reading 'Kim' Right* (1993) and *Karla's Web* (1994) add to our understanding of the matrix in which Canadian novels are published.

BEVERLEY DAURIO ¶ I'd like to begin by asking you a question raised for me by the opening pages of *Canadian Literary Power*, and pointed to by your publication of the books *Reading "Kim" Right* and *Karla's Web*: "'They think we have power— all we have is the power to bend spoons,' bpNichol would often lament... when he encountered yet another comment about the 'influential' Coach House Press, the 'dangerous' *Tish* group, or was told by an unpublished writer that he should read his or her manuscript— 'because you have power.'" In *Canadian Literary Power*, power is addressed conceptually and contextually, but the number of people wielding it, the extent of its influence, and other such aspects— its materiality, if you like— is not surveyed or addressed. It seems to me that bp was right, and Canadian literary power is largely chimerical. Would you please comment on this?

FRANK DAVEY § I'm not sure whether your question is about "power" generally or "literary power." bp's lament was that in Canada, literary power— the power to ensure that manuscripts get published, that books get considered for awards, that writers' opinions get printed in literary magazines, that certain writers get to be editors or get contracts for new projects, that they receive grants or obtain enough income to be able to continue writing— is not only diffuse in itself but is also ineffectual as a general social power. Who are the

Canadian literary powers? Because our literary community is highly frag-mented— by gender, region, ethnicity, race, etc.— power tends to be specific and limited. Greg Gatenby has been called powerful, but not over writers who disdain the postnational celebrity and pro-Ontario politics of his Harbourfront readings. Among Toronto editors, Louise Dennys has been said to be powerful, but this is a power none of the writers I've been associated with have noticed. Robert Kroetsch has power in Alberta and Manitoba to help authors find publishers and books find readers, but I'm not sure that his endorsement would have effect in Atlantic Canada, or in many parts of Toronto. Roy Miki is listened to with respect in many racial or ethnic-minority writing communities. Jeanette Armstrong, through her teaching, writing, and publishing work, is similarly respected by many aboriginal writers.

Susan Rudy-Dorscht wrote last year in an essay on gender and Canadian criticism that Canadian literary criticism is dominated by "Frank Davey, Robert Kroetsch, W.H. New, Robert Lecker, George Woodcock, George Bowering, Barry Cameron, Terry Goldie, W.J. Keith, and Arnold E. Davidson"— by somewhat-alive white males (Woodcock died after her article went to press). I have trouble remembering her list, mainly because there are so many names that could be there and so few that stand out for me as being "inevitably" on it. The list very likely reflected Susan's personal experience of literary power. Would this be Bill Keith's list, Linda Hutch-eon's, John Metcalf's, Arun Mukherjee's, or Shirley Neuman's? Or outside the academic community would this be Robert Fulford's list, Alan Twigg's, Margaret Atwood's, Neil Bissoondath's? What can be said about the materiality of Canadian literary power is that it is mostly non-hierarchical, being exercised in distinct and only partly overlapping spheres. A lot of people wield limited amounts of it. The spheres of power differ considerably in size, from racial communities, the Queen Street arts community, the various regional communities, to the Toronto/international scene in which Ondaatje, Atwood, and Davies, Anna Porter, Malcolm Lester, and Louise Dennys are considered powerful names. The power is by and large a white power, with racial minority writers wielding power mostly within smaller, "alternate" organizations, and often circulating their writing mostly within their own communities. Despite its diffuseness, this can be a consequential power. Failure to be endorsed by one of these spheres can result in a writer receiving no grants, having weak credentials for obtaining teaching or editorial jobs, earning little money from writing, and possibly giving up in discouragement.

The other aspect of bp's remark was that all of this literary power was ineffectual as an influence within society generally. There is a crippling assumption in the general Canadian community that literary texts are aesthetic— decorative entertainments— rather than social and political. Interestingly, this is not an assumption shared by minority communities, where a text like Kogawa's *Obasan* or Marlatt's *Ana Historic* can inspire social action. To have political influence in the general Canadian social community, or even in regional communities, one must write an overtly political text, like Atwood's *Survival,* Persky's *Son of Socred,* Bissoondath's *Selling Illusions,* or Richler's *Oh Canada.* Why is this? In part, I think it's because minority communities have few political outlets, and thus read literature as larger communities read newspapers and books on politics. In part, also, it may be because smaller communities hope for change and larger ones resist it. A new book by Marlatt or Scott is news in most lesbian-feminist magazines and newsletters. A new book by Marlatt, Scott, Davey, Kroetsch, or Richler is rarely mentioned by most Canadian magazines and newspapers. When they are mentioned, it is not as news items but as literary objects for review in an entertainment section of the paper, carefully separated from the news and op-ed pages in which topics for social decision are debated.

DAURIO ¶ I should have worded this question better. What I was referring to is the illusion set around "literary power," materially. It is somewhat essentialist to consider, I think, in the current Canadian cultural environment, the power to decide which books to publish at an uncapitalized literary press, for instance, simply as *power,* or even as *literary power,* without addressing the material and other conditions in which power is exercised. The illusion of many writers is that purely mini-capitalist enterprises comprise the literary publishing community, that these organizations exist on a hierarchical entrepreneurial grid entirely collusive with large capitalist organizations, and that this grid's openings are entries into an imaginary "plenty" where the tracks lead toward greater capital accession (for one small example). If the decision to choose a text to publish is going to be considered "power," I think it's important to recognize and analyze the limits of that power. Very particular Canadian conditions are the result of a massive matrix of interwoven cultural, economic, belief system and other illusions and realities. For me it's horrific to watch people fighting over resources that are so tiny as to be non-existent. I think that a certain portion of the fighting would be better directed at increasing and enlarging the resources. (I am not speaking here of those fights engendered by exclusion, or enlightening arguments, but rather, for instance, the fighting *against* "Writing thru 'Race.'")

DAVEY § It's remarkable from what different viewpoints we could have looked at the "power" question. You are right that the dollars-and-cents level of materiality is crucial to whether most literary and critical things get printed, even before anyone exerts control over which individual texts are printed, which reviewed, which publicized, which selected for college or high school study. Which is why so many people are currently frantic with anxiety about cutbacks to SSHRC's funding of scholarly journals, to the Canada Council's periodicals and publishing grants, to the Secretary of State's publishing support programs, and about the freezing or eliminating of publishing support in Ontario. If there were no journals or book publishers to publish what they write or edit, whatever "chimerical" power Bill New or Linda Hutcheon presently have would be enormously diminished. The dollars-and-cents level was lurking in my response above in the differences in size I noted among "spheres of power": the commercial Toronto/international sphere is financed well enough to pay its editors for their labour, to pay its authors substantial "rewards of capitalism," and to operate independently of many government subsidy programs. But as I suggested, there are limits to this sphere's power. It is not powerful to those who can manage to disdain or ignore it. It also tends overall to limit its own power to maintaining rather than challenging existing social conditions.

Your description of what you say are the illusions of "many writers" is depressing. They may aspire to money, or "buying power," or to the power to be able to get their own work published, but they don't seem to seek the kind of power to contribute to social change that bp and I were thinking of above. For me, there is no greater *material* power than the power to be able to participate in and influence the social debates of one's culture. This power does depend partly on wealth— which is why Thomas Jefferson believed it would be undemocratic for the state to allow individual Americans to amass more than seventy-five thousand (nineteenth-century) dollars in personal wealth. But it depends also on education, gender, ethnicity, colour, professional position, sexual orientation, as you know. And it is a power to change material circumstances, even— in cases where it has incrementally contributed to women being viewed as "potential" professionals, or to racial minorities being viewed as unjustly excluded— to help alter distributions of wealth.

Regarding the specific economic observations you have made, I don't think they are "particular Canadian conditions." You would find them, perhaps in more extreme form, in most capitalist countries, and certainly in the US or Britain. The material problem with your own situation is how to operate a "business" based on conceptual and aesthetic values in a culture which offers its greatest material rewards to businesses which provide entertaining or pragmatic commodities and services. Most Canadian artists and intellectuals have faced this problem by basing their economic life not on the objects they produce (manuscripts or paintings or performances) but on the services they can provide as teachers, consultants, editors, or administrators, services to which the culture assigns pragmatic value. That is, they define their productivity not merely in terms of intellectual or artistic "property" but in terms of a range of social interactions. Unless you can become a producer of what *appear* to be entertainments, "good reads" (as Ondaatje or Atwood have, for example), or of art objects likely to appreciate (as Attila Lukacs and Joanne Tod have), you have in a capitalist society no other way of grounding your work economically. Your personal quarrel here is with capitalism itself. Apart from successfully lobbying for more government grants (something cyclically difficult in a capitalist economy), your only way of resolving the problem of resources would be to alter fundamentally the grounds on which wealth is distributed in most of the industrially developed world. That is going to have to happen, as automation increasingly makes most remunerated work obsolete, but only as public opinion is changed by people like us over the long term.

DAURIO ¶ In addition to being a professor of English, you are a widely published poet, a small-press activist, editor and publisher of an innovative scholarly magazine, and editorial board member for two literary presses. In certain circles, writing books about general cultural issues— the "meanings" of "Kim Campbell" in *Reading "Kim" Right*, or the social and cultural implications of the Bernardo trial in *Karla's Web*, for instance— are extremely transgressive acts. Among certain groups of Canadian literary practitioners— including "apolitical" liberals and "anti-ideological" vanguard writers, the idea of textually entering popular discourse is regarded as a kind of personal artistic desecration. However, it seems to me that such interventions are extremely important reclamations of intellectual territory. Have you been criticized for these books on this basis? Do you see any conflict between a position on the editorial board of Underwhich Editions— for instance— and such work?

DAVEY § My wife muttered when I began *Reading "Kim" Right* that I was putting my literary "reputation" at risk, but if there have been criticisms that this and the *Karla* book are ones a serious writer should not have undertaken, I haven't seen or heard them. In the universities, where cultural studies advocates have been arguing for wider definitions of what it is that scholars study, those books have been seen as expanding the kinds of texts an English department can study. They've also been seen as demonstrating the continuing relevance of university research to society generally. As for those "anti-ideological" writers or "apolitical liberals" you mention, they didn't respond to the *Kim* book, and to the *Karla* offered mostly nuisance commentary— commentary that ignored or dismissed (like Fraser Sutherland in *Books in Canada*) the cultural issues.

Robert Lecker has written that the two books represent my turning away from an elitist view of literature and literary criticism as "private" within a small intellectual community to a view of literature and criticism as public actions. I have trouble with his terms "public" and "private," because he seems to assume that there is only one "public" and that any splitting of this public results in the creation of "private" constituencies. ("Private" for Lecker seems to be a synonym for right-wing "special interests" or "special interest groups"). In fact, since human public culture began, there have been numerous publics, divided by language, nation, region, gender, colour, ethnicity, by the institutions they employ, and by the interests their particular circumstances have generated. When I began writing in the early 1960s, poetry in North America was a circulating social discourse, a discourse that had impact on various publics' views of racism, war, nationalism, and social justice. One couldn't hope to address Lecker's "the public," in the sense of hoping to reach all citizens of Canada, or of North America, but one could address *a public* that bought books and went to readings, gallery openings, and anti-war demonstrations. That public hasn't shrunk so much as divided along regional, gender, racial, ethnic, and otherwise ideological lines, and re-combined with publics little interested in literature. This division has been useful in helping the new groupings to develop more specific vocabularies and more focused social analyses. But it has made it difficult for writers, inside or outside the new groupings, to address a large public. I see all of my writing and publishing as having been "public," but directed toward smaller or larger publics. As for deciding whether to write to larger publics, I don't think one has much choice. The larger affects the smaller. The larger publics are also the ones within which we must live (we can choose our smaller publics). If a writer wants to participate in the political activities of his own culture, and to help shape the general contexts within which an Underwhich Editions or Talonbooks has to operate, he or she has no choice but to attempt to write for the larger spheres. Reclaim intellectual territory? All public "territories" are potentially intellectual— and should be, unless we prefer Bosnia.

DAURIO ¶ You have described a curious and uniquely Canadian mechanism, the "mismatch between... free-market booksellers and a Canadian publishing industry in which nearly every literary title receives government subsidy [that] has made it difficult for new or generically dissenting texts to get out of publishers' warehouses and into Canadian bookstores, let alone into a canon." Many of these texts— and many of their publishers— are, of course, either openly or obliquely opposed to and critical of the very capitalist matrix into which these books are sent. At the same time, this tension helps to maintain the chasm between the literature produced here and its potential readership. You have had a great deal of experience in dissenting publishing in various forms: have solutions or partial solutions to these problems of dissemination occurred to you?

DAVEY § Once a government makes a decision to subsidize— and I think multinational capitalism, with its disregard for local culture and its confusion of culture and advertising, makes subsidies to cultural activities essential— it has to carry any subsidy program through all production and distribution levels. It makes no sense to subsidize writers if there are no publishers who can afford to publish them. It makes no sense to subsidize publishers if there are no bookstores that can afford to stock their books. In Canada we have chosen to subsidize artists, and to subsidize or regulate some of their distributors— publishers, alternate galleries, theatre companies, radio stations. For play-wrights, musicians, and visual artists, this intervention continues right up to the point where the art reaches its publics, but for writers, except during Ontario's "Half/Back" program in the 1970s, it has stopped short.

The need to subsidize bookstores— by perhaps renting shelf-space in them for Canadian books— becomes increasingly urgent as chain and big-box booksellers dominate more and more of the retail market. Smith-books and Coles, now merged as Chapters, have had little interest in books that they are unlikely to sell one thousand copies of, or that have only regional market potential. Wal-Mart is unlikely to be much different. These high-volume booksellers are now starting to influence the editorial deci-sions of some of the large publishers. A book which cannot be "pre-sold" to Chapters will, in many cases, be rejected.

Canada remains the only industrial country in the world where domestically produced books constitute less than a third of bookstore stock. A government program should be modelled on radio broadcast "Canadian content" rules, and aim to have a minimum of 25% of the stock of Canadian bookstores Canadian produced.

DAURIO ¶ In *Canadian Literary Power*, you comment that "A good deal of the contention and conflict is kept hidden... A pluralist may offer 'happy family' images of Canadian writing or criticism in public but in the privacy of an awards jury make condescending comments... etc." "Many of us have heard legends about quantities of radical criticism in Canada that cannot find publication... In my own experience as an editor who has searched for this homeless criticism, it does not exist." Referring to Lorraine Weir's consideration of this "civility," you note that when false harmony subsumes open discourse it can be crippling. It seems to me that the failure to create open fields of dialogue, argument, and criticism not only has been severely unhealthy for the development of Canadian literature, but that it also fosters a kind of private animosity which would be better transformed into open public discourse. I also think that this lack of healthy bellicosity in ideas makes far too much public literary discussion unrelievedly boring. Do you agree? How do we develop a more open and argumentative discourse in Canadian letters? Is it even possible?

DAVEY § Yes, and in addition I think that this insistence on civility has contributed to the fragmentation of public discourses into separate black, aboriginal, feminist, lesbian feminist, physically handicapped, gay, South-Asian, Japanese-Canadian spheres. What cannot be said or will not be heard within the necessarily "happy family" will create its own space to be said and responded to.

It seems to me there are at least two aspects to this problem. One is the unwillingness of humanist pluralists to listen to dissent. The dissenters are patronized and smothered with praise and comments like, "I know you don't really mean that" (a classic of this is Laurie Ricou's responses to Weir's criticisms of *Canadian Literature*). Or they are variously vilified and marginalized— called irrational, odd, unpredictable, uninformed. Their public spaces are called "private." Their language is labelled as substandard, or jargon-ridden. (Jack David's vilification of Barbara Godard in the twentieth anniversary issue of *Essays on Canadian Writing* is a recent example of this.) This unwillingness can cause the dissenter to withdraw to smaller cultural spheres. The other aspect is the hypocrisy it engenders when superficial politeness results in grant or award sabotage during arts council jury meetings. If the dislikes and reservations were routinely public, councils could at least make more informed jury selections.

What to do? I think writers have to learn to separate philosophical disagreements from friendship— to be able to respect each other when they differ, or perhaps because they dare to differ. Because of the small size of the Canadian literary communities, we are still distantly tied to the "good-ol'-Ned-Pratt" school of criticism that dominated Victoria College in the 1950s. I think more people like myself have to take the risk of publicly disagreeing with writers and critics who are also our friends and colleagues. I know that I have struggled repeatedly to retain the right to ask awkward or difficult questions about the writing of my friends, in order to be able to continue to be able to write credibly about them: Bowering, Barbour, Nichol, Marlatt, Lecker, Kroetsch, Godard among them. In most cases they have treated me the same way. Another part of this involves being able to disagree or dissent without adding insult and personal attack. Avoiding Weir's discourse of civility, as I understand it, doesn't require criticism to become yellow journalism. Indeed, insults eventually lead back to civility and hypocrisy.

DAURIO ¶ The preface to *Canadian Literary Power* presents a non-Toronto-centric vision of Canadian letters, but appears to collapse "downtown Toronto" with the "national" media based in Toronto and their bland and mushy conceptualizations of "culture." Downtown Toronto artistic communities operate in much the same ways that other regional communities do— they share the same lack of presence in and influence over the Toronto "national" media, for instance. In other words, what is reflected on the national CBC, in the *Globe*, *Saturday Night*, etc. usually has as little to do with the dissenting Toronto scene these media are geographically close to as they do with similar communities in say, Victoria, Montreal, or St. John's. But Toronto does not seem to recognize itself as a region, or behave as the other regions do. Do you think this is a fair assessment? If so, do you think it is a problem?

DAVEY § Yes, that's a fair assessment. One reason that Toronto (understood as the "national" media and publishing companies) is merely another region rather than an imperial centre controlling its far-flung regions is that it has so little influence on culture outside itself, whether that outside is Toronto's feminist-of-colour Sister Vision Press, or the Saskatchewan Writers' Guild. There's an additional question of what Toronto is a region of— I think it's both a minor region of multinational industrial culture and a region within Canadian culture. Is this a problem? Is it a problem that many Toronto "mainstream writers" (to distinguish these from Toronto's dissenting or less circulated writers) know and care much more about what is happening in New York or London than they do about what is happening in Fredericton, Montreal, Winnipeg, Calgary, or St. John's? Or that some of the best known write fiction whose geographic fields routinely include Toronto, New York, and various European cities but rarely include a city west of Hamilton or east of Oshawa? Maybe the difficulty lies in what this phenomenon says about Canadian cultural interactions. [...]

DAURIO ¶ "Does [the critical essay] construct the text and its author as isolated, 'unique,' praiseworthy or blameworthy occurrences, or does it construct them as part of ongoing intertextual and discursive histories?" I find the inherent value judgements implied around these issues in *Canadian Literary Power* extremely interesting. What do you think the major elements of literary criticism should be?

DAVEY § It's no secret, Bev, that the national media, the public school systems, and the scholarly criticism popular with textbook producers like McClelland and Stewart and ECW Press all prefer to view authors as heroic, remarkable individuals. They create an author-centred view of literature in which authors are cuddly and fascinating and in which "Alice Munro's world," or "what Margaret Laurence meant" is more important than the books they wrote, than a reader's encounter with them, or than the relationship between the books and Canadian cultural history. The author-centred focus is part of a general commercialization of literature and education. Publishers will tell you that if you want teachers or students to read books you first have to interest them in the personalities and faces of the writers. If you confront them on this issue— on their romanticizing of authors— they will reply, "Don't you want people to read?"

There are a number of serious problems with this approach. One is that it dehistoricizes and depoliticizes literature, encouraging a view that remarkable authors are ahistorical flukes that simply "occur" from time to time. Another is that it isolates literary works from the social and political discourses that nourish them, and which authors re-shape and transform, often unconsciously, in their literary writing (so perpetuating the rigorous separation between literature and politics). One more is that the various ways in which complex social developments influence the perspectives of people who become writers, and make certain books possible, in a sense partly "writing" them, become lost to readers. Would Laurence's *The Diviners* exist as we know it if there had not previously occurred the "hippie" and "back to the land" movements of the 1960s?— no chance. Yet another is the way this view reinforces the crippling free-market social view prevalent in our culture that all of us are autonomous entrepreneurial individuals, beholden to no-one, each trying to realize our peculiar and competitive geniuses. In fact, most of our celebrated writers today wouldn't even be writers had the Canada Council not been founded, and publishers and theatre groups encouraged and funded. Shakespeare's plays would not exist had there not been a Renaissance in Europe, wealth in Elizabeth's court, and a theatrical tradition developing in London.

The question is not so much what criticism should "do" as how large the range should be of the criticism that shapes our popular and public school views of literature. Keep some author-focused criticism (how authors interact with and re-shape the discourses and values they inherit *is* interesting), but make it one of several.

DAURIO ¶ "... limitations of a criticism focused on individual authors do abound... on another hand that national sign ['Canadian'] appears to be the only thing holding back an engulfing tide of international textuality..." Could you please explain a bit what you mean by this?

DAVEY § I was pointing to one of the contradictions within the stories critics tell about Canadian literature. All of the criticism that focuses on single authors (usually with a flattering photo of the author on the cover) and all of the criticism that reads an author's work as developing from their biography tells readers (quite often students) that poems and novels are the inspired and/or hard-won achievements of struggling individuals. This is the dominant critical mode, at least in Canadian high schools. Margaret Laurence or Morley Callaghan (substitute Margaret Atwood, Robertson Davies, Alice Munro, Robert Kroetsch, Timothy Findley, Alden Nowlan, etc.) make personal statements in their work. They are "trying to say," "trying to show," creating their "world," their "view." Everything in the text returns to *their* credit as special individuals who have had visions or insights. Yet this kind of interpretation occurs under the sign "Canadian literature," in a criticism that recurrently sees "Canadianness" as a property which a poem or novel is going to have whether or not an author has wanted it to. (Critics as diverse as Mandel, Frye, Thomas, Atwood, Jones, Kroetsch, McGregor, Hutcheon, and myself may have disagreed bitterly on how this occurs, but have nevertheless kept agreeing that it does.) "Canadianness" here is viewed as a cultural force, a complex of unanalyzed assumptions that colours what is thought, said, written, and done in the northern half of North America because the people who live here absorb it in their schoolyard games and family repartee. That is, much of what makes a text "Canadian" is seen as transcending individual design.

Why such theory? Because it's powerful and credible. Authors indeed appear to be "written" and enabled by the generic conventions they inherit, the literature their culture teaches them to read, and (like all people) by the specific cultural (including legal and economic) conditions and relationships they learn to take as "normal" as they grow. But why has this theory been given such prominence in Canada? Because unless Canadian authors bear such indelible inherited marks of their Canadianness, why should what they write be more relevant to Canadians than the writing which you quote me above as calling "the engulfing tide of international textuality?" Why not read Jeanette Winterson, Martin Amis, Hong Kingston, Adrienne Rich, and Toni Morrison instead of David Adams Richards or Aritha van Herk? The international titles cost less, they're easier to find, they carry the prestige of big country importance. Does Canada even need to produce literary texts when so many people elsewhere are writing and marketing them so cheaply and conveniently?

The view that writers are remarkable individuals undercuts the arguments that Canadians can benefit from reading the writing of *their own* remarkable individuals. If writers *are* only remarkable individuals, and work in utter disconnection from cultural determinants, does Canada really need to produce any? Doesn't the world supply enough already, and at a better price? We no longer grow sour cherries in Canada because Californians can grow them more cheaply— why grow writers?

DAURIO ¶ In a reading of criticism of *For Me and My House* (by Sinclair Ross), you offer "a particularly vivid example of how literary power is socially constituted, how it is the interaction between the signs a text deploys and the discursive context in which they are read that this power arises." This seems to me to be one side of a project of needed criticism, the other being the capacity to read texts as they demand to be read. Outside a very few specialized journals in Canada, there is no excitement about or even understanding of most literary texts produced here. What do you think of the current state of Canadian newspaper and magazine book reviewing?

DAVEY § What book reviewing? There are the few weekly pages of reviews in the *Globe and Mail* (with most of the books reviewed being international), the somewhat fewer weekly pages in the *Toronto Star,* and a weekly handful of reviews in papers like the *Montreal Gazette,* the *London Free Press,* the *Vancouver Sun,* the *Ottawa Citizen.* Then there are all those more numerous dailies with not even a fragment of a book page. Apart from *Books in Canada* and *Quill & Quire,* magazine reviewing is even more limited. *Maclean's* may have one book review in an issue. *Saturday Night* more likely has none. Literary journals often publish reviews three years after a book's publication. The reviewers tend to be very young people making hopeful starts as writers or journalists, but whose youth means that they haven't read nearly as much as have the writers whose work they are reviewing. They miss allusions, misunderstand genre conventions, overlook how books interact with others an author has written— they miss reading the text that is there to be read. (Most of the reviewers of *Karla's Web,* for example, excitedly discussed it as if it was my first book rather than my thirty-second.)

One of the big problems for reviewing in Canada is that writers and experienced critics have to do so many other literary tasks just to make sure they are done. We lack the depth of supply of professional editors, critics, reviewers, and publishers that many other literatures have— most likely because we remunerate these tasks so poorly. So you, Bev, edit and write for *Paragraph,* and edit Mercury, as well as do your own writing. A novelist like Kroetsch or van Herk writes criticism and reviews, and occasionally edits collections. Very few reviews are now written by the critics and writers who are most active or influential elsewhere in the literature— probably because they are over-extended by other activities. I know that I am— that to write a review means writing one less poem or essay, or not reading a novel ms. for a publisher, or a critical ms. for the Humanities Federation. On the other hand, there are people around who could do useful reviewing. Many doctoral students at universities (editors could inquire of grad program directors), faculty at smaller universities, high school department chairs... but this would require the book review editor to be pro-active, rather than leave books in a box for volunteer reviewers to browse in. And this editor may be as over-extended as I am.

DAURIO ¶ Reading your highly layered analysis of Margaret Atwood's "Notes Towards a Poem That Can Never Be Written"— taken together with the relating, for instance, of physical and social bodies in your work, I was struck forcefully with the notion that such cultural analyses draw people together through what could be characterized as "practical" use of "theory"— where, for instance, social, political and other lines are drawn like wire between elements of public experience, providing both understanding and strategies for avoiding being either tripped or tied by them; such connectors offer valuable ways of "knowing" social relations. Could it be that the resistance to "theory"— and you have quoted, for example, several paranoid pronouncements on the evils of postmodernism— could it be that this resistance has its roots in protection of the notion of bourgeois individuality?

DAVEY § Is the pope, etc. Yes, resistance to theory can "be" a lot of things— resistance to having social relations known, to having positions of interest exposed— but it very often can be resistance to having the limits of bourgeois individuality made known. I don't think the latter is necessarily always based on conscious investment in a theory of an independent self-made bourgeois subject, as a businessman's "I believe in an unregulated marketplace" might be. Some people who have grown up believing in the illusion that they are freely choosing individuals are genuinely shaken by being made to look at the web of connections that have helped shape them. Their self-confidence or self-esteem is threatened, that "I'm okay" fantasy that some need in order to be productive. Giving up the illusion of personal autonomy may give them anxieties that they may have been born in the "wrong" place, exposed to the wrong influences, through no fault of their own. Our culture produces a lot of people who can't work without feeling in control.

This dependence on illusions of personal autonomy often overlaps with resistance to feminism— by women who experience themselves as having struggled independently to achieve success, and who discount the ways feminist efforts to diminish systemic anti-woman discrimination has helped shape both their expectations and the opportunities they've encountered. You can see a lot of that sort of self-reassuring blindness in some of the contributions to *Language in Her Eye*. It also overlaps with the "political correctness" paranoia, as in various writers' attacks on the "Writing thru 'Race'" conference, or in some of Timothy Findley's and Alberto Manguel's comments on the Canada Council's evaluation criteria ("political correctness stinks," Findley told a Canadian Studies conference last year in Venice). Some writers seem to love unregulated cultural "marketplaces" because, like self-made Uncle Ben in *Death of a Salesman,* they have a desperate need to believe they've conquered the jungle by themselves.

DAURIO ¶ With the sale of the Mounties' copyright to Disney, there almost seems to be a public expectation that anything Canadian that is "worth" anything will be so acknowledged by its American purchase— that is, it will be so marked by its value translation into capitalist terms, and by the stripping away of its Canadian "meaning": in the case of the Mounties, the excision of the irony the Mountie image holds, for instance. There is also the very odd question of who owns and who has the right to sell such things. Do you think that the lack of a strong and viable Canadian popular culture is perhaps a greater cultural threat than Canadian artists have tended to acknowledge heretofore?

DAVEY § Yes, but there is also a problem with popular culture itself, which once was understood as having some connection with the populace with which it was popular— as being in some way produced by it. Today popular culture is largely a commercial culture, with pop-culture markets created by advertising, and by competition between advertisers. Culture by Disney, Mattel, Sony, *People* magazine, supermarket tabloids. Its funky moments are the products of opportunism as commerce appropriates the small lives of Amy Fisher, John Bobbitt, Michael Jackson, or Julia Roberts. And there is little that artists can do about this, even in the US, except perhaps to attempt to reach pop culture consumers by working with the corporations that manage what is popular. In licensing the Mountie image to Disney, our government is, I suppose, trying to control something that it knew was going to happen anyway.

There is an increasing economy of scale at work in pop culture, as technology allows fewer images to be the pop culture of more communities. So it is not merely the cultures of countries like Canada that are at risk, it is also the cultures of various regions within the US, who now receive most of their world and national news not through the interpretations of regional newspapers, or a choice of national networks, but of CNN. The fact that many people across Canada now receive their printed news from the *Globe and Mail* rather than a local newspaper may foreshadow a time when there is no *Globe and Mail,* only a *USA Today* or *International Herald-Tribune* on most Canadian doorsteps.

What this reduction in images often occasions, however, is a rebellion of the local, as new small cultural producers move into the niches created by the alienation bland, standardized cultural products lead to. We've seen that phenomenon with the bland beer of Molson's/Labatt's leading to the establishment of local micro-breweries. But the power of multinational corporations is such that they can often buy out these new operations, or attack them by faking similar "dissident" products, as in Molson's release of Red Dog.

I think that one can trust the productivity of people at the grass-roots local levels, and the alienation created by mass products, to keep this process or cycle going. There's a lot of evidence that globalization does more damage to nation states than it does to local cultures, and that by weakening the nation state globalization may even stimulate local cultures. There are desires all the marketing skills of the multinationals cannot satisfy, thankfully. The displacement of the *Globe* by *USA Today* could bring renewed life to local and regional newspapers.

DAURIO ¶ "The aerial battle on the cover of [George Bowering's *At War with the U.S.*] may as easily be one between two Canadians over how 'American' Canada should be— a Canadian civil war— as one between two countries." This domestic positioning of the responsibility for US cultural domination of Canada seems to me an extremely healthy one: the problem seems to be that, for the most part, only the nationalist side knows that it is fighting. Do you think it is possible to rehabilitate nationalist arguments in the current climate?

DAVEY § The most recent nationalist conception in Canada that has had any resonance is Joe Clark's "community of communities." The world to come is likely to be one or more large marketplaces dominated by a dozen or so global companies, with weak nation states, but strong regional and special constituency cultures. We can get a glimpse of this in the European Community, where national governments no longer can have independent economic, social, or labour policies, but where Welsh and Scottish and Flemish communities, and European "Green" parties, have become noticeably stronger. The only role for a nation state in such a world to seek is the facilitating of the separate and "special" goals of its constituent parts— its cities, regions, ethnicities, women, etc.— and to do this better than does multinational economics. If the state can't do this new job, it will either disappear or fade into irrelevance, as many of its sub-groups find ways to manage their own lives.

For Canadian nationalism to be rehabilitated many different constituencies that have been in recent times luke-warm toward nationalism are going to have to re-invent it to serve their own causes.

DAURIO ¶ "... especially transformative was the media's treatment of two social tragedies as provocative and continuing entertainments" leading back "to the mediatization of our own lives where we are no longer certain whether we are acting or experiencing life... transgression and violence become quick and addictive antidotes for anxiety and boredom." "All announced to Canadians that something fundamental had changed in our culture... some new multinational, private-enterprise system of interpretation seemed to be about to take over aspects of their lives that had previously been interpreted by our national and provincial governments, by our laws, and by historic cultural conditions... if it could transform the lives and deaths of Mahaffy and French... it could take over the lives of anyone." How do you think this transformation alters everyday Canadian life?

DAVEY § All of us live alongside narratives which variously guide and interpret us, telling of our place in the world, what we would like to do, and how we relate to others. The more narratives we have, the more freedom, in that we have more options for choice or for combining narrative elements. If deprived of narratives, or relentlessly taught the superiority of a few, one could come to a point where one "automatically" turned on a TV set in order to find what one was next going to do.

Three of the treasured objects I inherited from my dad are a child's rattle, crudely but cleverly carved out of a single piece of wood, a hand-carved wooden monkey, its limbs assembled on scraps of wire, that does acrobatics when its frame is squeezed, and a hand-stitched double-wedding-ring quilt. There was a moment in Canadian history when mail-order catalogues first arrived, offering machine-made toys and games, machine-made bedding, factory-made boats. At that moment the production of objects such as these three of my father's began to slow, and the expectation began that someone else would imagine and produce the objects one "desired."

Something similar to this has been happening to the meaning of our lives. Less and less does it come from our families, or our communities, or our cultural institutions, and more and more it comes from commercially produced news/entertainments. How does this alter everyday Canadian life? Look at how rapidly "populism," with its suspicion of government as something alien to the people, has spread in Alberta and other parts of Canada as that paranoid American view of government is increasingly marketed in entertainments like the Batman movies, *The X-Files* or *The Net*. Look at how Toronto's infatuation with blockbuster theatrical entertainments— *Cats, Miss Saigon, Les Misérables, Beauty and the Beast*— has decimated its small theatre scene.

DAURIO ¶ Much of your critical work in prose embodies the idea that meaning is to be argued over, constructed, and reconstructed, and this approach is also applied to the Canadian nationalist project: Canada, the state always in the process of its own construction. I like the idea of an open-ended, mutating, alterable Canada very much. But do such arguments imply that we are only intellectually compensating for the lack of a centre?

DAVEY § I don't see social debate as an intellectual compensation. For me, a national state is never more than a discursive site, a context in which the various elements in a society continuously negotiate and re-negotiate their relationships. It is not a "centre" either geographically or ideologically, with all the stillness that a word like "centre" implies. If you regard a nation as centred, you get into those idealisms that can paralyze social debate by blinding people to changing particulars— the kind that in 1965 saw numbers of Canadians defending the old red ensign with arguments that Canada was necessarily British. The recurrent search for something quintessentially Canadian, a Canadian "identity," has reflected one of these silly idealisms. In fact, Canada has been visible all along, in its economic and social history, in the accommodations its various inhabitants have had to make with one another, in the arguments and negotiations we continue to have. That is why it is so important that we continue speaking, writing, and listening to one another rather than only tuning in to CNN, renting Hollywood videos, reading transnational fiction, watching the Simpson trial. When we stop arguing with each other, Canada stops.

SELECTED CRITICAL BOOKS BY FRANK DAVEY:

Five Readings of Olson's "Maximus." Montreal: Beaver-Kosmos, 1970.

Earle Birney. Toronto: Copp Clark, 1971 (*Studies in Canadian Literature* 11).

From There to Here: A Guide to English-Canadian Literature since 1960 (Our Nature/Our Voices, Vol. 2). Erin, Ont.: Press Porcépic, 1974.

Surviving the Paraphrase: Eleven Essays on Canadian Literature. Winnipeg: Turnstone Press, 1983.

Margaret Atwood: A Feminist Poetics. Vancouver: Talonbooks 1984.

Reading Canadian Reading. Winnipeg: Turnstone Press, 1988.

Post-National Arguments: The Politics of the Anglophone-Canadian Novel Since 1967. Toronto: University of Toronto Press, 1993.

Reading "KIM" Right. Vancouver: Talonbooks, 1993.

Canadian Literary Power. Edmonton: NeWest Press, 1994.

Karla's Web: A Cultural Examination of the Mahaffy-French Murders. Toronto: Viking/Penguin, 1994.

Notes on Contributors

JOHN CLEMENT BALL is assistant professor of English at the University of New Brunswick, specializing in post-colonial literatures. His writing has appeared in numerous academic and literary journals, including *Canadian Literature, ARIEL,* and *Open Letter.*

CLINT BURNHAM is a Vancouver writer whose books include *Be Labour Reading* (ECW); *Airborne Photo & Other Stories* will be published by Anvil Press in 1999.

JEFFREY CANTON is the national director of "Word on the Street." His writing has appeared in a variety of publications, including *Xtra!*

BARBARA CAREY, poet and critic, is the author of several books of poetry, the most recent of which is *The Ground of Events.*

KEVIN CONNOLLY is the author of *Asphalt Cigar,* and is an editor at the Toronto weekly *Eye Magazine.*

BEVERLEY DAURIO has edited more than one hundred books, including this collection of interviews.

JANIETA EYRE is a Toronto writer and photographer whose photographs have been exhibited in various places across North America, including the Garnet Press Gallery and the Power Plant.

CARY FAGAN is the author of several books, including the novel *Sleeping Weather.*

VICTORIA FREEMAN is a Toronto writer.

ROBYN GILLAM is an Egyptologist with an interest in studies in popular culture. Her writing has been widely published.

MELISSA HARDY is a London novelist.

SALLY ITO is the author of two books, including *Floating Shore.* She lives in Edmonton.

MARILYN SNELL is a freelance writer based in San Francisco, and has worked as an editor at both *Mother Jones* and the *Utne Reader.*

Acknowledgements

Most of these interviews first appeared in *Paragraph: The Canadian Fiction Review*, between 1990 and 1998. I would like to thank all of the authors of these interviews for their cooperation in the publication of this book, especially Barbara Carey and Robyn Gillam.

— *Beverley Daurio*

Jeannette Armstrong: *Paragraph*, 1992
Marie-Claire Blais: *Paragraph*, 1995
Dionne Brand: *Books in Canada*, 1993
Nicole Brossard: *Books in Canada*, 1993
Carole Corbeil: *Paragraph*, 1992
Timothy Findley: *Paragraph*, 1994
Douglas Glover: *Paragraph*, 1991
Janette Turner Hospital: *Paragraph*, 1997
Thomas King: *Paragraph*, 1994
Joy Kogawa: *Paragraph*, 1996
Steve McCaffery: *Paragraph*, 1992
Michael Ondaatje: *Paragraph*, 1990
Althea Prince: *Paragraph*, 1997
Nino Ricci: *Paragraph*, 1991
Mordecai Richler: *Paragraph*, 1998
Veronica Ross: *Paragraph*, 1991
Gail Scott: *Paragraph*, 1993
Makeda Silvera: *Paragraph*, 1992
Audrey Thomas: *Paragraph*, 1996
Lola Lemire Tostevin: *Paragraph*, 1992
Jane Urquhart: *Paragraph*, 1991
M.G. Vassanji: *Paragraph*, 1994
A Conversation with Frank Davey: *Paragraph*, 1996

Interview with Margaret Atwood reprinted with permission from *Mother Jones* magazine, © 1997, Foundation for National Progress.